Impressionist Paris

Impressionist Paris

THE ESSENTIAL GUIDE
TO THE CITY OF LIGHT

by

JULIAN MORE

PAVILION

For Camilla

Museum note: works exhibited in Paris museums are indicated O for Orsay or, for the smaller collections, by the whole name, e.g. Petit Palais.

Price code: Restaurants (per person, meal only): (**C**) 150F and below, (**B**) 150F–300F, (**A**) 300F–1000F. Hotels (per night, two sharing): (**C**) 500F and below, (**B**) 500F–800F, (**A**) 800F–2500F.

☆ indicates hotel or restaurant of impressionist or period interest.

First published in Great Britain in 1998 by Pavilion Books Limited

London House, Great Eastern Wharf, Parkgate Road, London SW11 4NQ.

Text © Julian More 1998

All translations by the author

Maps © Venture Graphics

Photography © Julien Busselle

Copyright details of all paintings reproduced are given on page 208.

The moral right of the author has been asserted.

A CIP catalogue record for this book is available from the British Library.

ISBN 1 85793 832 1

Editor: Emma Tait

Picture Research: Lynda Marshall

Design: Ben Cracknell and Bernard Higton

Set in Bodoni

Colour reproduction by DP Graphics

Printed and bound in Spain by Egedsa

2 4 6 8 10 9 7 5 3 1

This book may be ordered by post direct from the publisher. Please contact the Marketing Department. But try your bookshop first.

CONTENTS

ACKNOWLEDGEMENTS

Many unnamed people with local knowledge - waiters, barmen, museum attendants, passers-by, and others casually encountered - helped with the making of this book. More specifically, I could not have embarked upon it without the permission of Henri Loyrette, curator of Orsay, to research books and documents in the museum library (unequalled for impressionist period information), where the staff were most attentive.

I was initially pointed in the right direction for the on-the-ground research by Edgar de Bresson with his eclectic knowledge of Paris and its art history. Lucy Degrémont was a generous hostess and informative guide in Marly-le-Roi, Louveciennes, and Auvers-sur-Oise. Guy and Anne Wolfers kindly entertained me at Bougival, and told me about the dedicated fight for conservation of impressionist sites on the River Seine by the Association des Sablons. I was lucky enough to have an art historian neighbour in Provence, Anne Macrae, to check the text for accuracy. And another Provence friend, gastronomic writer Patricia Wells, helped with the choice of restaurants.

My thanks to Jacki and Jean-Jacques Clerico for inviting me to the perennially marvellous show at the Moulin Rouge; to Michel Landureau of the Conseil Municipal at Maincy for guiding me to Cézanne's elusive bridge there; to Lucien Curzi of Argenteuil's Bureau Culturel for a most erudite exposition of the town's development; to Geraldine Salle of the Centre Culturel at Gennevilliers and Mr Duroche, Archivist of Asnières.

The following tourist offices all gave excellent advice and information: Barbizon, Moret-sur-Loing, Marly-le-Roi, Montmartre, Pontoise, Auvers-sur-Oise, and the main Paris Office du Tourisme on the Champs-Elysées was, as ever, most helpful.

Co-explorer on the impressionist trail was my wife, Sheila, who also originated the maps. She read different versions of the text with great patience, and I am most grateful for her many perceptive suggestions.

My publisher, Colin Webb, gave much practical and creative encouragement throughout; he and his wife, Pam, made a special trip to Paris to pioneer one of my walks. Ben Cracknell's design is all I could wish for. Steve Dobell did an excellent job editing my text, while Emma Tait has seen the book through meticulously as managing editor. And many sleepless nights were avoided thanks to the support of my agents, Sandy Violette and Abner Stein.

INTRODUCTION

An impressionist painting draws me into it. Its representation of the here-and-now, a specific time and place, has me asking a number of questions. Who are all those people having such a good time in Renoir's *Luncheon of the Boating Party*? Does his favourite Restaurant Fournaise still exist? Where is Pissarro's *View of the Tuileries Gardens*? Or Manet's concert there? If I stand on a platform at the Gare St-Lazare in these smokeless days, will it look anything like a Monet? Is the Boulevard de Clichy today just one big sleazy sex show, or would Degas still find models willing to contort themselves for hours into poses for nudes at their toilet, 'seen through a keyhole', as he described it?

The late nineteenth-century times that were 'modern' for the impressionists have distinct resonances for us today. Behind the apparently bland bourgeois bliss, a certain malaise lingered, a disillusionment with the industrial revolution's failure to live up to its promise of everlasting bounty (members of Sisley's and Degas's families experienced financial ruin, the upwardly mobile stockbroker Gauguin was victim of a volatile market). In our own *fin-de-siècle*, eat-drink-and-be-merry mood, we are quick to blame the technocratic society for not delivering, the computer terminal for a merchant bank's downfall. We suffer from a similar malaise. As the century rambles to its close, we share the same kind of escapist urge for distraction, a leisure-drive with which the impressionists were instinctively in tune.

Their Paris was a stunning façade. Not just in the beauty and charm of the parks and bridges, the avenues and river, but in the people, too. There was instantaneous energy in the movement of Degas's ballet dancers, jockeys and cabaret singers, Manet's suburban oarsmen and their girls, Renoir's Montmartre dancers. On the rural fringe of the city Pissarro delighted in the double movement of town to country (a factory in a riverside meadow) and country to town (peasants coming to market). Occasionally an impressionist would reveal the downside behind the façade: Degas with a bleak absinthe drinker, or yawning laundress; Manet with a bloody drawing of death at the barricades. On the surface, it was a carefree world – in sunshine, snow or flood – with children cavorting through poppies, and couples in pursuit of love. Rarely was the squalid no man's land of the outskirts' shanty towns depicted, until later with the post-impressionist pessimism of van Gogh, and Lautrec's portrayal of brothel girls with a bitter-sweet, caricatural intimacy.

Today, like the ornate pleasure-dromes of the more luxurious brothels (briefly revived by Madame Claude), much of impressionist Paris has fallen victim to the moralist and the bulldozer, but much is still there, often as the artists painted it. Places where they lived and had their studios, even a few bars and restaurants they frequented, sites they depicted – from Montmartre to Moret-sur-Loing, Bougival to Boulevard Haussmann, Pontoise to the Pont-Royal – are surprisingly intact and visitable. I shall also warn of the disappointments, notably Argenteuil, whose Second World War German aircraft factories led to its destruction by Allied bombing and which now boasts Monet's painting-boat as its single impressionist relic.

These 'sensationalists with rainbow palettes', as Kenneth Clark described the impressionists, were a varied clan (see 'An Impressionist Who's Who', p. 198) – from tailor's son Renoir to millionaire Caillebotte, local government worker Guillaumin to salon hostess Berthe Morisot, anarchist Pissarro to royalist Degas. They were united in their early days by a vigorous mutual support system (though not a mutual admiration society), working together, arguing together, sharing each other's failures and rare public successes. Together, they made common cause against a philistine art establishment, rising above the contempt of a myopic French public and incomprehension of foreign artists such as the niminy-piminy Dante Gabriel Rossetti. Between 1874 and 1886 they held eight group shows before an inevitable parting of the ways.

The watershed year was 1886, when Vincent van Gogh came to Paris and many new movements began. Whatever the artist's individual approach, it was still often a question of capturing the spirit of the age on canvas, the Paris scene as it was happening at that very moment. Post-impressionists Lautrec and van Gogh, Bonnard and Matisse, Derain and Vlaminck walked the same alleys and avenues as their predecessors, however different the eye and the look. The city and its surroundings seemed inexhaustible as a source of material, if not riches.

How did Paris come to be the spectacular boom town that inspired them? Thanks to France's industrial revolution (which the impressionists chronicled in images of trains, iron bridges, factory chimneys, coal barges being unloaded and urbanization), Second Empire Paris was the success story of Europe.

Napoleon III initiated massive town planning. Much of Paris was still a medieval city of stinking narrow streets, unsalubrious drainage, and traffic jams of defecating horses. In 1853 Baron Haussmann, the Prefect of the Seine département, was ordered to open the city up by building more railway stations, more markets, and great arterial boulevards, with underground sewage, water and gas. The poor were bustled out of the city centre to appalling shanty towns on the outskirts. Cynics claimed the wider avenues were mainly to enable the militaristic Emperor to rush troops across the city in the event of yet another popular uprising and the hurling of newly laid paving stones. One wit mocked a typical Haussmann avenue for being 'marvellously accessible to air, light and the infantry'.

They also became accessible to the new young artists, who began to see the possibilities of this modern, fast-moving City of Light – with countrified outskirts like Montmartre on its hill, and Bougival and Argenteuil villages by the river. In city or outskirts they found vantage-points at which to set up an easel, on riverbank or city balcony. Or make sketches and return to complete the work in the comparative comfort of the studio – if coal could be afforded in the all too frequent freeze-ups of cash flow.

Napoleon III saw himself as the French artists' benefactor. His Salon des Beaux-Arts, the annual exhibition that afforded the only opportunity for an artist to become known, was the almost exclusive domain of officially accepted artists, *pompiers* as they were caustically dubbed by their detractors, pumping out well-crafted but totally uninspired 'pomp' for provincial museums. Sentimental, melodramatic painters stuck with worthy but dull traditions like Meissonier (*The French Campaign of Napoleon I* – O), Bouguereau (*Day of the Dead*) or Cabanel (*Birth of Venus* – O) were anathema to young artists eager to get out in the open air and paint the real world as they saw it. The Salon des Beaux-Arts held its annual exhibition, appropriately for such a conveyor-belt of mass production, at the Galerie des Machines in the Palais de l'Industrie. In an enlightened move for a dictator, Napoleon III decreed in 1863 that those artists rejected by the academic jury should have their own Salon des Refusés next door. It was to change the history of art. Manet exhibited a shocker: *Le Déjeuner sur l'herbe* (O).

Howls of contemptuous laughter greeted it. What jarred was not so much that the lunching lady was naked or her bathing companion in a see-through shift, but that their two gentlemen were wearing everyday clothes instead of togas or shepherds' tunics. It somehow suggested the prelude to an orgy in a forest glade. Then, in 1865, Manet added insult to injury with *Olympia* (O) at the official Salon. Olympia was a common name among Paris prostitutes, and his nude reclining on her bed was far from Olympian in the classical sense: a contemporary Parisian *cocotte*, emanating whoredom from her used-looking flesh and world-weary, contemptuous gaze. In the voluptuous chiaroscuro, a black maid offers flowers from an admirer while a black cat watches from the foot of the bed. Savage cartoonist Daumier showed two members of the lumpen bourgeoisie, trying to make sense of it at the Salon, commenting: 'Why the devil is that woman called Olympia?' 'My friend, perhaps it's the name of her cat.'

These scandals marked the beginning of the impressionist group. After the humiliating defeat of France in the Franco-Prussian War (1870) and the exile of Napoleon III, they had hopes of a more democratic art policy from the Government of the Third Republic. But the *pompiers* were still pumping out the pomp and as influential as ever. The rebel painters decided to go independent. A generous photographer-balloonist, Nadar, offered his studio at 35 Boulevard des Capucines for an exhibition to combat the continuing philistinism of the Salon. It was 1874. Renoir, Degas, Monet, Cézanne, Pissarro, Morisot and Sisley all contributed works.

Although the pickings were as slim as the mockery was large, it was notable for the sale of one particular picture, Monet's *Impression, Sunrise* (Marmottan-Monet) at the highest price of 3500F. Art critic Leroy, using the heavily ironic device of imagining himself accompanied by an outraged artist of the nymphs-and-togas school, has the venerable old ass comment: 'Impression, certainly. And I'd even go as far as to say, because I'm impressed, that there just has to be an impression in it!' Less dottily, journalist Jules Castagnary, who frequented the Café Guerbois, haunt of Manet and other artists, used the word 'impressionism' in an article for the first time.

So arrived the most instantly memorable and least accurate art label of all time. No two painters could have a more different style than Degas, the indoor realist with his classical lines, and Monet, the confirmed *pleinairiste* with loose, quickly applied small brushstrokes. Renoir considered -ists and -isms to be purely for art historians. 'Impressionism', however, conveniently captured the mood of a group of artists working very differently but to the same ends. Pissarro, Cézanne and Sisley had each his distinct approach to outdoor phenomena, light, colour and image at a precise moment; Manet, Degas and, later, Toulouse-Lautrec recorded indoor impressions of a Parisian's momentary mood a fat man drinking beer, a girl having a pedicure, the fleeting motion of an acrobat.

With the reviving fortunes of Paris in the Belle Epoque, the gathering momentum of the impressionists, no longer a group, eventually found its public and, more importantly for the artists, buyers beyond the small but loyal group of Paris collectors consisting a couple of doctors, a publisher, an opera singer, a customs official, an art-shop owner, even a pastry-cook. Americans, liking what they saw, began buying into impressionism, even if the French museums did not.

It was not long before impressionism spawned other groups and -isms, either rebelling against or deriving from it: divisionism, pointillist painting with dots, by Seurat and Signac; Les Nabis (the Prophets), a group led by Pierre Bonnard and Maurice Denis experimenting with highly decorative, almost medieval or Japanese-influenced figures in stylized settings; and fauvism, the natural development from Gauguin's 'pure colour', which influenced Derain, Vlaminck and Matisse.

Paris was still the centre of these movements, even if Gauguin found his inspiration in the South Seas and Matisse on the South Coast. As art historian Clive Bell suggests: 'Impressionism leads straight to Picasso.' Picasso's first visit to Paris was in 1900, and in the decade to come he and others would begin to explore the next major art revolution, cubism.

Art history labels are notoriously slapdash, and borderline cases between one -ism and the next emphasize the importance of influences while an artist found himself. What went before and what came after the impressionists are naturally touched upon here: the early *pleinairistes* in Fontainebleau forest (Corot, Courbet, Millet), and post-impressionists Lautrec in Montmartre, van Gogh at Auvers-sur-Oise, Chagall, Léger and Soutine on the Left Bank. Modernist experiments in La Ruche reflect Monet's movement towards abstract art in his *Water Lilies*. (Chapter Eight, p. 181). I have no hesitation in including such a rich cross-fertilization in the book.

My walks and drives give suggested routes, but I have purposely avoided too-precise distances and timings. They are more contemplative rambles than heavy hikes or tours, to be taken at your own speed and leisure. I have arranged the walks in Paris city, for instance, so that the foot-weary can peel off to nearby Métro stations to reach wherever they're staying and, once rested, begin again where they left off.

Destinations out of Paris should not take much more than an hour to get to from the city centre, in reasonable traffic conditions. Visits can be done in a day or longer, according to time available. Walks are full day or half-day(with plenty of stops for refreshment). In each chapter there is an Information section that indicates places, some with a period ambience, to eat, drink and stay in near the route of walks or drives; and the local tourist offices (some very helpful, with impressionist maps and guides). A list of relevant Paris museums to be visited separately from walks and drives is given on page 194.

In Chapters Three and Five reproduction panels are mentioned. These are copies of an artist's work, often reproduced full-scale, placed outdoors at the spot where the artist worked on the subject. Intriguing comparisons can be made between now and then. Locations of the panels are indicated on maps available from local tourist offices.

A note on prices. Paris is one of the most expensive cities in the world, but paradoxically you can still find good value for money in restaurants and, particularly, in hotels. Fluctuating currencies don't always help. Visiting off-season always does: prices slump between October and Easter. Of course, accommodation and food can cost considerably less than I have suggested, but I wouldn't vouch for the quality. In categories of restaurant (per person, meal only), (C) means 150F and below, (B) between 150F and 300F, (A) between 300F and 1000F (e.g. Pré Catelan, p. 138). In categories of hotels (per night, for two sharing), (C) means 500F and below, (B) between 500F and 800F, (A) between 800F and 2500F (e.g. L'Hôtel p. 166).

Suggested itineraries outside Paris are by own transport. For public transport (where not indicated), call the relevant tourist office (numbers in the Information sections), as this can be complicated in the Ile-de-France.

I have set out my journey geographically rather than historically. As film director Jean-Luc Godard once said: 'A film should have a beginning, a middle and an end, but not necessarily in that order.' Consequently, for convenience of itinerary, the reader will find Sisley's last days at Moret-sur-Loing (Chapter One) before his student days on the Left Bank (Chapter Seven). Although much will be said about the artists' lives and loves and daily habits, spirit of place and painting takes precedence over art history. The image is the word.

So this is a book mainly about looking. Looking at paintings, looking at town and country, absorbing a distinct atmosphere that still exists. An echo of the past resonates in the present, imbuing us with the life force of the City of Light and the artists who celebrated it.

Julian More, Visan

FONTAINEBLEAU FOREST

A creeper-covered house at Barbizon.

If Paris nurtured the mind of the impressionist revolution, its heart and body took shape in the surrounding countryside. And its birth occurred some thirty miles south of the city in the forest of Fontainebleau.

In less than an hour from central Paris, soon after taking the Fontainebleau exit from the A6 autoroute, I was in one of the first landscapes to attract the impressionists with its specially clear light. It was a journey that took the young Renoir, unable to afford the train fare to Melun, two days. He would overnight in a barn where Orly airport's jumbos have long since replaced the flight of doves. Surprising how quickly I seemed to be out of town, suddenly crossing the flat, fertile Plaine de Chailly, vast hedgeless cornfields with clumps of pre-forest trees where Millet's devout, resigned peasants once guarded their twilit flocks or gleaned the corn from golden stubble.

'I detested Millet,' Renoir told his *cinéaste* son, Jean. 'His sentimental peasants always made me think of actors dressed up as peasants. I loved Diaz. I understood him. I told myself that if ever I became a painter, I would want to paint like him and perhaps I could do it. Because I very much like it when, in a forest landscape, I can imagine water. And with Diaz often you smell mushrooms, leaf mould and moss. His pictures reminded me of walks with my mother in the woods of Louveciennes, and the forest of Marly.' (From *Renoir, My Father* by Jean Renoir.)

Nevertheless, the pre-impressionists of the Fontainebleau school – Millet, Theodore Rousseau, Daubigny, Corot, Courbet and Diaz – showed the open-air way to the fledgling painters. In the forest and fields of their predecessors, Renoir, Sisley, Monet and Bazille were to explore key elements: the play of light and shadow, the contrasts of changing luminosity; colour that did not follow the confines of drawn lines but commanded the whole image as observed by an all-seeing eye at a given distance from it; space expressed with new angles, breaking the rules of traditional perspective, going beyond the confines of foreground and horizon; painting outdoors; painting the instant; painting with the new, easily transportable zinc tubes of oil paints instead of pots of pigments that had to be mixed – no joke beneath an umbrella in a sudden rainstorm; and, above all, subjects that expressed the new modernity – a look at the real world of nature in an actual place on the map called 'Fontainebleau forest', not some mythic woodland glade with the sound of the merry, merry pipes of Pan called 'Arcadia'.

The best of the pre-impressionists were not gentleman painters, any more than the peasants of the Plaine de Chailly were gentleman farmers. They were of the earth, earthy. Some, like Millet and Courbet, took pride in humbler origins than were generally acceptable at the Salon des Beaux-Arts. Count

Nieuwerkerke, the imperial Director of the Académie des Beaux-Arts, declared unequivocally: 'It is the painting of democrats, of men who don't change their underwear, who wish to impose themselves on society; their art displeases and disgusts me.'

Lowering the tone while heightening the colour gave the Fontainebleau school its social shock value. As early as 1834, Corot, on a painting trip south, had gone only thirty miles out of Paris when news of a cholera epidemic in Italy made him change his plans. And where better to be stranded than this virgin forest so near home? Paintings like *The Clearing* (O), with the play of light and shade on mysterious primeval shapes, sunlight cast through the pale green trees of springtime, were to influence the young Renoir's *Clearing in the Woods* (1865) and the early work of Pissarro in the forest of Montmorency, north-west of Paris. Though Renoir found Corot's circle of Parisian friends totally inane and out of touch, he always remembered the master's advice to go back to the same place and copy the same tree every year. It was never the same.

For artists in search of *plein air*, not so far from Paris as to be out of touch with the opinion-makers, the simple life in the hamlet of Barbizon with its whitewashed, thatched cottages was cheap, if not particularly cheerful. The early *pleinairistes* responded to the romance of the names on the map with their strange, medieval vibrations: The Fairies' Marsh, the King's Highway, the Cow's Gateway, the Heights of Jean de Paris, Great Huntsman's Cross, the Rocks of the Beautiful Thorn-Bush, the Gorge of the Wolves. Millet and Daubigny followed Rousseau, who, disillusioned by failure at the Salon, had settled there in 1836. And in the wake of Parisian painters with names now long forgotten came daubers of varying talent from Bucharest and London, New York and Buenos Aires. A commune with a population of a hundred or so in the 1830s swelled to 300 by 1872; 147 lived by the land and 100 by painting it. A few painters had it both ways by growing asparagus and raising chickens against the frequently rainy days when the Salon once more refused their work.

Finding Barbizon too crowded, with its trendy amateurs in smocks and floppy velvet berets and bourgeois rustics playing at the peasant life, the future impressionists sought out less popular villages like Chailly-en-Bière and Marlotte. Alfred Sisley was the first to discover Barbizon in 1861, and the only one to stay there. He was also the last to have connections with the forest of Fontainebleau, dying in 1899 at Moret-sur-Loing.

Sisley, despite his Parisian upbringing, looked every centimetre the dashing young English gentleman artist. Though cross-Channel smugglers could be boasted on both sides of his family, William Sisley père was – just as he appears in Renoir's genial portrait (O) – a respectable expatriate businessman who made his fortune exporting artificial flowers to South America. For business training Alfred was sent to London, where he discovered Constables and Boningtons were more to his taste than Lloyds and Barings. His father saw this was going to get neither of them further in artificial flowers, so he generously set his son up at Neuilly with a substantial allowance.

Sisley's golden boy beginnings hardly prepared him for the suffering to come. His Anglo-French background had already created a certain schizophrenia. Which landscape tradition did he belong to? The skies and clouds of a Constable, whose painting he had absorbed in London? Or the lyrical reverie of a Corot? It was as 'pupil of Corot' that he signed his first acceptance at the Salon of 1866 with *Fontainebleau Forest*, and there can have been no question of his allegiance when he first came to Barbizon.

WALKS AND DRIVES

IN

FONTAINEBLEAU FOREST

Steamboats on the Loing *by Sisley (1877).*

INFORMATION

Itinerary

Allow 2 full days, either making day trips from Paris or staying overnight. *Drive time* approximately 1 hour Paris–Fontainebleau forest.

Day 1

Paris–Barbizon via autoroute A6 to Fontainebleau exit, then N37 to D64.

Barbizon and Forest Walk.

Drive Barbizon–Chailly-en-Bière (D64, N7).

Lunch.

Visit Chailly.

Drive Chailly–Marlotte (N7, D58).

Visit Marlotte.

Drive Marlotte–Moret-sur-Loing (D58, D104).

Overnight Moret.

Day 2

Walking the Sisleys – morning.

Drive Moret–St-Mammès (5 minutes).

Lunch.

St-Mammès Walk – afternoon.

Drive St-Mammès–Maincy (D39 to Melun, then D408).

Visit Maincy Bridge.

Return Paris (autoroutes A56, A4).

Refreshment, Meals and Overnight

Barbizon

☆ Hôtellerie du Bas-Bréau (Relais et Châteaux, gastronomic), **(A)**, 22 Rue Grande.
Tel. 01.60.66.40.05.

Chailly-en-Bière

☆ Lion d'Or (village restaurant), **(C)**, 2 Route Nationale 7.
Tel. 01.60.66.43.12.

Moret-sur-Loing

Auberge de la Terrasse (hotel), **(C)**, 40 Rue Pêcherie.
Tel. 01.60.70.51.03.

Auberge de la Palette (restaurant), **(B)**, 10 Avenue Jean-Jaurès.
Tel. 01.60.70.50.72.

Auberge du Soleil (riverside restaurant), **(C)**, Moret–St-Mammès road.
Tel. 01.60.70.53.31.

Thomery (near Moret)

Le Vieux Logis (hotel), **(B)**, 5 Rue Sadi Carnot. Tel. 01.60.96.44.77.

Jean & Regine Farnault (b & b), **(C)**, Thoméry. Tel. 01.60.70.07.23.

Brigitte Stacke (b & b), **(C)**, Thoméry. Tel. 01.60.96.43.96.

Museums and Sites

Auberge Ganne Museum of Barbizon School, 92 Rue Grande, Barbizon, and Rousseau's House, 55 Rue Grande, Barbizon. Open daily (except Tues) 10–12.30, 2–5. All day Sat, Sun and hols. Joint entry: 25F.
Tel. 01.60.66.22.27.

Millet's House, 29 Rue Grande, Barbizon. Open daily (except Tues) 10–12.30, 2–5. All day Sat, Sun and hols. Entry free.

Medieval Town, Moret-sur-Loing.

Tourist Offices

Office du Tourisme, 55 Rue Grande, 77630 Barbizon.
Tel. 01.60.66.41.87.

Office du Tourisme, Place de Samois, 77250 Moret-sur-Loing.
Tel. 01.60.70.41.66.

Barbizon

half-day

The Painters' Village, as it cutely advertises itself, is now one of the tourist hypes of the Paris region, containing pleasant surprises behind the arty-chic façade.

First impressions are best in **Rue de Fleury**, which extends north from the busy **Grande Rue** where most of the pre-impressionist action is. Turning right at the crossroads where the Paris road enters the village, I found myself in a cobbled country street with a smell of woodsmoke and manure.

Unpretentious farm buildings showed signs of life beyond the heavily restored commuter homes. And I half expected to see Sisley at his easel painting the Corot-like courtyard of Le Rosier, an old farm entered by a fine stone gateway. A few hundred yards up the street, the open country of the plain began.

It was an auspicious start. That was what the Grande Rue must once have been like. Walking its many attractions from north to south, I found it still had much charm on an uncrowded day.

Auberge Ganne (No. 92). After lavish restoration the famous artists' inn has recently reopened as the municipal museum, a treasure house of pre-impressionist memorabilia. It was once the only pub in town, launched in 1822 by former country policeman François Ganne and his wife as a grocer's shop cum cabaret. Cabaret meant country bar, where singing by the guests was not only allowed but encouraged. Corot entertained with lusty pro-monarchist songs, and even had the job of waking hungover artists with his rich, fruity voice.

Apart from Sisley's brief stay at the Auberge Ganne, the only record of an impressionist at Barbizon concerns a memorable lunch endured by the young Monet and Renoir at the Restaurant des Artistes. 'We should have been warned,' Renoir recounts. 'The word artist always hides something louche!' An old grandmother had been left in charge while the family were at Melun. She could make an omelette, she said, only the eggs might not be fresh because her grandchildren were trying to get them to hatch chicks. She was very sorry – her daughter, who normally did the cooking, was at Melun hospital because of a difficult pregnancy. So heart-searing were the old crone's stories of premature births and children born dead that Renoir and Monet hadn't the heart to run for it before the grisly omelette made its appearance.

It is a warning to beware Barbizon restaurants even today. There are a lot to choose from. And although they won't serve omelettes with rotten eggs, their tourist menus are often a rip-off – with one notable exception (Relais et Châteaux) to be mentioned later (p. 22). Better to picnic in the forest or save lunch for Chailly-en-Bière.

Rousseau's House and Museum (No. 55). The truth is that the pre-impressionists only made sketches outdoors, and the main work was done in the studio. Spirit of place was mostly generalized – for instance, *Road in the Forest of Fontainebleau, Storm Effect*. Specific places like *The Bodmer Oak* were rare. And Theodore Rousseau was no exception.

One of the first to use the i-word, he spoke of the forest giving 'a virgin impression of nature'. As an early environmentalist, Rousseau persuaded France's last king, Louis-Philippe, to do the one useful thing of his reign: protect the forest of Fontainebleau. And his two-storey, creeper-covered village house bears witness to the simplicity of his life there, although disappointingly there are no Rousseaus on view. Corot's lovely etching of a man in a punt and his almost menacingly dark forest scene show the quiet power of nature. The studio Rousseau made for himself in the barn, reached by an outside stone stairway, is opened up on request. Barbizon houses, even the humblest like this one, had small back gardens where workaholic artists could escape stuffy summer studios for a breath of forest air without being trampled underfoot by ubiquitous rivals.

Overleaf: Pre-impressionist Millet's The Angelus *(1857), the world's most reproduced picture after the Mona Lisa.*

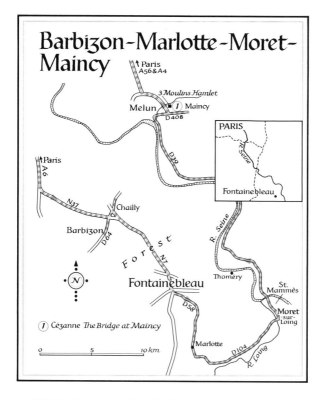

Barbizon-Marlotte-Moret-Maincy

(1) Cézanne *The Bridge at Maincy*

Millet's House and Studio (No. 29) is an even more basic nineteenth-century labourer's cottage: three rooms – kitchen, living room, bedroom – and an attic studio. A photo of Jean-François Millet shows him with a wife and four children, none of them looking specially happy.

You don't pay to see his home; it is privately owned, with a military-moustachioed custodian. He proved to be full of unexpected information. Seurat, that most revolutionary of impressionists, had apparently once painted at Barbizon.

The rooms are a homely clutter of pictures, sepia photos and faded memorabilia. An old stovepipe climbs to the ceiling in the room where sketches for *The Angelus* (O) are informally propped up on chairs.

The most interesting item is a composite display showing all the movements of physical labour that Millet so graphically captured: sweeping, sewing, chopping wood, beating linen, spinning, scything, threshing corn, constant bending and stretching. Later, Degas would do for Parisian laundresses and poorly paid corps-de-ballet dancers what Millet did for Fontainebleau peasants, however sentimental they may have appeared to Renoir. If it did not exactly improve their lot, their sweat is at least recorded for posterity.

The **House of Diaz (No. 28)** cannot be visited, but it is good to see that the fruits of Barbizon labour were rewarded. Beyond the plaque, stating that 'Narcisse-Virgile Diaz de la Peña lived here', a large (by Barbizon standards) front garden runs along a handsome, stone-carved Renaissance house with lattice windows.

Diaz's aristocratic Spanish-sounding name should fool no one. He began as poor as the rest of them, to become one of the group's most respected and influential members. Though his subjects were the usual lichen-covered rocks, gnarled old trees and heathery clearings, Diaz was one of the first to experiment with eliminating black and bitumen from his palette, as Pissarro and the impressionists would later do entirely. In Diaz's *Fontainebleau Forest* (O), painted in 1867 when Sisley, Monet, Renoir and Bazille had long since begun painting there, the shade is coloured – one of the hallmarks of the lightening-up process in impressionist works.

Hôtellerie du Bas-Bréau (No. 22), originally the Hôtel Siron, seduced the flusher clients, including Napoleon III and his Empress, in need of Monsieur Siron's superior comfort and less monotonous fare than the Auberge Ganne offered.

Renoir, late in life, was deeply suspicious of any temple of gastronomy bearing the newly fashionable word *hôtellerie* ('a word that never escapes my lips'), and the sight of false beams, studiously cracked plaster, carefully exposed bricks, and a *sommelier* sporting a genuine winemaker's blue smock and white cotton bonnet had the old painter shaking with ill-disguised mirth.

The Forest. To get a feeling of the forest as the impressionists knew it, a short walk near Barbizon is not too strenuous. Where Barbizon's **Grande Rue** ends, the forest begins. The **Allée des Vaches**, where once cows were driven to ponds or pasture, leads down a dead-straight avenue to the car park at the **Carrefour du Bas-Bréau**. All over the forest, at similar large clearings where tracks and roads converge, Peugeots and Renaults are neatly parked and Parisians lunch at tables – not on the grass and all respectably clothed.

I tried to identify Monet's *The Bodmer Oak at Bas-Bréau* but failed. The sturdy, hundred-year-old tree (according to its appearance in the painting) had no doubt long since been replaced. Alternatively, it might be somewhere else entirely. Identifying painting sites is often like detective work: instead of 'the bullet was fired at the victim from here', I deduce that 'the painter was here and the subject there'. Perhaps Monet's painting was done nearer **Chailly**, where he was staying at the time – in the area of the **Maison Forestière du Bas Bréau**. I could find no witness who knew the precise whereabouts of The Bodmer Oak. It was missing, presumed dead.

Chailly-en-Bière

1 hour

By whichever of several roads from Barbizon that you choose, **Chailly** is not more than a few minutes by car. Best to approach it from the N37, turning right on to a small access road with village church tower as a landmark. A perspective reminiscent of Millet's *The Angelus*, painted from a similar viewpoint on the plain.

From his own country childhood, Millet remembered his grandmother making him and the other children pray for the dear departed whenever the angelus-bell rang – three times a day. Renoir's distaste for Millet's sentimentalizing of poverty did not stop him from joining Monet, Bazille and Sisley at Chailly.

As art students they joined forces at Gleyre's studio in Paris (Chapter Seven, p. 160). Like four musketeers, they were already scheming to swashbuckle their way into the art establishment to save a duped public from its crimes. Each had his own favourite Barbizon painter: Monet did not agree with Renoir about Millet; Sisley was attracted to Corot's poetic classicism; Renoir veered between Diaz and the realist Courbet. None of their mentors, however, painted exclusively outdoors, as they were about to do.

Monet and Bazille spent the Easter vacation of 1863 in the forest of Fontainebleau. There were already more artists than tourists at Barbizon, and false Millets at dinner were worse than false peasants on canvas. They settled for the comparatively banal but more prosperous stagecoach post of Chailly, one and a half miles away. Bazille had a handsome allowance. Until the egalitarian student life of recent years, it was the habit of better-off students to subsidize the poorer, and Monet saw to it that they both lived in the style to which Bazille was accustomed.

The inns of Chailly – on the main road (N7) from Paris to the south via Fontainebleau – were like the Ritz compared to the Auberge Ganne. Picturesqueness was unimportant – they just wanted good bed and board within hiking distance of the forest. Over the next few years the four musketeers made several stays at both the **Auberge du Cheval Blanc** and also the **Auberge du Lion d'Or** in Chailly.

Both are still extant, nearly opposite each other on the busy main street. One is well worth visiting, the other a disaster area. **L'Auberge du Cheval Blanc** displays its old coaching inn sign but that's about all. I also took in the modest but famous **Church**, standing on a rise near the car park; the devout of Chailly are proud of *The Angelus* and still respond to its bell.

Monet's The Chailly Road, Forest of Fontainebleau *(1865) (O), once the woodcutters' log route to Paris, now the N7 racetrack for competitive commuters.*

The Fontainebleau Forest can still be seen as it was in Monet's day.

Monet's version of Déjeuner sur L'Herbe *(1866) (O), unlike Manet's studio work, was done largely from outdoor sketches. Also unlike Manet, Monet preferred his picnickers clothed.*

Millet and Rousseau are buried at the **Cemetery** on the Melun road.

Bazille wrote to his mother of that first Easter visit: 'I was with my best friend, Monet from Le Havre, who is very strong in landscape and has given me very helpful advice.' Monet had already begun one of several versions of *The Chailly Road, Forest of Fontainebleau* (O), a wide avenue thrusting straight as a royal ride through the tall trees.

In 1864 Monet persuaded the three other musketeers to accompany him to Chailly. Bazille and Sisley had some landscape experience in the field, Renoir very little. Monet, from his friendship in Normandy with older landscape painters, Jongkind and Boudin, was ahead of the game.

Their temperaments were as different as their styles later became. Monet was fiercely ambitious, Bazille eager to please. Sisley passionately serious. Amid the intensity at Chailly, Renoir had a refreshingly relaxed attitude. He was neither ambitious, eager to please, nor even particularly serious about his art. 'Too much like hard work' was his attitude to humping easel, canvas and paints for miles into the forest, and he persuaded his brother, Edmond, to be his 'bearer'.

One forest expedition nearly ended in disaster. Renoir was busy on a painting, experimenting in direct application of paint with his palette knife, a technique which gave the dark, solidly naturalistic look of a Courbet. He was not happy with the effect. And even less so when a group of day-trippers, loud-mouthed office clerks and drapers' assistants showing off to giggly milliners, made fun of the blue smock he wore as a porcelain decorator, his Paris job at the time.

Renoir, intent on his work, ignored the increasingly provocative louts. So he was unprepared for the boot that suddenly kicked the palette off his thumb – to a roar of mocking laughter and cheers. That did it. Renoir lost his cool, went for the lout, and was set upon by the whole gang. The milliners seemed intent on poking an eye out with the sharp points of their parasols.

Suddenly, out of the bushes limped a huge man. He had a wooden leg, but it didn't stop him laying into the louts,

and not even the girls' parasols were a match for his flailing stick. The day-trippers fled.

The man helped Renoir up, his eyes turning with interest to the painting in progress. 'You are very talented,' he said, 'but why do you paint so black?' Renoir replied that it didn't hurt Courbet to paint black. But the man pointed out how even the shadows of leaves caught the light, the trunk of a beech tree, too. 'Bitumen is finished! Lighten up your palette!'

The one-legged saviour turned out to be none other than the distinguished Diaz. Now Renoir respected him more than ever. It was advice he acted on. And, although that year (1864) he was accepted at the Salon for the first time, he later destroyed the work as too old-fashioned.

L'Auberge du Lion d'Or is still a typical, small nineteenth-century hôtel-restaurant, with a façade as unpretentious as its welcome is warm. The kind of place I love to discover on these explorations – somewhere pleasant to relax at lunchtime and sort out my impressions over a *salade paysanne* and *faux-filet au poivre vert*, with a bottle of the *cuvée du patron* at a most reasonable price.

In 1865 Monet had the pleasant added expense of Camille Doncieux, an artists' model with whom he had fallen in love. He ran up bills at the Cheval Blanc that he couldn't possibly pay, so he and Camille were forced to do a moonlight flit to the Lion d'Or. As the second inn wasn't even a hundred yards away, the proprietors must have known he was a bad risk. It says much for Monet's devious and determined charm that Mère Barbey and her village blacksmith husband accepted him. Luckily, he was also accepted at the Salon that year, a boost that his large ego badly needed.

At the same Salon, Manet was also represented – by *Olympia*. A friend told him a picture of his was causing a stir, and he thought the friend must mean *Olympia* – which did just that. Not a bit of it. The picture was *The Lighthouse at Honfleur*, a subject he had never painted in his life. Who was this talented Monet, with a name so close to his? Although his pride was hurt by the savaging of *Olympia*,

Manet generously encouraged Monet to attend his Café Guerbois evenings.

Now Monet wanted to pay homage to the master with his own *Déjeuner sur l'herbe*, inspired by Fontainebleau Forest. Hence the expanded vision of the picture, the vastness of its canvas – 'I can do bigger and better than Manet,' it seems to say – at approximately thirteen feet by nineteen feet, depicting twelve picnickers instead of Manet's intimate foursome.

On a visit to the Lion d'Or, Courbet gave Monet some welcome advice, as the picture was of the same dimensions as his *The Painter's Studio* (O). He was not at all sure that Monet could bring it off, but did not want to daunt the enthusiasm of a 25 year old. Among his models were Camille and Bazille, who posed for at least four of the men in the picture. Courbet is also included, sitting on the ground, looking towards us.

Misfortune, which was to blight much of Monet's early life, took over. First, a short-sighted British discus-thrower fractured Monet's shinbone in a forest clearing. Laid up at the Lion d'Or, Monet was ministered to by Bazille, who had been a medical student. In Bazille's *The Improvised Ambulance* (O), the versatile painter has fixed up a large earthenware pot above Monet's leg, an ingenious system of weights and pulleys to ensure the bruises were drip-cooled. He was back in the forest within a few days.

Then Monet was once again out of funds for his hotel bill. This was more serious. Already his small allowance had been cut off by his father, who had intended his son to be the new Winterhalter or Cabanel, painting pallid portraits of the Empress Eugénie or prurient, milksop nudes for lecherous provincial notaries at thousands of francs apiece; a generous Le Havre aunt's contribution had been spent on painting materials; and Bazille was temporarily skint himself. So Monet had to leave the sketches with Mère Barbey as surety for the unpaid bill.

Later he redeemed them. But the three completed segments of the vast painting also had to be surrendered to a creditor. In 1884 Monet found them rotting in an Argenteuil barn. He preserved the two good segments and destroyed the other. They were sold separately. The sale led to much controversy in the art market: a Lebanese collector had one segment, which he wouldn't part with, but Georges Wildenstein presented his segment to the State. Wildenstein's generosity helped secure the second segment, and thanks to him we can now see them both at the Orsay. A small study of the whole is at the Pushkin, Moscow, a living proof that the Lion d'Or at Chailly had seen the first signs of a master of sensuality, the serenity of sunlight filtering through leaves on to long, taffeta dresses and a heart with an arrow carved in the silvery bark of a tree.

Marlotte

half-hour

Marlotte, a later haunt of the four musketeers, lies on the southern edge of the forest. The N7 took me speedily to the **Carrefour de l'Obélisque**, a roundabout on the outskirts of **Fontainebleau** where six roads meet, of which the smallest is signposted to Marlotte.

The narrow forest road dips to cross the **Gorge aux Loups**, a favourite painting area, before entering the long **Rue Murger**. Apart from containing the two important impressionist sights, the street is named after Henry Murger, whose bestselling short stories, *Scenes of Bohemian Life*, predated the impressionists by a decade.

L'Auberge de la Mère Antoni (No. 37) is recognizable by its rusty old inn-sign and plaque: 'Pierre-Auguste Renoir stayed at Marlotte 1863–1868 and there created his famous picture "The Cabaret of The Red Clog".' Dates and title are misleading. Renoir stayed only intermittently, first with Bazille and Sisley, to escape the overcrowded folksiness of the Barbizon area.

The picture's title better fits the exaggerated description by the Goncourt Brothers: 'It appears that, twenty-four hours round the clock, *chez* Antoni is like a wedding party in the Paris outskirts . . . guitar music, plates smashing on heads, and sometimes a knife fight.' And maybe even a Red Clog Dance? Renoir hated

picturesqueness, and his painting, usually known simply as *Mère Antoni's Inn*, shows behaviour that would not disgrace a *salon de thé* in Trouville.

Murger peers somewhat caustically at the unbohemian artists from a drawing on the wall behind. Nana, *la patronne*'s daughter, clears the table of what could be teacups for *le five o'clock*: Sisley was there, with Monet (in a typically rakish straw hat) and Renoir's architect friend, Jules Lecoeur. Lecoeur is the only unbearded one; he lived down the street and had better access to hot shaving water. Forest artists were known as *les bisons*, because of their perpetual hairiness.

Sisley is next to Nana. She was only too willing to add to his rake's reputation. And easy virtue led to literary fame: Zola is alleged to have borrowed her name for his most famous *cocotte*. A sheet of the newspaper Zola wrote for, *L'Evénement*, serves as a tablecloth. The realist Zola not only championed the impressionists' rebellious beginnings in print, but himself stayed *chez* Mère Antoni while writing *L'Assommoir* to get the right atmosphere for his low-life pub in the novel. Zola had a thirst for material like a *bison* for booze. Friendship with artists – he was at school with Cézanne in Aix-en-Provence – gave him the background for his later novel set in the Paris art world, *L'Oeuvre*.

Now all that can be seen of Mère Antoni's pub is badly in need of a little care and attention. An entrance from the street took me into the romantic remains of the Renaissance garden, where painters and writers relaxed, drank, played and vied for the favours of Nana.

Jules Lecoeur's House (No. 16). Continuing past a beautiful seventeenth-century stone house with a tower, I came to Jules Lecoeur's, also with a tower, constructed by an eccentric Venezuelan painter who liked to sleep beneath the stars on its roof.

The house had romantic associations for Renoir. It was here that he met the first great love of his life. Eighteen-year-old Lise Tréhot, a postmaster's daughter, was sister of Jules Lecoeur's companion, Clémence. In the next four years of struggle and poverty he was to paint twenty pictures of her, many of them with Fontainebleau forest motifs – as Diana the Huntress, a nymph, and most notably *Lise with Parasol*, which was accepted for the Salon of 1868. With the portraits of Lise he abandoned traditional clichés and began to find himself as his own painter.

The women in their lives helped give the future impressionists a modern look. As models, they were an inspiration; as companions, they were brave to take on such precarious lovers. They had staying power. Even Renoir's Lise lasted six years.

For Camille, Monet's companion, it was a life sentence. Not only was she a striking, dark model whose portrait in a flowing green dress was accepted at the Salon in 1866, but her even temperament saw them both through highs and lows with extraordinary equanimity.

Then it was Sisley's turn. Around the time of painting everyday village life – a man chopping wood, women going about their daily chores, *A Street in Marlotte* in the grey-gold light of early autumn – he met, in Paris, Marie Lescouezec, a slight brunette from Meurthe-en-Moselle. She came from a middle-class family fallen on hard times, and modelled to support herself. Renoir said of Sisley: 'He never could resist a skirt. We were walking in the street, talking about the weather. Suddenly, no more Sisley. I would find him making out with a girl.' Marie was not just any girl; Renoir's portrait of the couple shows Sisley, metamorphosed from rake to perfect English gentleman in velvet jacket, gazing at her with the total concentration of serious involvement; in her candy-striped dress, she leans on his arm with the confidence of a woman who knows she has tamed him. The couple lasted a lifetime.

This right bank viewpoint of Sisley's The Bridge at Moret *(1893) no longer has the big millhouse blocking the medieval Porte de Bourgogne. Sisley painted many versions of the bridge.*

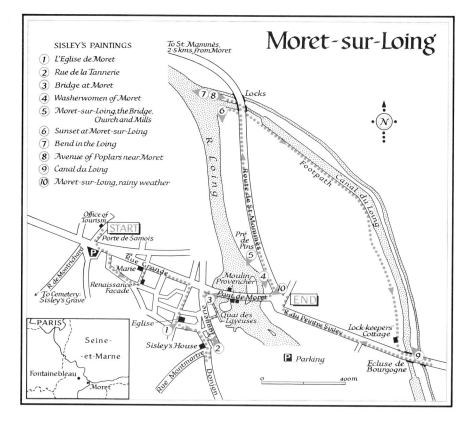

SISLEY'S PAINTINGS

1. L'Eglise de Moret
2. Rue de la Tannerie
3. Bridge at Moret
4. Washerwomen of Moret
5. Moret-sur-Loing, the Bridge, Church and Mills
6. Sunset at Moret-sur-Loing
7. Bend in the Loing
8. Avenue of Poplars near Moret
9. Canal du Loing
10. Moret-sur-Loing, rainy weather

From Marlotte days on, the survival of the young impressionists in their struggle for recognition was greatly helped by these women. But there was nothing yet that had the makings of a group; Manet was somewhat aloof and Degas wittily contemptuous of *pleinairistes*: 'If I was the Government, I would have a brigade of gendarmes keeping a watch on those who paint landscapes from nature. Oh, I wish no man death; but I wouldn't be against them putting a little shot in their guns for a start.'

Although their style was not yet truly impressionist, the four musketeers of Fontainebleau forest had at least begun, as Monet so perfectly put it, 'capturing the light and throwing it on canvas'.

Moret-sur-Loing

overnight

Next stop was a flash-forward to the fraught, final nineteen years of Sisley's life, spent at various times at **Moret-sur-Loing** and the nearby village of **Veneux-Nadon**, while he also worked at the Seine-side barge port of **St-Mammès**. Never achieving the later financial security of Monet or Renoir, Sisley found living near Paris at Marly-le-Roi too expensive. If Moret was the scene of debilitating disappointment, the body of work Sisley accomplished there shows a deep, sensitive love of its unusually varied landscape. He did for the east Seine what Monet did for the west.

A tributary of the Seine, the Loing's limpid waters earlier inspired Corot. The D104, which runs between the edge of the forest and the river, via the riverside town of **Montigny**, took me from Marlotte to Moret in twenty minutes.

Moret would be worth visiting without the Sisley connection. On a small river near its confluence with a great one, its medieval splendours are bathed in a limpid light that attracted a great colourist like Sisley with its infinite changes. From June to September an inventive *son et lumière* show dramatizes Moret's past glories and those who passed through it – the mystic Saint Louis, Henri IV thwarted in love, Napoleon returning from Elba, and First World War Prime Minister Clemenceau, who was Monet's close friend (Chapter Eight, p. 184).

The **tourist office**, near the bust of Sisley in **Place de Samois**, put me on the right track with an excellent illustrated booklet and itinerary for following the Sisley trail.

Walking the Sisleys

half-day

The twelfth-century gateway, **Porte de Samois**, leads into the main street, and I was too close to the town hall gardens to pass up Moret's most important non-Sisley site. An ornate, stone-carved Renaissance façade sumptuously adorns a house where the ubiquitous François I lived. It was definitely worth the detour.

L'Eglise de Notre-Dame. Sisley painted a series depicting its flamboyant Gothic façade in all lights and seasons, his easel planted on the doorstep of a corner house by the marketplace. This was Sisley's church round the corner – he makes us feel it.

Sisley's House (No. 9 Rue du Donjon) is sizeable, standing in its own garden. Now privately owned, it has a plaque over the front door but this is indistinct. A sense of brooding melancholy hangs over the place: it is where Marie died of a terrible cancer of the tongue. As Renoir described it: 'Her pretty little face was all deformed. And from so little!' A mere three months later, Sisley himself died of cancer of the throat. The serenity in the paintings gives no hint of fate's injustice, the final agony of an ill-starred, loving couple. They are buried together in **Moret Cemetery**.

Rue de la Tannerie. At the bottom of the steps from **Rue Montmartre**, the view of the street and church is almost exactly as in the 1892 painting. I took a detour down an alley to **Quai des Laveuses** to get the feel of Moret's waterfront – weir, bridge, the mill on its island, and the tree-lined Loing disappearing into the forest.

Pont de Moret. On the right bank several of the painter's angles were easily detectable from the illustrations provided in my booklet: *The Washer-women of Moret* on a grass bank where there is now a willow tree, downstream of the bridge; *Moret-sur-Loing, the Bridge, the Church, and its Mills* from the shady riverside meadow **Pré des Pins**; that painting, and others from this viewpoint, show the **Moulin Provencher** much larger in those days – two big white buildings with red roofs and mill-wheels in mid-river – than it is today.

A ten-minute walk down the St-Mammès road leads to where the **Loing Canal** joins the river. Reached from the road bridge, a path continues to the tip of a narrow island with three viewpoints: upstream, *Sunset at Moret-sur-Loing*, a wintry scene with the town shrouded in mist; downstream, *Bend in the Loing* towards the railway viaduct, with men fishing; and *Avenue of Poplars near Moret*, looking back towards the canal lock – early autumn sunshine turning the shadow on the bridge mauve.

After a stroll along the pedestrians-only canal towpath to **L'Ecluse de Bourgogne** (Burgundy Lock), I was at the scene shown on a 1989 French postage stamp, celebrating Sisley's 150th anniversary. Though the poplars along the towpath have been regrettably savaged since *Canal du Loing* (O), the little lock-keeper's house is still the same. From there, **Rue du Peintre Sisley** leads back to the roundabout on the town bridge's right bank and my favourite *Moret-sur-Loing, Rainy Weather*. All the familiar landmarks are bathed in a glistening, sepia glow. It is painfully sad, a visual epitaph.

St-Mammès

1½ hours

The frugality of Sisley's last years made anything but a simple lunch seem like bad taste. On the short drive to **St-Mammès**, just before the railway viaduct, the riverside Auberge du Soleil looks old enough to have been there in Sisley's time. A few parked trucks are always a good sign. 'They've got *coq au vin* today!' a departing truck-driver confided. Another good sign: three generations were eating in the kitchen of this family restaurant.

Port de la Batellerie. Sisley found further inspiration on the river port's quayside. Inland water transport, now sadly in decline, was then in its heyday. The painting of two barges – done from the war memorial by the bridge – shows the busy action of the Seine as a

Overleaf: Water, as a Cèzanne subject, was usually southern and warm. Cool water bubbling under The Bridge at Maincy (1879) (O) near Fontainebleau Forest was an exception.

transport artery and the forest of Fontainebleau in the distance.

Quai de la Croix Rouge (No. 19). A curved archway leads off the quayside into a replica of Sisley's *Farmyard at St-Mammès*, a whitewashed, red-tiled décor with higgledy-piggledy roofs and rickety wooden balconies. Riverside farmyards were convenient gathering spots for fruit and vegetables grown directly behind the farmhouse and transported by boat to Les Halles market in Paris.

Les Coteaux de la Celle-sous-Moret. Across the river, upstream of the bridge, Sisley's golden, autumnal slopes are reflected in barely rippling water. From the right bank of the Seine at least four paintings show the long waterfront of two-storey houses, church and barges.

Sisley remained a true impressionist long after the last group show of 1886. His contemporaries had moved on, but he remained, his detractors claimed, stuck in a rut. Not for him the backbiting and infighting of the art world; he just got on with the only work he knew and loved. It was both a strength and a weakness. True to himself, he lost touch with friends and dealers. He wasn't envious of others' success, just perplexed by his own apparent failure. Monet, by then doing well, visited him a week before his death, to settle the future of his children and say goodbye.

In the sale of the Chocquet collection only a year later, *The Seine at Billancourt* was expected to fetch about 500 francs. It went for 6000 francs, an untold sum for a Sisley. But now, posthumously, he had scarcity value. Another collector, the pastry-cook Mürer, called him 'the subtlest of the impressionists, with a poet's soul and paintbrush'.

Maincy

half-hour

Devotees of Cézanne should take a leisurely route back to Paris, via **Melun**, where the meridional artist stayed from May 1879 to February 1880 and painted the definitive *Bridge at Maincy* (O). It is a pleasant drive, with the D39 hugging the serpentine Seine's right bank as far as Melun, where you take the D408 to the village of **Maincy**. Later you can speedily bypass the dull outskirts of Paris by using autoroutes A56 and A4 for the return to the city.

Cézanne made several visits to the forest of Fontainebleau, staying at Marlotte with the four musketeers. He had met Monet at the Académie Suisse as an art student; the other connection was his schoolfriend Zola, and *Forest Scene*, painted in the 1860s, shows the influence of the Barbizon school, particularly Courbet. After his initiation into landscape impressionism with Pissarro at Pontoise (Chapter Five, p. 108) in the Seventies, Cézanne landscapes more usually depict the dry, hot Provençal country.

Not merely ahead of its time, the picture is ahead of Cézanne – with hints of cubism in the reflection of bridge and lush green foliage in water. It is a wild, savage, poetic place that he depicts, and I couldn't wait to find it.

This was easier said than done. The village of Maincy is near the seventeenth-century château of Vaux-le-Vicomte, where the elaborate waterworks (imitated by Louis XIV at Versailles) of the Le Nôtre gardens are fed by the tiny River Almont. So far so good. The Almont was clearly the river, but which was the bridge? After sleuthing my way beyond a modern concrete excrescence and another bridge that was little more than a few stepping-stones, I discovered that Cézanne's was not strictly at Maincy at all. From Maincy Church take the Trois Moulins road for about one and a half miles. At the Château des Trois Moulins, near the entrance gate, a lane descends to a bridge badly damaged by recent floods, famous on canvas but little known even to the locals. A certain Colonel Johnson, an Englishman who lived in a nearby manor, built it so he could cross the river on foot. The mystery was solved.

LES BATIGNOLLES–PIGALLE

The nineteenth-century details remain at Gare St Lazare.

The first Paris centre of impressionist action lay to the south of the hill of Montmartre, between the Parc Monceau's mock Gothic residences of the *nouveaux riches* and the bohemian cafés of Place Pigalle. An expanding village known as Les Batignolles neighboured the railway tracks and bridges of the Europe quarter and the narrow residential streets of St-Georges. Not to mention a few threatened fields with cows where could be heard the occasional sound of a property magnate's hunting horn. According to Renoir, priceless eighteenth-century furniture, found in old buildings being torn down, was used by wealthy scrap-metal merchants for firewood.

By mid-century, cornfields had made way for the Gare St-Lazare, terminus of the first French railway (1838). Two years earlier King Louis-Philippe had closed the gambling dens of the Palais-Royal, and the louche life of Paris also moved north-west. Artists, perennially attracted to their Sohos and Greenwich Villages, moved with it. For cheap living and studios, the poorer artists followed the trajectory of the Palais-Royal prostitutes, up the still countrified hill; nearer to the new Gare St-Lazare that allowed Monet, Renoir, Pissarro and Sisley to travel quickly by train between their painting grounds in the country and the Paris powerhouse of avant-garde art. Streetwalkers benefited, too, from a lucrative flow of comers-and-goers a discreet distance from the station, in the warren of streets around the church of Notre-Dame-de-Lorette. They were known as *lorettes*.

What would the impressionists have made of today's Boulevard de Clichy? In its sex shows and videos, art can be said to have lowered its sights. Yet apart from one comparatively short stretch of boulevard and a few back alleys of melancholy lubricity, Les Batignolles–Pigalle still has many period enclaves: narrow streets, hidden studios, shady little squares, wide tree-lined avenues with nineteenth-century ashlar buildings as depicted by the wealthy Gustave Caillebotte, whose family lived at 77 Rue Miromesnil.

Artists and writers flocked there. Young journalist Emile Zola espoused the cause of Manet and followers, mainly to stir up the stuffy and help get himself known as a rebel. In 1869 Manet painted his portrait (O): although Zola's apartment on Rue de Clichy was the scene, details reveal the painter's own self-obsession – a copy of *Olympia* on the wall, nineteenth-century Japanese prints, the pamphlet Zola had written about Manet peeping from behind a pen's feather. 'That portrait isn't bad,' Zola later commented, 'but Manet was not a very great painter; his talent never fully developed.' And in 1902 he confessed: '. . . I can't really get excited about painting.'

Manet and Zola were both *habitués* of the Café Guerbois. There was a saying: 'Cafés fly a flag and you judge a man in Paris by the one he frequents.'

It is still true. From the Parc Monceau to Pigalle, a vigorous spontaneity was to be found in its café life, and Manet preferred to be known as *spontanéiste* rather than *impressioniste*. In search of low-life inspiration came the talented slummers rich and poor: writers Maupassant and Daudet; poets Mallarmé, Verlaine and Rimbaud; and, of course, Monet, Renoir, Pissarro, Bazille and Sisley, with their eye for life as it was lived and whoever it was lived by. In tandem with the impressionists' close observation of life, there was vociferous participation – in passionate debate of the latest artistic scandal at the Guerbois, where Manet held court, or later at the Nouvelle-Athènes, where Degas took over as an acerbic godfather, respected but feared for his savage tongue.

Heads reeling with impressions, and sketches complete, the pre-1870 urban painters – notably Manet and Degas – would return from cafés and streets to a bourgeois formality after a brief skirmish among the proles.

The lifestyles of artists in Les Batignolles varied widely. By the 1880s rich official artists had invaded the Parc Monceau and the Avenue de Villiers, and some, like Carolus-Duran and Gervex, even mingled with the rebels at their cafés, in order to be aware of the enemy. Meissonier, known for his military epics, lived at 131 Boulevard Malesherbes and had a street named after him. In 1886, when van Gogh came to Paris, Meissonier paintings sold for 840,000 francs. And soon 202 painters had the Légion d'honneur – including Manet, the first of the rebels to be officially recognized.

Manet led a double life, one *bon chic, bon genre* as a family man at his town house in Rue des Batignolles, the other as a gentleman bohemian holding open house for models and artists after work at his studio in Rue de St-Petersbourg. Favourite models were women who were painters in their own right, socialite Berthe Morisot and Spanish journalist's daughter Eva Gonzalès. Manet was a vocal upholder of a woman's right to a career, believing women to be too much under the clergy's influence with their eternal do-gooding. In one Manet portrait of her, Morisot hides with ironic modesty behind a fan. The mockery of a duenna indicates an intimate, comic understanding between them.

Her friendship with Manet was more than a young girl's crush on an older man she admired as an artist. Less blatantly sexual than the demi-mondaine *Lady with Fans* (O) and *Portrait of Jeanne Duval* (Baudelaire's mistress), his *Repose* (1870) shows Morisot's large dark eyes fixing us – or rather Manet painting her – with lovelight in them. In virginal white and discreetly upright on her brown plush sofa, Berthe seems languidly available, the nice girl from Passy who knows the sign language of a dangling fan. She describes Manet in a letter to her sister Edma: 'I have never seen such an expressive face: he laughed, a little embarrassed, swearing that his picture was very bad and would therefore be extremely successful. I find his disposition charming and infinitely pleasing. His painting still evokes an impression of wild fruit, sometimes a little green.'

Whether they made love, which is improbable but not impossible, we shall never know. Manet's philanderings were hush-hush and Berthe had the extreme discretion of her class. Safely accompanied by her parents, she attended the more elegant evenings, when the Manets were at home to princes and bankers, and Suzanne Manet entertained at the piano, playing Beethoven, Schumann and the new rage, Wagner. Berthe married Eugène Manet, the painter's brother, who was the next best thing to the painter. For the Manets and the Morisots, it was a very small world within a much larger one.

Salons were the thing in Les Batignolles. Every Tuesday the symbolist poet Mallarmé entertained the upcoming and the arrived, including the symbolist painter Odilon Redon, the Manets, Berthe Morisot, Renoir and, of course, Degas. Anywhere Manet went, you were likely to see Degas. They were of the same cloth, and only the best tailors cut it. Their friendship, however, was as volatile as the Paris stockmarket.

More travelled in his youth than any of the young impressionists, thanks to prosperous Neapolitan relatives, Degas had an early acquaintance with Italian classical art. 'Oh Giotto, don't prevent me from seeing Paris,' was his silent prayer, 'And Paris, don't prevent me from seeing Giotto.' The conflict between classicism and modernity was a natural paradox, for in spite of his youthful travels Degas was the most 'local' of the impressionists. Born a banker's son in 1834 at 8 Rue St-Georges, he died near-blind and resembling a *clochard* in 1917 at 6 Boulevard de Clichy, a ten-minute walk away.

Oddly for a banker at that time, Degas's father gave him every encouragement to become a painter, even providing helpful critical and technical advice. Hilaire Degas had singers and musicians among his close friends, though Edgar's upbringing was every bit a gentleman painter's of the period. There was a naturally rebellious side to him: a dashing self-portrait (1862) shows his youthful posture of renegade, shirtfront open, challenging the art establishment. He teased Manet about his relentlessly bourgeois aspirations and constant hankering after official recognition; Manet teased him about his fraught relations with women.

As Berthe Morisot was to Manet, so Mary Cassatt was to Degas – model and protégée. Morisot versus Cassatt is a constant argument among impressionist buffs; Cassatt wins on points, partly thanks to a most assiduous taskmaster in Degas, who depicts her with her sister Lydia, studiously consulting a guidebook in the Louvre. Later in life the American artist bridled at the unflattering realism of *Miss Cassatt Sitting, Holding Playing Cards*. Of this she wrote: 'It has qualities of art, but it is so hard to take being shown as such a repugnant personage that I do not wish anyone to know that I posed for it.' Their long-lasting, tempestuous friendship is probably the nearest Degas ever got to love.

The most permanent woman in Degas's life was his housekeeper, Zoé. At the home he inhabited longest – in Rue Victor-Massé, where he lived for twenty-five years on three floors – she was instructed never to shake the priceless oriental carpets nor dust too vigorously the Louis-Philippe salon furniture inherited from his father, nor his private collection: 13 works by Delacroix, 6 Corots, 7 Cézannes, 8 Gauguins, 8 Monets, 20 Ingres and 1800 Daumier lithographs. Nor was Zoé ever to attempt to put any semblance of order into his chaotic studio with its huge zinc tub in which the model posed for *After the Bath* (O). Paul Valéry described it as 'an old bachelor's home where dust is happy'.

Before the 1870 war the well-to-do of the Batignolles group were Degas, Manet, Cézanne, Sisley and Bazille. Caillebotte joined them later. The poor members were Pissarro, Monet and Renoir.

Renoir's easygoing sociability, however, made him a natural for the salons where he looked for buyers for his paintings. The tailor's son crossed class barriers as if they didn't exist. His companion, Aline, a Burgundian winemaker's daughter with lush beauty and a peach-plump, glowing skin texture that presaged the Renoir Nude, was a great asset. Aline wore her clothes with style and, when Renoir began to have a little success, she too was as much at ease with chic nights *chez* Charpentier, Renoir's publisher patron, as at a riverside boating party.

Their meeting was romantic. With a little money coming in from his assiduous dealer, Durand-Ruel, Renoir rented a studio in Rue St-Georges. He lunched every day at a dairy opposite. Madame Camille, *la patronne*, didn't mind giving him credit; she had eyes on Renoir as a prospective husband for her daughter. But in an unguarded moment she introduced him to a couple of Burgundian dressmakers, mother and daughter, who also lunched there. Soon Aline was modelling for Renoir. She was his ideal – an attractive country girl who loved good food and was not too fussy about her waistline.

In his memoir of his father, Jean Renoir describes Renoir's presentiment that he and Aline would meet. 'Since the moment he had held a paintbrush, perhaps even before, in his childhood dreams, thirty years before knowing her, Renoir created the portrait of Aline Charigot.' When he worked as an apprentice to a porcelain decorator, she was the Venus on a painted vase. She was the Marie Antoinette on a painted box, her retroussé nose quite at odds with the royal likeness. And now here she was, an image made flesh. Oscar Wilde later reassured Renoir, there was an artistic precedent for this: 'Before Turner, there was no London fog'.

And before Monet, there was no Paris train smoke. The painter who was to immortalize the Gare St-Lazare was, like Renoir, on the wrong side of the tracks. His shuttling back and forth by train between Les Batignolles and Le Havre, Bennecourt, Bougival and Argenteuil would have been easy for a well-to-do bachelor like Degas. Monet had a family to support and no family money to support it with. Just possible if you were as frugal as Pissarro; tough if you had the best tailor in town and were determined to be a two-studio artist – one in the country, one in town.

Monet drove himself hard, and his sufferings were never from laziness. Monet and money were quickly parted, and he had no compunction about hustling his richer friends with begging letters. Bazille bought *Women in the Garden* (O) for an over-the-top price of 2500 francs, which he could ill afford on his small allowance; Monet rode over him like a one-man Norman conquest every time he was late with the 50-franc monthly instalments. His Parisian peregrinations were legendary – all in the Batignolles area, new escape routes from old debts: Hôtel de Londres et de New York; 8 Rue d'Isley (1871–4), near the Gare St-Lazare; 17 Rue Moncey, rented in Caillebotte's name (1877); after expulsion from his Argenteuil home, an apartment at 26 Rue d'Edimbourg (1878); and, finally, a studio at 20 Rue de Vintimille – after his family had moved once more to the country at Vétheuil.

Monet's ability to detach from the trials of family life showed a certain ruthlessness, for which he had frequent pangs of remorse. Who would detect the troubled man behind *Parisians Enjoying the Parc Monceau*, painted in 1878? *Enjoying* is the key word. It shows the bourgeois pleasures of family life in a prosperous neighbourhood's park. A volume of space enclosed by trees is filled with colour-bearing, filtered light, turning the path pink, the grass a vivid green and yellow speckled with bold, dark shadows, the faces of the people red – presentiments of the non-realistic colours of Gauguin and the fauves.

The *Gare St-Lazare* series (O) best represents Monet in his Batignolles life, and the station is a convenient place to begin a walk. It took me a full day, with leisurely stops for refreshment and a slow-food lunch.

A Walk

IN

Les Batignolles–Pigalle

Manet's Gare St-Lazare (1873), more accurately called The Railroad.

INFORMATION

Walk (full day).

Start: Métro Gare St-Lazare. End: Métro St-Georges. **Lunch**: Rue Cavalotti–Place de Clichy area.

Refreshment, Meals and Overnight

Restaurants, Bars and Cafés

Wepler (café-bar, shellfish), **(B)**, 14 Place de Clichy.
Tel. 01.45.22.53.24.

Charlot (shellfish), **(B)**, 128bis Boulevard de Clichy.
Tel. 01.45.22.47.08.

Galère des Rois (restaurant), **(B)**, 8 Rue Cavalotti.
Tel. 01.42.93.34.58.

Le Bouclard (bistro), **(C)**, 1 Rue Cavalotti. Tel. 01.45.22.60.01.

☆ La Joconde (bar), junction of Rue de la Rochefoucauld and Rue Notre-Dame-de-Lorette.

A la Place St-Georges (bar), Place St-Georges.

Hotels

Mercure Montmartre, **(B)**, 1 Rue Caulaincourt. Tel. 01.44.69.70.70.

☆ Concorde St-Lazare, **(A)**, 108 Rue St-Lazare.
Tel. 01.40.08.44.44.

Hôtel Aurore Montmartre, **(C)**, 76 Rue de Clichy.
Tel. 01.48.74.85.56.

Museum

Gustave Moreau, 14 Rue de la Rochefoucauld. Open 10–12.45, 2–5.15; Mon, Wed, 11–5.15. Closed Tues. Entry: 17F.
Tel. 01.48.74.38.50.

Tourist Office

Office du Tourisme, 127 Avenue des Champs-Elysées, 75008. Open daily 9–8.
Tel. 01.49.52.53.54.

A view along the Rue de Vienne.

A Walk in Les Batignolles–Pigalle

whole day

Gare St-Lazare. Conveniently served by three Métro lines, the station dominates the heart of Haussmannland and the *grands boulevards*. A suitably period décor of brass banisters, marble steps and Venetian lamps greeted me at the Place de Rome entrance for the suburban lines.

It is a big station by Paris standards, a vast hangar instantly recognizable by the canopy's apex at the Pont de l'Europe end, where the wide expanse of curving rails narrows in a mesh of points to be funnelled under the bridge. With more than an echo of London's Crystal Palace, the glass, iron and stone structure also mirrored the triangular apex of architect Victor Baltard's church of St-Augustine, built in 1860. The railways were the religion of the century and deserved their 'cathedrals of the new humanity', as Théophile Gautier described these monumental termini.

Monet's motive was less grandiose. Far from deterred by critics sneering at the mists obscuring the boats and harbour of Le Havre in *Impression, Sunrise* (Marmottan-Monet), he would go one better: the thick smoke from railway engines as they got up steam for departure obscured practically everything in sight. The play of sunlight on billowing smoke was an enchantment, he told Renoir. 'They'll have to delay the Rouen train half an hour,' he said. 'The light is better half an hour after it's left.' Renoir thought he'd gone crazy.

Although broke, he had his least shiny suit pressed. Camille repaired the lace cuffs of his least frayed shirt and, rapping on the door with a gold-topped cane, he swaggered into the offices of the Director of the Western Railways. 'I've decided to paint your station,' he loftily informed the Director, who was too scared to admit he didn't know Claude Monet from a Rouen assistant signalman. 'For a long time, I've been hesitating between the Gare du Nord and the Gare St-Lazare, and I've decided yours has more character.'

What was to be the first Monet 'series' fuses people and machines and buildings in perfect symmetry. Figures are dwarfed by great clouds of steam, by the engines, by the vastness of the station and the hazy apartment blocks. The cliff-like buildings beyond the station are as awe-inspiring as the cliffs at Etretat that Monet painted at the other end of the line.

Place de l'Europe. Reached by **Rue de Rome**, the bridge beyond Monet's train smoke was one of the engineering feats of nineteenth-century Paris – massive masonry piers and iron trellises carrying no fewer than six intersecting streets over the rail tracks.

Manet's rather more intimate, gentler view of *The Railroad* shows a summery little girl watching the trains beyond the garden railings, in the charge of Manet's favourite model, the versatile Victorine Meurent – Olympia one day, Nanny the next. The gardens survive, with manicured lawns and trim conifers, and the neighbourhood around the bridge is still residential. For work on his *Pont de L'Europe* Caillebotte constructed a special glassed-in omnibus from which he painted the bridge and its passers-by in all weathers. In those days, without fear of a parking ticket.

As a naval engineer, Caillebotte was ingenious. He was also the richest of the group by several million francs. Surprisingly, he was one of the most socially aware. Workers sweat in *Planning the Floor* (O). His mother and brother in the heavily *haut bourgeois* scene depicted in *Lunch* (1876) do not appear to communicate, his brother cutting his meat on a table covered with crystal while his mother, many silver dishes away, is served by the butler. In the midst of plenty, Caillebotte understood the alienation of classes and generations. His 1994 retrospective, described as 'The Modernity of an Unrecognized Artist', had people astonished at just how modern he still is. Alienation is a malaise of the technocratic society, too: for all its architectural splendours under the Mitterrand reign and before, new Paris today often has the same chilling anonymity of Haussmann's stark new streets and boulevards, a mechanical precision where man becomes just another solitary machine in a cityscape.

For as long as Monet took to paint eight masterpieces, the Gare St-Lazare (1877) was his. He planted his easel on platforms, between the rails, in the engine sheds. Trains were delayed, coal was not spared, engines delivered smoke to order.

From his Rue de St Petersburg balcony opposite Rue de Berne (then Rue Mosnier), Manet did Laying Paving Stones in Rue Mosnier (1876), also the street decked with flags for the fourteenth of July. War damage repairs and a man on crutches are reminders of the Commune uprising.

A late arrival in the group, Caillebotte did not give up his law studies for the Beaux-Arts till 1870, while continuing to pursue his passion for sailing and boat-building. Monet met this man of many parts at Argenteuil and found that the playboy façade hid an artistic sensitivity. Monet helped him overcome his reticence about painting, and Caillebotte helped Monet construct his painting-boat. He also put together the largest early impressionist collection, later bequeathed to the State amid much controversy (Chapter Seven, p. 176). Of the sixteen Monets, three were of the Gare St-Lazare.

Rue de St-Petersbourg runs from Place de l'Europe to **Place de Clichy**. At **No. 4**, Manet had a ground-floor studio, at the junction with **Rue de Berne** where a gap in the tall buildings opposite let in the light. It was a vast, opulently decorated salon with gilt wood panelling, which the painter kept sparsely furnished apart from hundreds of paintings and drawings on the walls. Manet used much of the space to exhibit works of colleagues, hoping one of his rich friends might buy.

On his shady balcony Manet had three friends pose in a strangely formalized group: landscape artist Antoine Guillemet, violinist Fanny Klaus, and Berthe Morisot ('I look more peculiar than ugly – a bit of a *femme fatale*'). His palette is restricted: beautiful blacks and whites interspersed with occasional eye-catching colour – the man's blue silk tie, green railings, shutters and parasol. Again, like Caillebotte's people, Manet's group in *The Balcony* (1869) (O) do not communicate. They appear at first sight to be meaningless, just unrelated figures in a cityscape. Yet we know they can't be unrelated in this particular spot. It creates an atmosphere of tension, malaise. Manet creates the same subtle alienation effect in *Lunch* (1868), where the cook is an impartial witness to Manet's son Léon who, for some reason, is not talking to a guest, the amiable opera singer Faure.

Léon had most inauspicious beginnings. As a young merchant seaman, Manet met a Dutch piano teacher, Suzanne Leenhoff, and got her pregnant. His mother heard of it and made instant plans to hide it from Monsieur Manet, who would have had apoplexy. Madame Manet sent Suzanne away to give birth. By fiddling of legalities in high places baby Léon was registered as Suzanne's son by an unknown father, thereby losing one parent; at his baptism Léon was given the fictitious surname Koella, with Suzanne and Manet registered merely as his godparents, thereby losing his second parent. To make doubly sure of the cover-up, Léon was boarded out with a nurse. Manet's father died in peace, without ever knowing of his grandson's existence. And Léon, aged ten, could safely return to the bosom of his absentee parents, who then married at last.

That was not the end of it. With the date of his birth clearly indicating conception before his parents' marriage, Léon was always introduced as Suzanne's younger brother – even to Picasso.

This black Feydeau farce was played out in Les Batignolles. Manet's second studio in Rue de St-Petersbourg, **No. 51**, is opposite the present Maison du Lait, and his last home, **No. 39**, a once *grand standing* apartment block, is now to be found between a little brasserie and a cobbler's. In 1883 he died there of creeping paralysis, the legacy of a dose of syphilis caught as a merchant seaman in Brazil.

Avenue de Clichy. In **Place de Clichy** I noted two convenient lunch stops for later: the art deco Charlot Le Roi de Coquillages and the Café Wepler, where the oysters juiced up Henry Miller for his quiet days in Clichy. Period charm of any period gets hard to find around here. Tour buses head up towards Montmartre, and Paris by Night is a hectic bustle of light and sound.

Across the street from **No. 7 Avenue de Clichy** a sinuous lane is called **Passage Lathuile** in memory of the popular restaurant made famous by Manet. In *Chez Père Lathuile* a raffish young layabout (modelled by the owner's son) is making out with a rather prim tart (modelled by Judith French, a relative of Offenbach) at lunch in the restaurant's garden. This

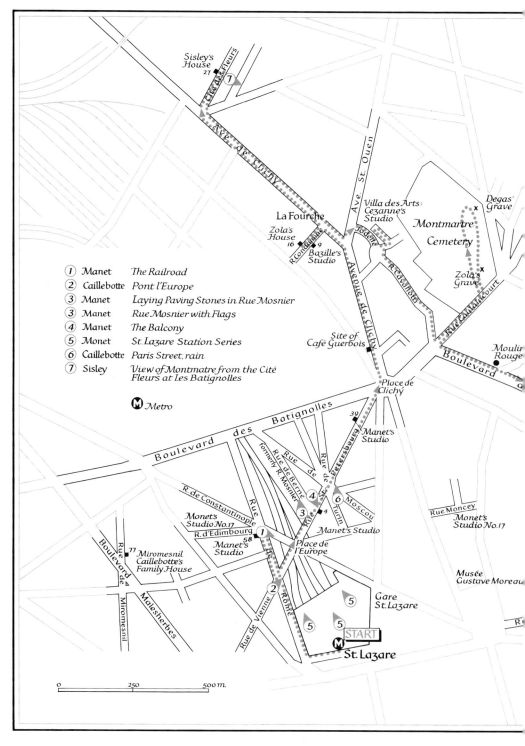

Ⓜ *Metro*

1878 prelude to love in the afternoon, observed by an envious waiter carrying a bock, riled the critics but clearly shows the influence of the impressionists on Manet.

In another famous Manet portrait, *Le Bon Bock* (1873), the genial, beer-bellied President of the Bon Bock Society sits smoking a clay pipe, poised to drink his beer at the **Café Guerbois**, formerly at **No. 9 Avenue de Clichy**. On Thursday night Manet would hold court with his younger admirers. The click of billiard balls and the clatter of bocks on marble-top tables punctuated the polemic; huge gilt mirrors with pegs for the top hats of Degas and Manet reflected the animated group at the two tables reserved for them in the front room.

Eldest was Pissarro, two years Manet's senior; his calm, patriarchal bearing made him dean of the group, much admired for his philosophical acceptance of hardship and his quiet good humour. As a socially-conscious

Les Batignolles-Pigalle

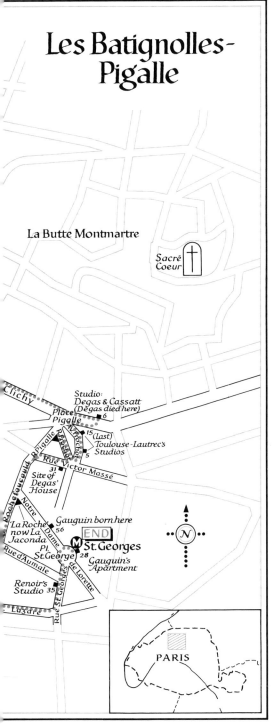

La Butte Montmartre

Sacré Coeur

Clichy

Studio:
Degas & Cassatt
(Degas died here)

Place Pigalle 6

15 (Last)
Toulouse-Lautrec's
Studios
5

Rue Victor Massé

31
Site of
Degas'
House

Gauguin born here
56

'La Roche
now La
Jaconda

END
St.Georges

Pl.
St.George
28 Gauguin's
Apartment

Rue d'Aumale

Renoir's
Studio 35

Lazare

PARIS

---

art was instinctive. Life was to be absorbed unconsciously, not grasped at with the mind. 'I'm not interested in what goes on in my head. I want to touch . . . at least, to see . . . !' Monet, not yet thirty, was also a silent but attentive listener to his peers; trouble with his art was best kept to himself, his spare energy devoted to gardening.

Both relished the clashes, however. Mostly they involved Manet who, after a few drinks, revealed the verbal prize-fighter behind a kindly, modest façade. The usually benign critic Duranty had the misfortune to take a mild swipe in print at Manet's *The Music Lesson*, quoting a spectator who had referred to it as 'a debauch'. This led to a duel in the forest of St-Germain, with Zola as one of Manet's seconds. The two contenders, though totally inexperienced at fencing, fell on each other with such vigour that, when Duranty was slightly wounded, the seconds could hardly separate them. That night, at the Café Guerbois, Manet analysed why Duranty had lost: his boots were too tight. As the champagne of reconciliation flowed, Manet generously gave the critic his own superb, softly fitting boots, handmade in London.

'Nothing was more interesting,' Monet said of the Café Guerbois, 'than these discussions with their perpetual clash of opinions. I sat there expectantly, spurred on to research ever more deeply for our common cause, provided with enough enthusiasm to keep me going week after week until an idea took shape. I always left feeling better nourished, my will firmer, my thoughts on a sounder, clearer track.'

La Fourche, the fork where Avenue de Clichy and Avenue de St-Ouen separate, was dangerous, according to Renoir, the haunt of knife-brandishing apaches and their slit-skirted girls. Nowadays commerce is safe and varied. Portuguese cab drivers brush up their *fados* and Tunisians sell deliciously honeyed and fattening pastries at all hours.

Rue de la Condamine. One block farther up the left side of Avenue de Clichy is the street where Bazille worked at **No. 9** (entered at **No. 7**) and Zola lived for a time at **No. 16**.

anarchist, he found it hard to take Degas's tease about 'the unsuitability of making art available to the lower classes and allowing the production of pictures to be sold for thirteen sous'. Yet he could empathize with Degas's defence of fellow artists, his admiration for the meticulous endeavour that made painters like Pissarro such stayers. 'If it wasn't trouble,' Degas said, 'it wouldn't be fun.'

Renoir didn't agree. Whatever financial trouble he may have had, his

Caillebotte's Pont de L'Europe *(1876) proves that grown men, not just Manet's little girl, enjoyed watching the trains go by. Different ages, same fascination. Iron, steam, power. Today's electric trains seem bland by comparison.*

Bazille's studio took a bit of finding. Beware: some buildings on the impressionist trail have coded entry bells. No use coming at weekends, holidays or in the evenings, when these protect the residents' security; on weekdays, a press on the button will usually click open the door. On this occasion, I was challenged by a sleepy concierge in the entrance hall. '*Où est l'atelier de Bazille?*' I asked. He looked blank. '*Bazille? Bazille? Il n'y pas de Bazille ici.*' As if to confirm the absence of Bazille, he pointed to the mail-boxes. When I explained my quest, he was most co-operative, pointing down a long glass-roofed corridor linking the street with the back garden.

In the enclosed garden stood a gem of a two-storey Restoration house where Bazille lived and worked in tree-surrounded seclusion. Neighbour Zola used Bazille as the model for a character: 'Blond, tall and slim, very distinguished. A little the style of Jesus, but virile . . . all the noble qualities of youth: belief, loyalty, delicacy.'

Bazille's studio was open house for Renoir and Monet in their poorer days. In 1867 Monet had to leave his companion Camille and the newborn baby Jean in Paris without resources, while he lodged with an aunt near Le Havre to continue painting on the Normandy coast.

Monet made frequent trips to Paris in an attempt to sell the Norman works. Bazille's painting *The Artist's Studio* (1870) shows a welcoming informality in harmony with the easygoing comfort of the room, its jumble of paintings, the stove, and big, casually curtained window. Zola, from the attic steps, chats with Renoir sitting on a table; Manet is giving a critical appraisal of the painting Bazille is poised to continue, while Monet smokes one of Bazille's cigarettes and Maître plays the piano. That very year, their generous young host was killed on active service in the Franco-Prussian War. His pictures – *Summer Scene*, *Bathers* and *The Artist's Family on a Terrace near Montpellier* (O) – were as full of sunlight and warmth as that studio in Rue de la Condamine.

The dull ten-minute walk up Avenue de Clichy is well rewarded with **Cité des Fleurs**, one of the most unusual residential streets in north Paris. No wonder Sisley lived here for a time. In a capital where private houses are rare, this 'garden city' is more like London than Paris.

Between 1867 and 1870 Sisley spent time at **No. 27** with Marie Lescouezec, whom he had met while she was working in Paris as a florist and part-time model. Their son, Pierre, was born here. They were not married until 1897, in Cardiff, while Sisley was on a painting trip to South Wales.

Now dilapidated, it is a four-storey house with a palm tree in the front garden. From it, Sisley made sorties in search of a Paris that was not merely picturesque: the Canal St-Martin, the Pont de Grenelle, and *A View of Montmartre from the Cité des Fleurs at Les Batignolles* (1869). The painting shows how countrified the area still was, reminiscent of a Corot landscape, green in the foreground and a scattering of white buildings at the bottom of the hill, which does not yet bear the landmark of Sacré-Coeur. A man with a horse and cart drives by.

Perseverance is now needed to foot it back to La Fourche, cross Avenue de St-Ouen and burrow into a warren of backstreets – **Rue Etienne-Jodelle** to the intersection of **Rues Pierre-Ginier** and **Hégisippe-Moreau**.

Villa des Arts. Cézanne, though he dressed like a starving bohemian, was hardly from a poor family. Son of a hatter who founded a bank, he played the part of strong, solitary Provençal determined not to be put down by Parisians who mocked his accent.

Unsurprisingly, he did not come to terms with Les Batignolles until the end of his life when, for his trips to Paris from Aix, he rented a studio in the enchanting Villa des Arts, on the lower western slope of Montmartre hill. Its imposing wrought-iron gateway leads to a tranquil, leafy courtyard little changed; a building with twelve north-orientated studios faces a low, long house with *oeil-de-boeuf* windows, where Cézanne had his base. I entered to find a perfect Belle Epoque hallway – parquet floors smelling of beeswax with a double staircase lit by a bronze nude balancing a glass globe. I half-expected Cézanne, mellowed by late recognition, to invite me into one of the studios at the back and show me his progress on *Portrait of Ambroise Vollard* (1899) (Petit Palais). Here Cézanne painted *Portrait of Ambroise Vollard* (1899) (Petit Palais), the hirsute, swarthy Réunionais art dealer who suffered from sleeping sickness, would no doubt be taking a well-deserved nap during one of his astonishing 115 sittings.

And it was here that Cézanne's war with Paris ended peaceably. It had begun at the Café Guerbois, which he attended mostly to please his friend Zola, and as infrequently as possible. He was in awe of Manet the artist, whose *Déjeuner sur l'herbe* had encouraged him to lighten his heavily dark palette, and he kept his irritation with Manet the man in check. Artists in gloves and top hats were not for him: 'All bastards! They look like a bunch of lawyers!'

In an attempt to get him launched, Zola took his uncouth friend around the salons where the habit of taking his jacket off, revealing a none too clean shirt, hardly endeared him to prospective patrons. Cézanne preferred the company of Monet and Renoir, or the solitariness of his studio. 'I'm sticking to still lifes,' he told Zola. 'Female models terrify me. The bitches pounce on you in a moment of feebleness. You have to be on the defensive the whole time, and the painting deserts you.'

Eventually he lived with a model, Hortense Fiquet, had a son by her and even married her. At the Villa des Arts, with the confidence of old age and success, Cézanne returned to the nudes of his Paris youth. Between 1872 and 1906 he did around forty variations of female and male bathers: the *Grandes Baigneuses* and others were worked on here and in Aix, so he could keep the theme going at both ends of the line. Earlier bathers are stumpy little creatures by comparison, and Cézanne seems to have become less of a misogynist with age; they are masterworks of composition, symmetry and drawing. Their serenity blends sky, trees, water, vegetation and figures in a miraculous landscape far, far from Paris.

Rue Cavalotti has a number of convenient restaurants for lunch,

including the Galère des Rois. My choice was Le Bouclard, a *fin de siècle* bistro, with a 55-franc lunch menu including *rillettes* and duck breast with blackcurrants. Afterwards, a left on **Rue Caulaincourt** brought me to the scene of a difference of opinions that may well have continued even beyond the grave.

Montmartre Cemetery boasts the graves of Fragonard, Berlioz, Dumas, Feydeau, the brothers Goncourt and Guitry, Gustave Moreau, Offenbach and François Truffaut. I was there for Zola and Degas. Zola has star position overlooking the *rondpoint* near the entrance, reached by passing beneath the iron-structured Pont Caulaincourt. Above red-speckled marble a verdigris-covered, leonine head challenged me: what side would you have been on in the Dreyfus case?

In the courageous pamphlet, *J'Accuse*, Zola proclaimed the innocence of the Jewish officer sent to Devil's Island for allegedly selling military secrets to the Prussians. Degas, at rest in the much simpler De Gas family tomb with its bronze medallion of the artist, was anti-Dreyfusard, that being the entrenched attitude of his class. The same year (1896), anti-Semites like Athman ben Sala, a friend of Gide's, wrote to Degas: 'What I like about you is that you do not like the Jews . . .' A typically sweeping assertion of a bigot eager for old-boy-network allies in a seedy cause. Degas saw Dreyfus first as a traitor; that he happened to be Jewish was secondary. In fact, Degas's side got it wrong both ways: Dreyfus was proved not to be a traitor, and that he happened to be Jewish caused the spread of an anti-Semitic virus at its most contagious. 'The same eternal camps,' Renoir observed. 'Protestants versus Catholics, Republicans versus Monarchists, Communards versus Versaillais. Personally, I'm for Watteau against Bouguereau!'

Ironically, the quickest way to Degas's tomb in the cemetery's 4th Division (hard to find even with map provided at the gate) was via the Allée Halévy of Jewish tombs.

Boulevard de Clichy's neon lights flash *Cuir-Latex-Lingerie*, *Peepshow*, *Nu Integral*. A short stretch of sleazy boulevard is the most direct route from Montmartre Cemetery to the **Pigalle-St-Georges** area and at least passes Toulouse-Lautrec's **Moulin Rouge** (**No. 82**), best visited at night (Chapter Four, p. 105). Signac, who also had a studio at Villa des Arts, worked in 1886 at **No. 130** and produced a stunning snowy *Boulevard de Clichy* in the pointillist manner.

Beyond **Place Pigalle** is a building (**No. 6**) where Mary Cassatt worked and Degas had his last studio.

For a daughter of a Pennsylvania financier, it was a raunchy neighbourhood to choose. 'Mame' Cassatt's parents had taken an apartment in the wide, residential Avenue Trudaine nearby. It shows much family faith that her father, mother and sister crossed the Atlantic to chaperone her in Paris. They were convinced Francophiles. Her father, only moderately rich, was ambitious for his children to succeed at whatever they did: his son Aleck became a railroad company president; and faith in his, gutsy, horse-riding Mame, paid off, even though it shocked his Victorian standards. Her first solo show led Degas to declare: 'I am not willing to admit that a woman can draw so well.'

On the face of it, Mary Cassatt and Edgar Degas were an odd couple. Yet the American feminist and the French monarchist were rebels with the same cause – a revolution in art. Pigalle was its centre. Mary Cassatt could thank the day when a long-forgotten artist, Tourney, brought Degas to see her work in that modest studio in 1877.

Place Pigalle. On the site of La Narcisse, a bar-nightclub on the angle of **Rue Frochot** and **Rue Pigalle** showing the inevitable garish photos of sticky-looking bodies entwined, the Nouvelle-Athènes once stood.

In the post-war 1870s Degas took over from Manet as impressionist guru, and the Nouvelle-Athènes from the Café Guerbois as the artists' hangout. Its terrace, enclosed in winter, contained hothouse plants of all varieties, some requiring regular doses

of absinthe. For Degas's *L'Absinthe* (O) (1876), Comédie-Française actress Ellen Andrée acted suitably addled in front of her glass of 'the green fairy'; she is not speaking to her shabby but characterful partner, for whom Marcellin Desboutin posed. Desboutin was a talented engraver who had squandered a private fortune in Florence, tried his hand unsuccessfully at acting and playwriting, and was then the café's most popular layabout.

Degas's *Women in Front of a Café* (1877) are caught at a very specific moment; over an evening drink, before picking up a client, one woman is flicking her teeth with a gloved thumb at another. Degas observes with a ruthless eye the tough sign language of the streets, the prostitute's contempt for someone who has offended her.

The café was also where his cronies gathered, new young artists whom he was bringing on: the witty cartoonist Forain; the social realist Raffaëlli, recorder of desolate Parisian outskirts; the ebullient Italian Zandomeneghi, whose 1885 painting of the Nouvelle-Athènes made it look a lot more fun than Degas, however superior the master's disturbingly honest eye. His unswerving loyalty to these three led to several disagreements with colleagues about their inclusion in impressionist shows. Degas invariably prevailed.

Avenue Frochot and **Rue Victor-Massé**. Degas's old apartment block just off Place Pigalle at **No. 37** Rue Victor-Massé was pulled down in 1912. Opposite, not to be missed, is a short street where he also lived briefly, one of the most charming, unspoilt hideaways in Paris – a mere block away from the tawdriness of Place Pigalle.

Avenue Frochot is entered by a coded gate. I had been warned not to ring for the concierge, who would almost certainly refuse me, but discreetly to wait for the frequent coming and going of residents. Its solid town houses of dilapidated elegance, in nineteenth-century styles from mock Renaissance to Louis-Philippe, housed composers, actors, playwrights and Toulouse-Lautrec at **No. 5** and **No. 15**.

The driving necessity of Mary Cassatt's career which produced domestic masterpieces like Little Girl in a Blue Chair *(1878) was never fully understood by her American-in-Paris family. Degas worked on this picture with her.*

Another distinguished resident was Jeanne Samary, a beautiful and vivacious Comédie-Française actress whose portrait Renoir painted on several occasions. They became very close, but never permanently. 'Renoir is not made for marriage,' Jeanne reckoned. 'He marries every woman he paints . . . with his paintbrush.'

Rue Pigalle is named after an eighteenth-century sculptor. At **No. 28** post-impressionists Bonnard and Vuillard shared a studio in the 1890s. Struggling artists van Gogh, Seurat and Signac were allowed to exhibit their work at the **Théâtre Antoine**.

At the junction of **Rue de la Rochefoucauld** (named after an abbess of Montmartre) and **Rue Notre-Dame-de-Lorette** is a friendly little corner bar called La Joconde which used to be **La Rochefoucauld**, Degas's 'canteen', known by locals as 'La Roche'. Degas used to lunch and argue there with two symbolist painters: Puvis de Chavannes, known to his detractors as 'Pubis', whom Degas admired for his composition of figures (it would be impossible, he said, to displace one of Puvis's ethereal maidens a centimetre without ruining the group); and Gustave Moreau, a butt for his witty, anti-symbolist sallies ('Next you'll paint Christ with a watch chain!'). Down the road at **No. 14** Rue de la Rochefoucauld, the **Gustave Moreau Museum** at the artist's home houses an important collection of his works. *The Muses Leaving Apollo, their Father, to Go and Bring Light to the World* (birds leaving the nest), and all India synthesized in a valley of sacred lakes, temples and idols with Alexander the Great a symbol of imperial power – these and other vast, poetic works show how differently a contemporary of the older impressionists expressed himself, to great effect.

Rue St-Georges. At **No. 35** was Renoir's first of many studios in the neighbourhood. A mattress, a stove, a chair, a table and a cupboard were its sole furnishings. Brought up to respect order and cleanliness in the cramped conditions of his childhood, Renoir kept his studio cleaner and tidier than most. That didn't make living conditions easy. Even the most comfortable studios lacked running water; water closets were shared, on the landing between floors. Difficult, when entertaining. And Renoir, particularly prone to musical evenings, entertained frequently.

From the days when he and Bazille would go to Offenbach operettas and concerts of Wagner (whose portrait he later dashed off in twenty minutes at Palermo), Renoir had a passion for music. His companion Aline was a passable pianist, so he installed a piano for her. The composer Chabrier once gave such a spirited performance of his *España* that people in the street were stamping their feet, clapping, and shouting *Olé*!

The wealthy publisher and collector, Georges Charpentier, would drop by. In *The Artist's Studio, Rue St-Georges* (1876), Renoir captures the conviviality of gatherings there: painters brought friends, musicians would try out their latest numbers, and in the painting Pissarro, white-haired and balding at 46, has made one of his rare sorties to Paris from his home and vast family at Pontoise.

Place St-Georges. The eclectic, intimate little *rondpoint* manages to contain a bar, a theatre, a statue, a flea market and a crescent of elegant Louis-Philippe houses where, at **No. 28** Gauguin and his Danish wife Mette had a flat during his flush, money-market period. He was born up the street at **No. 56 Rue Notre-Dame-de-Lorette**, where a plaque can be seen above Restaurant Le Gauguin. The **Métro St-Georges** was then convenient for the journey home.

3

THE RIVER SEINE

Place de L'Abreuvoir, Marly-le-Roi.

To the west of Paris, Sequana's serpentine river traces a large inverted S on the map in honour of its patron goddess. Sensual bends with gently wooded slopes, long reaches, bosky islands and lively villages attracted the impressionists, along with a million others of the Second Empire's newly leisured middle class.

These were not the Elysian fields and romantic riverside hamlets painted by Turner when he came to Bougival. The 30mph, smut-fluttering, rattletrap train journey in double-decker open coaches on the first railway in France linked the capital with the important river port of Le Pecq for commercial reasons, not merely as a joyride to the intermediary station of Chatou for seamstresses and barons in search of a romp in the reeds.

On Sunday, however, the river was theirs. Shop assistants and landscape painters littered the riverbanks. So did the rinds of watermelon. As the church bells of Bougival rang out, raucous Parisian laughter could already be heard as the first day trippers disembarked from a riverboat. Bank clerks on a binge, bringing their city habits and jokes and songs with them, pretending not to be at a loss in what they believed to be the country. Laundresses had long since replaced shepherdesses in this no man's land of riverside villages, market gardens and factories. At the hundred-and-one *guingettes* along the banks and on the islands, corks began popping and the rabbit was put on to stew in rough Argenteuil wine. As the sun sank lower, so did the songs; the jokes were smutty as detachable collars grimed by train smoke. You lost your daughter in the forest, and your son-in-law in waterfront hotels.

Manet, despite his radical politics, looked warily upon the masses threatening the privacy of his sixty-acre family estate near the river at Gennevilliers. It was, however, where the impressionist movement began. Walking with a friend along the riverbanks, he was enchanted to see loose women, known as *grenouilles* (froggies), stripping off for a quick plunge in the Seine's insalubrious waters. 'I'm going to paint a nude in just such transparent light,' he declared, 'with people like those over there.' And their riverside boyfriends became the shocking modernly clothed gentlemen of *Déjeuner sur l'herbe* (O), which so upset Napoleon III.

Eager to see for himself whether such nudes posed in the flesh, the Emperor paid a surprise visit to the notorious bathing place cum restaurant, La Grenouillère (The Froggery), in 1869. Not a froggie in sight. Manet, anyway, had done his painting in the studio; and those of Renoir and Monet, done on the spot, were pictures of decorum.

As Mallarmé put it, Monet and Renoir were after 'painting not the thing, but the effect it creates'. A suggestion of joys hidden among the riverbank bushes, the dappled sunlight upon unspecific figures, cheap music and frying fish neither heard nor smelt but readily imagined.

Guy de Maupassant, sharp observer of the flora and fauna along the Seine's banks, paints La Grenouillère in rather more lurid colours than Monet and Renoir in his short story 'La Femme de Paul'.

The immense raft, covered with a pitch roof supported by wood columns, was joined to the charming island of Croissy by two footbridges, one of which penetrated into the aquatic establishment, while the other linked it, at the end, to a tiny islet planted with one tree called The Flowerpot and, from there, reached dry land near the bathing place. . . .

Not for nothing was it called The Froggery. By the side of the raft where one drank, and very near The Flowerpot where one bathed, women of an ample girth came to display their wares naked, and attract customers. . . .

The organizer of the can-can, majestic in his tired evening suit, faced all and sundry with the ravaged countenance of an old purveyor of cheap pleasures at bargain prices . . . they danced: couples facing each other capered about like mad things . . . women with disjointed thighs leaped up and down with skirts flying, showing their underwear . . . men crouched like toads, making obscene gestures. . . .

As Berthe Morisot's mother wittily warned her about the Seine on Sunday: 'You go there alone, but you come back at least two.' Considered a dilettante because of her class rather than her sex, Berthe may secretly have longed to join the froggies and shed her class label. Unless lesbian or fallen, however, women like Berthe never went near La Grenouillère. Staying with the Manets in Gennevilliers or later at her own summer home at Bougival, she continued to be the epitome of respectability. In 1874, the year of her marriage to Eugène Manet, her *Bridge near Paris* had the same sense of rural tranquillity as Sisley's *Bridge near Paris* of the year before.

Pioneer of remote sites, Sisley had discovered the Seine valley's special light and planted his easel near an *Avenue of Chestnut Trees at La Celle St-Cloud* (Petit Palais) in 1867. He also became the most subtle river impressionist. No longer the youthful skirt-chaser, now enjoying a steady relationship with Marie, he was not tempted by La Grenouillère. His inspiration came from the peaceful village streets of Louveciennes, the former royal retreat of Marly-le-Roi, and deserted stretches of river a mere fifteen-minute walk down the road at Port-Marly.

Sisley and Pissarro were the solitary introverts of the group. Portraits were rare and figures usually anonymous in their landscapes, in contrast to Monet's wife and son in a poppy field, Morisot's sister chasing butterflies, or Renoir's Aline lunching *chez* Fournaise. Pissarro's pleasure was capturing the truth of countryside at a given moment, a peasant's labour portrayed with a naturalism of which Zola approved: too busy with the practicalities of the potato crop even to hear the angelus, let alone pray for a dead granny.

Pissarro had spent much time exploring the environs of Paris before settling at Louveciennes in 1869. Like a true traveller from the West Indies and Venezuela (with relatives in England), he had already discovered such out-of-the-way river sites as the Marne at Chennevières, the Seine at La Roche-Guyon, and the Oise at Pontoise. His parents had returned from their St-Thomas hardware store to retirement in the forest of Montmorency, also near the Oise. On his small allowance he would stride out like some purposeful Wandering Jew in his big floppy hat with the edges turned down and his mountainer's boots, rucksack of materials on his back, a thumbstick calmly parting bushes, occasional burrs sticking in his beaver beard. He had to take his subject by surprise, be surprised by it himself, and capture it on the spot. Getting down to work was often delayed by agonizing appraisal of the subject, by which time the light had changed. 'It's the major difficulty,' he claimed. 'If you don't feel it, nothing, absolutely nothing, is worth while.'

With the modesty of his master Corot, he claimed to play only a small flute but always to try to hit the right note. In *The Wash-House*, *Bougival* or *Orchard at Louveciennes* (both 1872) a harmonious spirit of place prevails over detail. Pissarro's Seine valley, unlike Monet's and Renoir's, is more for work than play.

The Seventies became a golden age of river painting, even if not much gold came the artists' way. Monet, Renoir, Sisley, Pissarro and Morisot were to do some of their most distinctive group work, in accordance with definite aims they shared (Chapter One, p. 10). Even Manet was so fed up with Salon's refusal of *The Railroad* – an outdoor subject done in his Paris studio – that he decided to put his friends' *pleinairiste* theories to the test and joined Monet at Argenteuil. Although he had declined to exhibit in the first group show that same year (1874), his images of oarsmen, their girls, the river, and the Monet family have the authentic impressionist look without losing his own implicit social comment.

Monet, unlike the fundamentally city-bound Manet, became obsessed with Seine water under different conditions – ice-floes breaking up, the effect of summer ripples from a passing skiff or the wake of a barge. He spent seven years at Argenteuil, a record in his peripatetic life, and all his comrades came to stay with him there at some time or another. Generous with his own money when he had it and with others' when he hadn't, Monet took his place as the natural leader.

Argenteuil suffered from schizophrenia – half rural, half industrial. Monet managed to avoid showing the tannery or barges in his pictures, but a train streaks across *The Railway Bridge, Argenteuil*, disturbing the peace of the yacht basin on a summer's day. Trains every hour to Gare St-Lazare from 7.50am to 9.50pm in 22 minutes. Very convenient. Closeness to the city encouraged the *Société des Régates Parisiennes* to install their club there; mooring space was at a premium. While Pissarro favoured barges, Monet and Renoir preferred sailboats, setting up easels near each other as they had done pre-war at La Grenouillère: in Monet's *Regatta at Argenteuil* (O) sails and ochre villas shimmer in the water; in Renoir's *The Seine at Argenteuil* a golden yellow suffuses the racing boats and, below a pontoon, a man's long evening shadow ripples dark upon the water near the bank.

Across the bridge on the Seine's left bank, the tiny waterfront community of Petit-Gennevilliers saw the arrival of Caillebotte in 1877. His property was big enough to indulge the gentlemanly hobbies of gardening and boat-building, and nobody in those days was shocked by a young man living a life of so-called idleness. He had given up painting until a chance encounter with Monet fired his spirits and emptied his pockets – in the good cause of art. He did not just take up painting again; he took up the whole impressionist group as its most active funder, organizer and collector.

Renoir also had a permanent tie with the river. His parents had retired to Louveciennes before the war, and he had many temporary homes there. His favourite riverside haunt – still visitable with pleasure today – was the Hôtel-Restaurant Fournaise on the Island of Chatou. After most impressionists had moved and the group was fragmenting, Renoir did his masterwork *Luncheon of the Boating Party* there in 1881.

Two years later, following the S-bends nearer Paris, began the revolution which put paid to the impressionists' group shows. Reminiscent of the lithe, gay men bathing and romping in Bazille's 1869 *Summer Scene*, Seurat's *Bathers at Asnières* goes downmarket in its choice of men but is symptomatic of his ideal of Democratic Arcadia. The haze of a weekend heatwave envelops his clerks, fixed in time as they laze motionless in a variety of hats from bowler to boater, protecting pallid faces against the white heat. It was the prelude to the great pointillist experimental masterpiece *Sunday Afternoon on the Island of La Grande Jatte* (1886) (sketches at Orsay), and struck a final discord among the impressionists. Because of the presence of Seurat and his fellow neo-impressionist, Signac, there was a schism with Monet, Renoir and Sisley, who refused to take part in the last group show. Of the great river painters, only Pissarro and Morisot were represented. They had finally gone their separate ways.

The influence continued, however, as other movements took wing. A year later, post-impressionist van Gogh worked at Asnières. And in 1900, while Pissarro was painting the city and Renoir his voluptuous nudes, Chatou saw a revival of its artistic fortunes. Derain and Vlaminck made it 'The Argenteuil of the Fauves [Wild Beasts]'. A new school was born in a shared studio on the island, as the two friends worked with purest primary colours to produce canvases almost like children's paintings in their directness and brightness: Derain's *Bridge at Le Pecq*, *The Seine at Chatou* (O) and *Two Barges*; and Vlaminck's *Street in Chatou* (O).

Derain, son of a local shopkeeper, was the more restrained. Full of self-doubt, he needed to loosen up at the nearby Fournaise. A former street musician of Dutch origin, Vlaminck was altogether a wilder beast, squirting his paint direct on to the canvas from the tube, and boasting that he had never set foot in the Louvre.

They were the natural inheritors of the river that had been such an inspiration to their forebears. 'Take me as I am,' said Vlaminck, as though also making a plea for his beloved Seine, 'warts and all.'

My exploration took four days – warts and all.

WALKS AND DRIVES
BY
THE RIVER SEINE

Sailboats at Argenteuil *by Caillebotte (1888).*

INFORMATION

Itinerary

Allow 4 full days, either making day trips from Paris or staying locally for 2 nights at St-Germain-en-Laye or Bougival.

Day 1

Paris–St-Germain via autoroutes A13 or A14.

Visit St-Germain-en-Laye.

Drive St-Germain–Marly-le-Roi.

Lunch.

Marly-le-Roi Walk.

Day 2

(From Paris to Louveciennes via A13 to St-Germain exit, then N186.)

Louveciennes Walk.

Lunch.

Drive Louveciennes–Bougival via Rue de la Princesse.

Bougival/St-Michel-de-Bougival by car with stops.

Day 3

(From Paris – same route to Bougival as on Day 2 to avoid confusion, then head down to Ile de la Chaussée.)

Bougival–Port Marly round trip by car with stops.

Drive Bougival–Chatou bridge via N13, turning left at Avenue Albert 1er, which joins Avenue de Colmar.

Slipway off bridge to Fournaise.

Fournaise Museum and Restaurant (**lunch**).

Impressionist Island Walk.

Return Paris via Nanterre and La Défense (N190, N13).

Day 4

Strictly for aficionados as far as Ile de la Jatte. Industrial outskirts and Port of Paris, with a few charming enclaves. Expect heavy traffic.

(Same route from Paris to right bank side of Chatou bridge. Turn right.)

Drive Chatou–Carrières-sur-Seine via N321.

Visit Quai de Seine, Carrières.

Continue to Argenteuil via N321 and N311.

Argenteuil and Petit-Gennevilliers Walk.

Drive Argenteuil–Villeneuve-la-Garenne via autoroute A86 and N186.

Visit Villeneuve-la-Garenne/Ile St-Denis.

Riverside drive Villeneuve to Ile de la Jatte via Asnières-sur-Seine and Clichy, crossing from left to right bank by the Asnières bridge.

Lunch

Visit Ile de la Jatte.

Return Paris via Neuilly.

Public Transport

Paris–St-Germain-en-Laye by Express Métro RER (Line A).

St-Germain-en-Laye–Marly-le-Roi by local bus or taxi.

Marly-le-Roi, Louveciennes, Bougival-La Celle-St Cloud are on SNCF's St-Nom-la-Bretèche line from La Défense or Gare St-Lazare.

Bougival–Chatou by local bus or taxi.

Chatou by RER (Line A).

Argenteuil by SNCF's Pontoise line from Gare St-Lazare.

Ile de la Jatte by 82 Bus or Métro Neuilly.

Refreshment, Meals and Overnight

St-Germain-en-Laye
Hotels

Pavillon Henri IV, (**A**), 21 Rue Thiers. Tel. 01.39.10.15.15.

La Forestière, (**A**), 1 Avenue du Président-Kennedy. Tel. 01.39.73.36.60.

Ermitage des Loges, (**B**), 1 Avenue des Loges. Tel. 01.34.51.88.86.

Marly-le-Roi
Restaurants

Les Chevaux de Marly, (**B**), Place de l'Abreuvoir. Tel. 01.39.58.47.61.

Le Village, (**C**, lunch menu), 3 Grande Rue. Tel. 01.39.16.28.14.

Louveciennes
Restaurants

Aux Chandelles, (**B**), 12 Place de L'Eglise. Tel. 01.39.69.08.40.

Bougival
Hotels

Des Maréchaux, (**B**), (no meals), 10 Côte de la Jonchère. Tel. 01.30.82.77.11.

Forest Hill, (**B**), (no meals), 10–12 Rue Yvan-Tourgueneff. Tel. 01.39.18.17.16.

Restaurant

Le Camélia, (**B**), 7 Quai G.-Clemenceau. Tel. 01.39.18.36.06.

Port-Marly
Restaurant

Bistrot Italien, (**C**), Rue de Paris. Tel. 01.39.58.44.56.

Chatou
Restaurant

☆ Fournaise, (**B**), Ile des Impressionistes. Tel. 01.30.71.41.91.

Ile de la Jatte
Restaurant

La Guinguette de Neuilly, (**B**), 12 Boulevard de Levallois. Tel. 01.46.24.25.04.

Museums and Sites

Promenade Museum, Marly Park. Open Wed–Sun, 2–6. Entry: 30F. Tel. 01.39.69.06.26.

La Maison Fournaise, Ile des Impressionistes (Chatou). Open Wed–Fri, 11–5; Sat, Sun 11–6. Entry: 25F. Tel. 01.34.80.63.22.

Salle Jean-Vilar, Argenteuil. Monet's painting-boat. Entry: Free. Tel. 01.39.61.51.43.

Boat Trips

Check trips on the Seine and Canal St-Martin in 'Promenades' section of *Pariscope*, as these are seasonal.

Tourist Offices

38 Rue Au-Pain, St-Germain-en-Laye. Tel. 01.34.51.05.12.

2 Avenue des Combattants, Marly-le-Roi. Tel. 01.39.16.16.01.

Hôtel de Ville, Bougival. Tel. 01.39.69.01.15.

St-Germain-en-Laye

2 hours

Best to start at **St-Germain-en-Laye**, the most westerly town on the river's inverted S, and then work one's sinuous way upstream towards Paris, ending with **Ile de la Jatte** (no longer *Grande*) at Neuilly.

Avoiding rush-hour back-up on the often clogged St-Cloud viaduct, I made city centre to St-Germain in under thirty minutes using autoroute A13. The new A14 will be a lot quicker. St-Germain can also be reached by high-speed Métro (RER). For those relying on public transport (suburban trains and local buses), I have planned some round-trip walks to begin and end at stations, which are also practical for parking the car.

St-Germain is a good bet for overnight accommodation, and as one of the most spectacularly elegant eighteenth-century towns in France it is also a fine place to take one's bearings.

Château Gardens and Terrace. This classic French park, designed by Le Nôtre, with crunchy paths and neatly clipped conical box bushes, has a panoramic terrace high above the river. The view of Paris on a clear day is worth the trip. A helpful *table d'orientation* indicates three important areas of impressionist inspiration: Montmartre, the city itself, and the River Seine. Although the basilica of Sacré-Coeur (10½ miles away) was not completed when Sisley painted his *Terrace at St-Germain* in 1875, I looked down to a springtime river view that cannot have changed much: Le Pecq bridge, barges passing, a big house on the steep slope below. Upstream, a thickly wooded slope on the Bougival bend; downstream, the clear, straight reach towards Herblay, where, from a painting-boat, Signac immortalized the little hill town with its twelfth-century church reflected in the water.

And later still, on this same terrace, Maurice Denis (who lived in St-Germain) showed romantic girls in virginal white picking white flowers in *April, 1892*. Denis was a leader of the Nabis (the Prophets), the group that included Bonnard and Vuillard in a return to medieval-influenced and Japanese stylization. The movement owed much to the later developments of impressionism, and Denis's *Homage to Cézanne* (1901) deeply touched the maverick older artist, who had been far too long unrecognized.

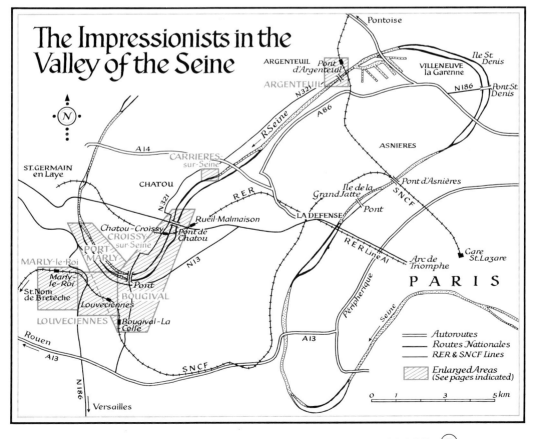

The Impressionists in the Valley of the Seine

Above: Pissarro's Entrance of the Village of Voisins *(1872) is an inviting prospect with the white château glimpsed through autumnal trees and the red roofs sloping with Voisins down its hill.*

Right: Probably the most famous Bougival painting is Renoir's Dance at Bougival *(1883), in which the adorable Suzanne Valadon has her arm languidly round her partner's neck as they dance at a leafy guingette.*

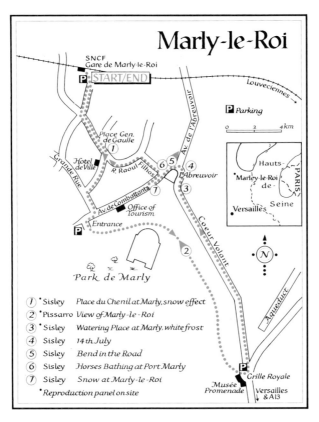

Marly-le-Roi

short half-day

I armed myself with the hefty but indispensable *Guide-Atlas de l'Ile de France*, which gives detailed street maps of the outskirts of Paris and the fastest or most attractive routes to get from one to another. Two and a half miles from St-Germain, at the bottom bend of the Seine's inverted S, are **Marly-le-Roi, Louveciennes** and **Bougival.** The three communes now overlap confusingly: woods, valleys, village streets, hills, waterfronts, country houses, gardens, orchards, purposely unmade-up roads. Unspoilt, recognizable impressionist sites survive in all three, and preserving them from the property developers is a continuous fight. This privileged residential area, which inhabitants such as fashion designer Agnès B and actor Gérard Depardieu wouldn't dream of calling suburbia, is a mere twenty minutes from the Arc de Triomphe.

Place Général-de-Gaulle (formerly Place du Chenil). Five minutes from Marly-le-Roi station is the first of several reproductions displayed on outdoor panels: Sisley's *Place du Chenil at Marly, Snow Effect.* Sisley moved to Marly from Louveciennes in 1875 and stayed until

1878. The ridge of the Louveciennes hill can be seen beyond the trees of Marly park. It was evidently a hard winter. The pleasant little town hall square looks much the same, even without the snow. Narrow, cobbled streets lead through the old town to the park.

Parc de Marly. At the **tourist office** on **Avenue des Combattants** I picked up a useful little book called *Dans les Pas des Impressionistes,* with illustrations to show where to find each painting site in the three communes, and a map of reproduction panels.

The park, another Le Nôtre masterpiece, slopes down from a romantic hill where once a cascade of the elaborate water garden tumbled. Nearby is a reproduction panel of Pissarro's *View of Marly-le-Roi* (1870). His cows no longer graze, though there is a three-day horse fair in the park every June. On the terrace of the watering-place where the park ends are two magnificent horse statues by Costou, their originals in the Louvre. The eighteenth-century house in the picture, **No. 9 Avenue des Combattants**, is still there, but summer foliage veiled it from me.

Pissarro's home on the Route de Versailles, Louveciennes (to be visited on another walk) was close to the park's entrance at the **Grille Royale**. Near this gate the **Promenade Museum** has a fine exhibition of Marly's history including the famous Machine, and many temporary exhibitions.

Le Coeur Volant. From the Grille Royale, the King's horses pulling his carriage from Versailles to his observatory at St-Germain or a hunt in the Marly forest had an easy descent to their watering-place at the bottom of the avenue where a reproduction panel shows Sisley's *Watering-Place at Marly, White Frost*. Several houses are still recognizable, especially the two to the right of the Ford garage, with red roofs and garden gates.

Place de l'Abreuvoir. Sisley never tired of painting the watering-place where four roads meet, to give different perspectives of this unusual pond surrounded by stone bollards for tethering thirsty horses. The King had such respect for his horses that he insisted the pond echo the magnificence of the park itself. The

terrace walls were decorated with seashells from the French Antilles.

Only the surrounding buildings have changed, not the ambience. With the aid of my little book I identified the sites of eight of the nineteen views Sisley painted from his house at **No. 2 Avenue de l'Abreuvoir**(no longer there). They include a rainy *Fourteenth of July*, with characteristic British humour showing Republican pennants near the last château built by a French king; and the familiar way to Port-Marly in *Bend in the Road*, down which he hurried the moment he heard of the floods. The little house at **No. 1** with its charming garden is still there.

Rue Raoul-Philos leads back to Place Général-de-Gaulle and the railway station. By car, Louveciennes is quickly reached by taking Avenue du Coeur-Volant, **Rue du Coeur-Volant**, and passing under the aqueduct on **Chemin de l'Aqueduc**. By train it takes a few minutes.

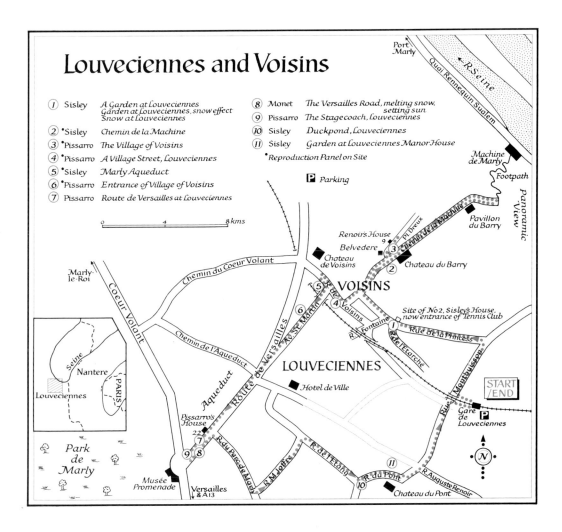

Louveciennes and Voisins

1. Sisley — *A Garden at Louveciennes / Garden at Louveciennes, snow effect / Snow at Louveciennes*
2. *Sisley — Chemin de la Machine*
3. *Pissarro — The Village of Voisins*
4. *Pissarro — A Village Street, Louveciennes*
5. *Sisley — Marly Aqueduct*
6. *Pissarro — Entrance of Village of Voisins*
7. Pissarro — *Route de Versailles at Louveciennes*
8. Monet — *The Versailles Road, melting snow, setting sun*
9. Pissarro — *The Stagecoach, Louveciennes*
10. Sisley — *Duckpond, Louveciennes*
11. Sisley — *Garden at Louveciennes Manor House*

*Reproduction Panel on Site

P Parking

0 ——— 4 ——— 8 kms

Sisley painted several versions of Flooding at Port-Marly *(O)
when the Seine broke its banks in 1872 and 1876.*

Morisot's summer holidays inspired over forty works like
Woman and Child in the Grass at Bougival *(1882).*

Louveciennes

long half-day

Louveciennes is the smallest of the three communes, with only 7000 inhabitants to Marly-le-Roi's 17,000 and Bougival's 8500. Its centre, the hamlet of Voisins, has the ambience of a country village. Yet it has the largest concentration of impressionist sites of the three, and the longest walk.

Station. On arrival you go straight into a time-warp that takes you back into the late nineteenth century. The red-and-white brick station, with its green fretwork frieze, is exactly the same as Tellier's 1888 picture with the aqueduct in the distance.

A few minutes' walk down **Rue de Montbuisson** lies more Sisley country (150 works at Louveciennes alone!).

Rue de la Princesse. After the collapse of his father's business in 1871 Sisley's comfortable Neuilly days were over, and with a wife and two children to support he settled for cheaper living in a spacious house at **No. 2** of this quiet village street, from 1872 to 1874.

The house, which burned down in 1978, has been replaced by the entrance to the tennis courts of a modern development, Les Granges du Barry. On its terrace overlooking the street Sisley was perfectly placed for the narrow country lane opposite, **Chemin de l'Etarché**, done in summer as *A Garden at Louveciennes* and the following winter as *Garden at Louveciennes, Snow Effect*. Another evocatively wintry scene shows the curve of his street with house and terrace, and in the background a house in **Rue de la Grande-Fontaine** that is still there.

Near where Rue de la Princesse meets **Chemin de la Machine** is the gatehouse of Madame du Barry's magnificent property, a gift from her royal lover, Louis XV.

Chemin de la Machine. I turned into the wide tree-lined, grass-bordered avenue that runs along du Barry's western wall.

The ingenious Marly Machine pumped water from the Seine to feed Louis XIV's fountains at Versailles and the new water gardens at Marly. A Belgian carpenter, Rennequin-Sualem, designed a system of fourteen wooden paddle-wheels and ducts, and 221 wooden pumps operated by windmills to bring the water up 535 feet to the Roman-style aqueduct.

One of Sisley's most famous paintings, *Le Chemin de la Machine* (O), rates a reproduction panel, and is instantly recognizable by the white house lived in by the Machine's first manager, Arnold de Ville, and later by Madame du Barry.

Follow the chestnut avenue for a panoramic view of the eighteenth-century ruins of the Machine's works directly below, the Ile de la Loge in mid-Seine, a cobbled pathway descending, a 200-year-old cedar of Lebanon, and ramparts with Madame du Barry's Pavillon de Musique on top, where concerts are regularly held.

Before leaving the Chemin de la Machine, turn right at the belvedere.

Place Ernest-Dreux. A reproduction panel shows Pissarro's *The Village of Voisins* (1872), with the ramp leading up to the belvedere. This was part of the Château de Voisins property belonging to the Princesse de Conti, the daughter of Louis XIV by one of his mistresses. The bourgeois house on the right of the picture still has its classic nineteenth-century Seine architecture – pinky-orange, wistaria-covered façade, and slate roof with fretwork frieze.

Place Ernest-Dreux's cul-de-sac is an isolated collection of ungentrified agricultural cottages. Storehouses that once had pulleys and chains show just how many market gardeners worked the land here. Pears were a Louveciennes speciality when Renoir lived at **No. 9** (an old foundry), during visits to La Grenouillère with Monet. Monet, in the direst of straits, was often sustained with leftovers and tobacco from Renoir's generous parents, who had retired to what Renoir affectionately called their *bicoque* (shanty) in Voisins.

In 1881 his sister Eliza moved to **No. 5 Place Ernest-Dreux**, where Renoir visited her during his most fruitful Seine period of *The Seine at Chatou*, *Luncheon of the Boating Party* (O), *Dance at Bougival* and *Dance in the Country* (O).

Rue de Voisins has the ambience of a sunny hillside fishing village much further south. I passed cobbled alleys, workmen's cottages coloured pink or yellow with blue or brown shutters, gardens bursting with flowers.

Place Fernand-Guillaume. Arriving at the T-junction, I looked back down Rue de Voisins to identify Pissarro's *A Village Street, Louveciennes*, with the servants' quarters of the Château de Voisins on the left, a kitchen garden on the right. 'Paint the essence of things,' Pissarro advised. 'Try to do it by whatever method, without thinking of the *métier* but painting what you observe and what you feel.'

Avenue St-Martin. Two reproduction panels are displayed here. North of the bridge over the railway, Sisley's *Marly Aqueduct* shows the dramatic structure coming to an abrupt end in the middle of fields. This can only be seen before spring, after which trees hide it until autumn. Water from the Machine, after passing along the Chemin de la Machine, was pumped by high pressure up to the aqueduct channel that took it to the Versailles fountains. A remarkable engineering feat by M. Rennequin-Sualem and Company.

South of the railway bridge is one of Pissarro's best-known Louveciennes works, *Entrance of the Village of Voisins* (1872). A horse and cart are approaching up the avenue, across which the shadows of tall trees fall. Two old women are walking towards the village, and I felt I would like to be with them.

Route de Versailles. Maison Retrou (**No. 22**) is familiar from Pissarro's *The Road to Versailles at Louveciennes* (1870), an unusual Pissarro landscape in that it shows identifiable people. Looking towards Louveciennes, on the left-hand side of the busy road is a large, maroon-shuttered grey house covered with Virginia creeper, big enough for his growing family (three children born, five more to come). The mother is Julie Vellay, formerly his parents' maid: running off put a stop to his allowance, but he married her the following year in Croydon, England. The others are his five-year-old daughter Minette, who died four years later, and her nurse.

Pissarro rented the Louveciennes house in 1869. Appearing in the later, peaceful painting *Chestnut Trees in Louveciennes* (1872) (O), it was a scene of catastrophe. Hardly settled in, the Pissarro family was forced to head for England by the dangerous proximity of the Prussians in the invasion of 1870. Pissarro had to leave almost his entire body of work since 1855. The Prussians requisitioned the house and used the studio to butcher meat. Imagine the artist's dismay in London on receiving this letter from his landlord: 'Prussians have caused plenty of havoc. . . . Some of the pictures we have taken good care of, only there are a few which these gentlemen, for fear of dirtying their feet, put on the ground in the garden to serve them as a carpet.' Only forty paintings remained.

Among the destroyed paintings were also some Monets. Pissarro had kindly stored them after putting up Monet and family when the debt-ridden artist was forced to flee creditors in St-Michel-de-Bougival. Together they had worked on the effect of snow: shadow cast by a coloured object on its whiteness contained some of that colour – it was not bituminous. Coloured shade was one of the impressionists' great discoveries. The fascination with different atmospheric conditions is evident in Monet's *The Versailles Road, Melting Snow, Setting Sun* and Pissarro's *The Stagecoach, Louveciennes* (O) (same direction as Monet's, cobble-stones shiny after rain. Paris coach arriving at the Hostellerie du Soleil Levant).

Continuing the walk, I took **Rue du Parc de Marly**. Nearly opposite Pissarro's house, the entrance of the road was a place from which to paint several views in this direction, taking in the still recognizable Mont Valérien and church spire of Louveciennes. He used to walk this way to kitchen gardens and orchards in **Rue du Maréchal-Joffre**. Now suburbia.

Rue du Pont. A bend in the road reveals an old stone bridge leading to the Château du Pont, and water with ducks very much like those in Sisley's *Duckpond, Louveciennes* (the manorial moat, in fact, not a duckpond).

Further on, at the junction with **Rue Pierre-Auguste-Renoir** and **Rue** de Montbuisson, another fine eighteenth-century house was the home of Renoir's painter-model friend, Jeanne Baudot, a local doctor's daughter. The view to the north of the village from here, only visible in winter with leafless trees, inspired no fewer than three painters in consecutive years – Pissarro (1871), Cézanne (on a rare visit, 1872), Sisley (1873).

Not Renoir. It may have been the presence of his ageing family at Louveciennes that made Renoir's output there comparatively small. He worried about their wellbeing. In 1900, old himself, he rented a house in Rue de Montbuisson, near Jeanne Baudot's. Suffering bad arthritis aggravated by a bicycle accident, he was recommended by Doctor Baudot to take frequent purges and physical exercise. Renoir's sense of absurdity was unimpaired: he took up juggling with three small balls.

Bougival

2 hours' drive with stops

Except for Renoir's *Dance at Bougival* (1883), nearly all the other paintings done locally are river subjects (Monet, Pissarro, Sisley, Vlaminck, Derain).

Bougival is an up-and-down commune, its village sprawling down a valley between two steepish hills and the only one of the three communes with a waterfront. Its impressionist sites are spread out but quite possible to walk. I decided to drive.

Seven minutes' drive from Louveciennes station, via **Rue de la Princesse** and **Rue du Peintre Gérôme**, brings one to the bottom of the Bougival valley.

Rue Kellner. No. 1 is an ugly barracks of a house; now offices, it was once the residence of Berthe Morisot. Her beautiful garden, in which she painted Eugène Manet helping their daughter Julie with her lessons, was destroyed to widen **Avenue de la Drionne** into a four-lane highway.

Morisot was a serious walker, exploring the network of footpaths that then linked woods and fields and river. *Woman and Child in the Grass at Bougival* (1882) evokes a hazy, lyrical summer's day; as do Julie and her nanny in *Pasie Sewing in the Garden*

and *Haymaking at Bougival* with its golden beehive haystack.

Morisot's work is often patronized as merely charming. It went much deeper. On her marriage certificate she was 'without profession'. Yet she consistently earned higher prices for her paintings than many of her male colleagues after her Salon debut in 1864. She resented being thought of as simply a talented Sunday painter.

'The singularity of Berthe Morisot,' wrote the poet Paul Valéry, who married her niece Nini, 'was to live her painting and to paint as if it were a natural and necessary function.' She was also adept at role-playing: flirtatious artist's model for Manet, hardworking daughter for her ambitious mother, devoted mother for an only child, and sensitive wife for a kindly but dull husband. As Manet's sister-in-law, however, she felt a secret sympathy with the Olympias of that world and their haughty independence. Morisot tells a revealing story. One day on the riverbank, Julie as a young child was asked her name by a passer-by and innocently gave herself a common cocotte name, 'Bibi'. 'I am Bibi Manet,' she announced confidently. According to Morisot, it made 'two cocottes out promenading on the riverbank laugh until they cried, since they doubtless took her for the child of the celebrated Manet, put out to nurse in the land of the boating girls.'

Bougival town and country. On the other side of the valley are a **Church** and the **Parc de la Jonchère,** its footpaths cutting through fifty acres of unspoilt woods with magnificent Seine views to the terrace of St-Germain-en-Laye downstream and the Ile des Impressionistes upstream.

St-Michel-de-Bougival. Returning to the Louveciennes side of the valley, the hamlet where Monet and family spent 1869 was a discovery. The best of Bougival. Without a car, it is an easy walk from the station of **Bougival-La Celle-St Cloud**.

These were fraught times for Monet. When he was working in Normandy the year before, his worries for Camille and Jean, who were not living with him, caused a suicide attempt. It was half-hearted, admittedly: throwing himself in the water was hardly the most effective suicide for a strong young man brought up by the sea. Monet was a confirmed self-dramatizer and, whenever the situation became drastic, he had no hesitation in laying on the pathos for his friends: 'Think of my position, a child sick, and not the smallest resources.'

At Bougival the family was reunited. Monet had been advised to be nearer to Paris. A collector had bought his portrait of Camille, *Woman in a Green Dress*, but he had not sold much more. Things should have improved. They did not. 'For eight days, no bread . . . no fire for the kitchen, no light,' he wrote to Bazille.

St-Michel-de-Bougival itself was some consolation. Monet lived at **No. 2 Rue de la Vallée**, still a steep, cobbled village street of houses with ramshackle courtyards. The copper beech in **Place de la Chapelle** catches the evening sun, and there is no sound of traffic. The chapel of St-Michel has been bought by the actor Gérard Depardieu, restorer of old properties in his spare time.

The best buildings are in **Place Couturier**: whitewashed, rose-covered houses with outside stairways, shaded by plane trees. An alley hung with vines, strings of onions and straw baskets sounds like a film set but manages to avoid gentrified rusticity. In June there is a picnic for all the community, sharing food and wine under parasols.

Bougival–Port-Marly

2 hours' drive with stops

This important short stretch of the Seine can be either walked or driven. Walking means you have to return the same way, but it is a different view, and the changing light changes the river accordingly. Allow three hours for the walk.

Ile de la Chaussée (known also as **Ile de Bougival**). Taking the slipway off the Bougival bridge leads to convenient parking. A reproduction panel on **Avenue du Commandant-Charcot** facing the town from the island shows Monet's *The Bridge at Bougival* (1869), then a much smaller structure. Otherwise, the view across to

the quayside seems hardly to have changed, the wooded slopes so far spared developments like La Résidence Fontaine-Monet at Chatou.

From my vantage-point on the riverbank opposite Bougival, two illustrations in my little book helped me link Morisot's impressionist *Banks of the Seine* (1883) with Vlaminck's fauvist *Banks of the Seine at Bougival* (1904) and arrive at a panoramic perspective of **Quai Georges Clemenceau**.

Quai Rennequin-Sualem and Quai Conti. Continuing along the main road in St-Germain-en-Laye direction, a ramp leads up to what used to be the managerial offices of the Marly Machine. A reproduction panel displays Vlaminck's *Restaurant, Marly-le-Roi*; though its venue is wrongly titled, a restaurant of sorts is still there. And another reproduction panel displays the reverse angle, back along the quayside to Bougival with another wrongly titled Sisley, *The St-Germain Road at Marly*.

On the left of the quay towards Port-Marly, nestling under the cliff, are ghostly buildings with fanlight windows where once the Marly Machine did its royal water-pumping.

Ile de la Loge. Immediately before the turning to the right over the bridge to the island, a reproduction panel shows Sisley's *The Weir and the Marly Machine*. Downstream of the weir, the view to the Parc de la Jonchère hill is recognizable, but the fine seventeenth-century building jutting out into the river and weir was destroyed in 1968 to make way for the new Bougival lock. All that remains is one small redbrick hut, but the big house with six windows is still there.

Easy parking on the island. The view downstream towards Le Pecq – wide, straight and leafy – is one of the most unspoilt, particularly on a balmy summer's evening or with autumn mists rising. You can visit the impressive modern lock. Sisley's *Boats at the Bougival Lock* (O) shows the smoking funnel of a barge tug emerging from the depths of the lock, industrial transport in a country setting. 'The subject, the motive must always be rendered in a way that is simple, comprehensible and attractive

Renoir's Luncheon of the Boating Party *(1881) chez Fournaise shows a rosy picture of riverside life in contrast to de Maupassant's acerbic short stories with the same setting.*

The attractive brickwork of the Hotel Fournaise.

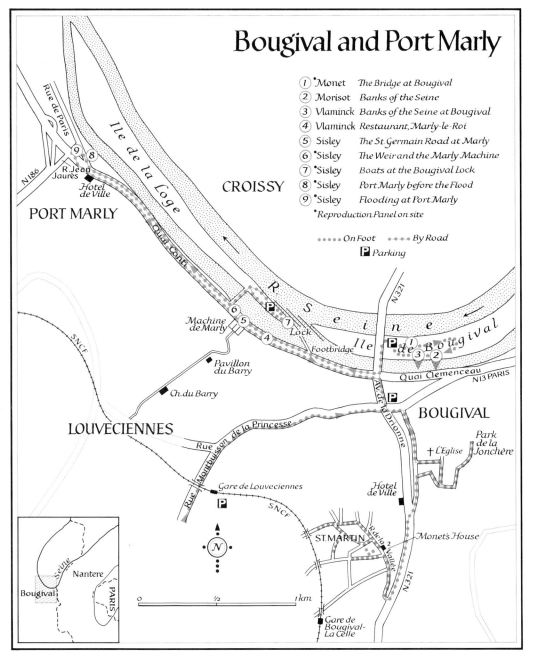

Bougival and Port Marly

①	•Monet	*The Bridge at Bougival*
②	Morisot	*Banks of the Seine*
③	Vlaminck	*Banks of the Seine at Bougival*
④	Vlaminck	*Restaurant, Marly-le-Roi*
⑤	Sisley	*The St Germain Road at Marly*
⑥	•Sisley	*The Weir and the Marly Machine*
⑦	•Sisley	*Boats at the Bougival Lock*
⑧	•Sisley	*Port Marly before the Flood*
⑨	•Sisley	*Flooding at Port Marly*

•*Reproduction Panel on site*

•••••• *On Foot* ◆◆◆◆ *By Road*
🅿 *Parking*

CROISSY

PORT MARLY

LOUVECIENNES

BOUGIVAL

ST. MARTIN

for the spectator' was Sisley's motto.

Beyond the reproduction panel of this picture, walkers will find a useful footbridge back to the waterfront; the foot-slogging can be reduced by making the island detour on the return journey from Port-Marly.

Port-Marly, scene of spectacular floods in 1872 and 1876. On **Rue de Paris** Sisley liked to lunch at the Auberge du Lion d'Or, now the Bistro Italien offering *pizza au feu de bois*. The old inn sign is recognizable from *Port-Marly before the Flood*. The river is very close, just beyond the trees where cars now park. The auberge on the corner of **Rue Jean-Jaurès** in *Flooding at Port-Marly* (O), now Le

Brazza, is where Sisley shows a punt and two men at the door – a calm, clear, limpid image with no sense of danger, almost as though this were an everyday occurrence, or Venice.

Impressionist Island

allow 1 hour for the Fournaise Museum before lunch at the Restaurant, a half-day for the walk after lunch

The park at Chatou called **Ile des Impressionistes** is at the north end of a long, serpentine strip of land linking the **Islands of Chatou, Croissy and Bougival**. The whole of it could reasonably be called **Impressionist**

Island. A ten-minute drive from Port-Marly via Rueil-Malmaison took me to the Chatou bridge. A slipway leads off it on your right to the best-restored impressionist site on the river.

Fournaise. Recently reopened as a restaurant-museum. Renoir's favourite is a bastion of charm holding its own against the aggressively inappropriate Rueil 2000, a Miami-sur-Seine horror on the left bank opposite. Close your eyes to it, and keep them firmly on the redbrick and white stone buildings with wrought-iron trimmings of its guest annexe, where Guy de Maupassant stayed while getting inspiration for 'Yvette' and 'La Femme de Paul': the yellow stucco with maroon shutters and the *guinguette's* terrace with its red-and-white striped awning and coloured light bulbs on strings, where Renoir painted his masterwork *Luncheon of the Boating Party*.

The **Museum** gives an enlightening who's who of the people having such a good time in the picture. On the left, leaning against the balcony rail, is Alphonse Fournaise, son of *le patron*, by Aline Charigot, later Renoir's wife, with her dog, talking to Caillebotte sitting astride a chair. Next to them, actress Ellen Andrée (Degas's model for *Absinthe*) is with an admiring Italian journalist, Maggiolo. With his back to us Baron Barbier (who with another friend, Prince Bibesco, introduced Renoir to the sybaritic pleasures of the Seine), in a brown hat, is talking to Alphonsine Fournaise, daughter of the house. Angèle, a florist and Montmartre painter's model, swigs a glass of wine before being seduced by the quiet, nondescript mystery man at her table: behind her, two much more interesting catches – the poet Laforge and the top-hatted banker, Charles Ephrussi, who was later director of *La Gazette des Beaux-Arts*. The trio behind Maggiolo are Lestringuez, civil servant at the Ministry of the Interior, and Paul Lhote, travel agent at Agence Havas, with his arm round Jeanne Samary, Comédie-Française actress. No painting of the period gives a truer key to the kind of men and women who frequented such places.

The museum pays tribute to Renoir's close friendship with the Fournaise family in no fewer than seven portraits of Alphonsine (O), and one of the likeable Père Fournaise, a pipe-smoking boatbuilder-turned-restaurateur.

When I was at Fournaise, the *bon riveur* Caillebotte was being celebrated rather more unusually. To raise money for Sequana (a Seine valley conservationist group), young boatbuilders were making a replica of Caillebotte's 32-metre sailing boat, *Le Roastbeef*. Each T-shirt bought by visitors paid for 10 centimetres of boat.

The **Restaurant** is not so much about *what* you're eating as *where*. Outside, opposite the riverbank, a reproduction panel shows Renoir's *The Boating Party at Chatou* (1879): Aline raising her skirt to get into a skiff from the pontoon, watched by the ever stylish Caillebotte.

'It was a perpetual holiday,' Renoir declared. 'I was always at Fournaise. I found as many superb girls as I wanted. But my friends knew that for me a girl was only a pretext for a painting.' Until he met Aline.

Post-impressionist Derain's studio, which he shared with Vlaminck, was in a shanty of a building (now also restored) behind the restaurant.

A Walk on the Island. After lunch, the walk began downstream under the road bridge. Two reproduction panels appeared almost at once: Vlaminck's *The Chatou Bridge*, over which the railway brought Parisians to their pleasure ground; and Renoir's different treatment of the same subject – its metal structure and the river glimpsed mysteriously through lush foliage in *The Railway at Chatou* (O).

On the other side of the island a footpath reveals countrified views towards Bougival and Port-Marly. The islands are joined by an isthmus where, when a barge goes by, water laps the path. Where the island swells out again, Le Golf de la Grenouillère is a far cry from 'The Froggery'.

Croissy and Chatou. Crossing the Bougival bridge, I returned upstream along the right bank's riverside road which is closed to traffic on Saturday and Sunday and leads to the reproduction panel of Monet's *La Grenouillère*.

In 1869 *fiacres* from Chatou station

Converted with Caillebotte's help from a coal-and-vegetable transporter, Monet's painting-boat was the subject of Manet's Monet Working on his Boat *(1874), accompanied by Camille.*

Morisot's Hunting Butterflies *(1874) (O) was one of her twelve paintings sold at the otherwise disastrous impressionist Drouot auction of 1875.*

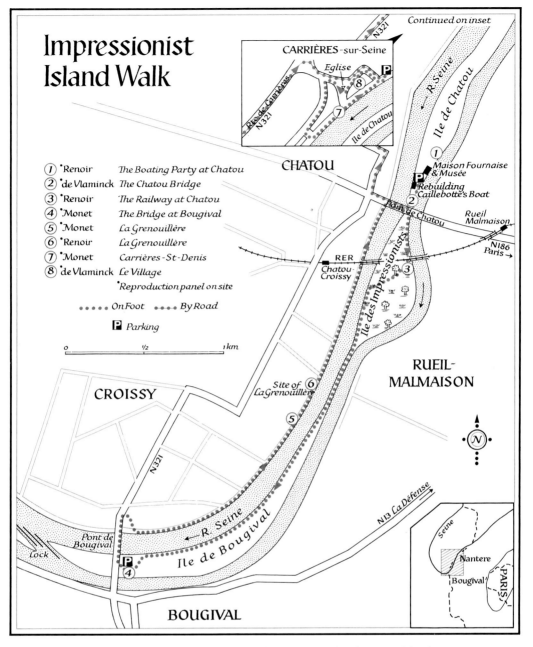

Impressionist Island Walk

CARRIÈRES-sur-Seine

Continued on inset

Eglise

CHATOU

① • Renoir   *The Boating Party at Chatou*
② • de Vlaminck   *The Chatou Bridge*
③ • Renoir   *The Railway at Chatou*
④ • Monet   *The Bridge at Bougival*
⑤ • Monet   *La Grenouillère*
⑥ • Renoir   *La Grenouillère*
⑦ • Monet   *Carrières-St-Denis*
⑧ • de Vlaminck   *Le Village*
　　　　　　　 • *Reproduction panel on site*

••••• On Foot   •••• By Road

🅿 Parking

0 ――― ½ ――― 1 km

CROISSY

Maison Fournaise & Musée

Rebuilding Caillebotte's Boat

Pont de Chatou

Rueil Malmaison

N186 Paris →

RER Chatou-Croissy

Ile des Impressionistes

RUEIL-MALMAISON

Site of ⑥ La Grenouillère

⑤

N

R. Seine

Ile de Bougival

N13 La Défense

Pont de Bougival

Lock

🅿 ④

BOUGIVAL

Seine

Nantere

Bougival

PARIS

lined the towpath, from which the bathing-place, restaurant and island were linked by pontoon. It is difficult to imagine the location as it was in the nineteenth century, because the riverbed has changed greatly; the 'dead' reach where La Grenouillère was situated is now busy with barge traffic.

Skint as they were, Renoir and Monet found mutual support in painting together. A little farther upstream is the reproduction panel of Renoir's treatment of the same subject. At first glance their approach seems identical: the effect of ripples in water, sunlight in foliage, boats, figures, reflections, the use of three primary and their complementary colours. A closer look shows Monet more sombre,

his figures on the Flowerpot Island more blurred. It is the darker image of a sufferer.

Monet raged against poverty, Renoir accepted it with humour. Although not as sure-footed as Monet's, owing to less outdoor painting experience, Renoir's *La Grenouillère* is altogether greener, lighter, sunnier and, in its sharper definition and greater variety of people on the Flowerpot, shows the artist already more interested in the pulse of humanity than the landscape.

The walk's sites end on Chatou bridge, where the downstream view is completely impressionist except for today's electric trains. I picked up the car at Fournaise and continued the drive up the right bank.

Carrières-sur-Seine

half-hour

A detour from the Argenteuil road down to the riverside promenade of **Carrières-sur-Seine** with its giant weeping willows was well rewarded. Fine bourgeois houses with big gardens and a municipal park stretch back to a cliff on which buildings cluster round the church like a hill village. No wonder *Carrières-St-Denis* (O) (as it was called in 1872) appealed to Monet, who painted the view, practically unchanged, from his painting-boat.

Argenteuil and Petit-Gennevilliers

2 hours

Monet's painting-boat, or rather a faithful replica, is one of Argenteuil's few remaining impressionist relics, displayed in the **Salle Jean-Vilar**. Convenient parking near the river makes it a good place to start the walk.

Argenteuil, an iron and steel town, provided the metal for the Gare St-Lazare. Even in Monet's day not much remained of the medieval town, where three religious orders cultivated wine, asparagus and figs. Nowadays the tiny, exquisite Romanesque Chapelle St-Jean-Baptiste is dwarfed by modern concrete blocks. A population of ten thousand in Monet's day has risen to ninety-six thousand, many residents working in the nearby aeronautical factories.

Argenteuil Bridge. Badly damaged in the Franco-Prussian War, it is seen to be under repair in Monet's 1872 painting. Now, walking across the new four-lane road-bridge is the only way to get an impression of the river's attraction at this spot. A perfect stretch for sailing and rowing.

Manet's father was mayor of **Gennevilliers**, an important industrial suburb on the other side of the river. The family property has long since been swallowed up in the urban development of the **Port of Paris**, and only masochists should try to locate it. Berthe Morisot, around the time of her marriage to Manet's brother in 1874, received a letter from him describing the plain 'looking pretty in every direction'. Her paintings are at odds with this: inevitable smoking chimneys and modern stucco villas are the background of *In the Corn*: *Laundresses Perch* has riverside washerwomen hanging out linen on lines near 730 acres of market garden irrigated by sewage from Haussmann's Paris. Only the lyrical *Hunting Butterflies* (O) escapes the tentacles of the urban monster.

Painters of the local gentry seem to have found the Sunday visitors somewhat absurd. Manet gives a flat look to his boating couple in *Argenteuil* (1874). The clerk and his girl, out for a good time, don't seem to know quite what to do with it: she in her fancy city hat; he, ginger-moustached, gazing at her vacantly. Caillebotte went one better the same year with *Oarsman in a Top Hat*, who at least has the sleeves of his striped shirt rolled up.

Petit-Gennevilliers. To visit Caillebotte country, after crossing the bridge I turned right in the downstream direction, where the riverbank was receiving a much-needed refit. It was once a community of some twenty-five bourgeois homes and boatyards. In *The Garden at Petit-Gennevilliers* (1885) yachtsman-horticulturalist-artist Caillebotte shows a beautiful white house with red roof and sunflowers; in another painting his beloved roses are being tended by a girlfriend. By turns humble and provocative, funny and angry, Caillebotte battled on behalf of his colleagues.

From this waterfront, looking across the river, Manet did *Argenteuil (Study of Boats)*, with the green avenue of trees in front of the Salle Jean-Vilar looking much as it does now. Monet captured Camille and Jean walking through *Poppies* (1873) (O) in the field behind (industrial now). Renoir, who frequently stayed with Caillebotte, made *The Seine at Argenteuil* (1874) almost violet, the banks autumnally brown, with a glimpse of the church spire in the distance.

Also still recognizable from Monet's paintings of the toll-bridge are the white, red-roofed cottage of the ferryman, and the taller red *octroi* gatehouse to the left of the bridge. *Octroi* was a tax on goods imported into Paris, and the uncategorizable primitive painter 'Douanier' Rousseau was so called because he once collected the money at just such a toll-gate. Rather than pay tax on *bleu d'Argenteuil*, as the cheap local wine was called, Parisians crossed the bridge to drink it on the spot, which may partly account for the success of its yacht basin and Monet's generous hospitality there.

Rue Pierre-Guienne. Once back across the bridge in Argenteuil, I headed towards the railway – Monet's favourite image of modernity.

Rented with the help of Manet in 1871, Monet's Maison Aubry was seventeenth century, a house of substance with a garden going down to the river. It no longer exists, but the present **Museum** in the same street is a former hospital building of the same period. After the war Durand-Ruel had bought heavily into Monet. For a time it was the lush life: Renoir and Sisley to stay, Camille lavished with clothes and perfume, Jean for once well fed. *Lunch* (O) in a sun-filled garden shows pure sensual happiness – the remains of a good summery meal on the table, Jean playing in the shade, Camille taking a stroll, a straw hat hanging on a branch. *Camille in the Garden, with Jean and his Nanny* (1873) is also very different from the tough year pre-war at St-Michel-de-Bougival. Proudly, Monet painted his garden, and Renoir painted him painting it. Manet, visiting, observed Renoir at work and whispered to Monet: 'Tell him to give up. That boy has no talent!'

Boulevard Karl-Marx. In 1874 Monet had to move round the corner to a more modest house that can still be seen at **No. 21**. A European recession hit France in 1874, and Durand-Ruel was forced to give up buying. Pissarro, Sisley, Renoir and Monet were all once again in financial trouble, and the group united to go independent with the First Impressionist Show.

Monet's second house was no *bicoque*. With a big garden at the back, it was Dutch-style, cream with brown shutters. The river was still only a few minutes' walk away, the railway running parallel with the avenue. Monet must have relished closer proximity to the steam and clatter; he

immortalized *Argenteuil Station* (1872) (Pontoise Museum) beneath a most evocative grey, windy sky, with the red lights of shunting engines, and the hills of the Cormeilles forest behind.

A ten-minute walk brought me back to Salle Jean-Vilar to pick up the car.

Villeneuve-la-Garenne

half-hour

Cutting across the top bend of the Seine's inverted S, I headed in a matter of minutes (via the A86 and N186) across industrial Gennevilliers to the pleasant surprise of **Villeneuve-la-Garenne** and **Ile St-Denis**.

From the **Quai des Saules**, on the island – where a charming clump of *fin-de-siècle* houses drew me back into period after the ugliness of Gennevilliers – Sisley painted *Village by the River, Villeneuve-la-Garenne from Ile St-Denis* (1872). Near the green bridge, cottages line a riverside avenue of neatly clipped trees.

Crossing back to the left bank at Villeneuve-la-Garenne, I drove south along **Quai d'Asnières** with its inviting view of the Ile St-Denis's barges, bistros and *bicoques*.

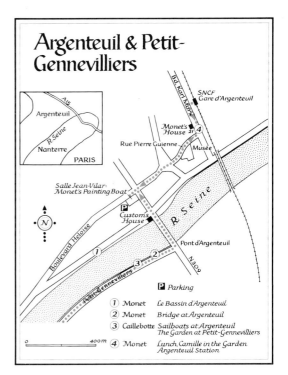

Argenteuil & Petit-Gennevilliers

Argenteuil
R. Seine
Nanterre
PARIS

Bd. Karl Marx
SNCF Gare d'Argenteuil
Monet's House 21
Rue Pierre Guienne
Musée
R. Seine
Salle Jean-Vilar: Monet's Painting Boat
Customs House
Pont d'Argenteuil
Boulevard Héloïse
N300
Quai de Gennevilliers

🅿 *Parking*

① Monet — *Le Bassin d'Argenteuil*
② Monet — *Bridge at Argenteuil*
③ Caillebotte — *Sailboats at Argenteuil / The Garden at Petit-Gennevilliers*
④ Monet — *Lunch, Camille in the Garden / Argenteuil Station*

400m

Controversy over Seurat's revolutionary Sunday Afternoon on the Island of the Grande Jatte *(1885) was a contributing factor to the break-up of the impressionist group in 1886.*

Asnières-sur-Seine and Clichy

half-hour

Asnières, as a late nineteenth-century suburb, was a cultural high spot. Sarah Bernhardt, composer Saint-Saëns and many musicians lived in its quiet, leafy backstreets. The rich and famous came there to have their favourite poodles laid to rest in the **Dog's Cemetery** (a worthwhile incidental visit). In 1887 post-impressionist Emile Bernard, whose parents lived at Asnières, invited van Gogh to the *Restaurant de la Sirène* (O).

Van Gogh painted the restaurant (no longer there) and the railway bridge from upstream, with the road bridge in the background and an elegant lady with a red parasol walking under it. Its wildness gives a hint of the swirling colour-shock of van Gogh that was later to influence Vlaminck and Derain – a turning away from the objectivity of impressionism to the subjectivity of expressionism.

Modern Asnières has pleasant enough enclaves of magnificent *fin-de-siècle* houses and gardens, but its riverside, apart from the park, is strictly for high-speed traffic. No point in searching for where Seurat painted his *Bathing Party*. And across the river in **Clichy**, today's gasworks will only attract the most dedicated of neo-impressionist buffs. Seurat's fellow pointillist Signac had *Gasometers at Clichy* in the Eighth Impressionist Show, and used to sail down to the Ile de la Grande Jatte with Seurat on his boat, *Le Hareng-saur épileptique* (The Epileptic Red Herring).

Nowadays the best way to see this busy, suburban stretch of river is by means of the canal-boat excursion from **Suresnes**, a leisurely, varied day trip passing through the locks of Sisley's *Canal St-Martin* (O).

I did discover where Monet painted his only industrial picture showing men at work. Just south (upstream) of the Asnières bridge on **Quai Michelet**. *Men Unloading Coal* (O) for the Clichy gasworks are suffused in eerie green. When he painted it in 1875 Monet could relate to the daily grind, having fallen once again on rough times after his brief period of financial security.

Beyond the tip of Ile de la Jatte, which van Gogh rendered in *The Levallois Bridge*, the riverscape changes from mundane industrial to fashionable residential. There is easy parking on Quai Michelet near a footbridge over to the island.

Ile de la Jatte

1½ hours

Although the island is in the shadow of La Défense's skyscrapers, with any vestiges of Seurat's park confined to its two tips, a quality of leisure survives. The Neuilly *jeunesse dorée* play tennis and hang out in its trendy bistros, and a genuine rivery smell rises from the quiet, canal-like reach where only houseboats and ducks may float.

More than a century ago, capitalist leisure was the theme of Seurat's masterwork *Sunday Afternoon on the Island of La Grande Jatte* (sketches at Orsay), which took from 1884 to 1886 to complete. High summer with heavy traffic on the river: sailboats, rowing four, skiffs, ferry with tricolour, tug. People seem alienated from one another: girl meditating upon bunch of flowers; giantess too tall to communicate with small girl; man playing a toy trumpet alone; little girl skipping alone; couple not talking, he smoking cigar, she walking a lemur. Seurat's image is not of tranquillity at all: a storm seems about to break, or the stockmarket to crash again.

A stroll down **Boulevard Georges-Seurat** and **Boulevard du Parc** reveals an exclusive island of plant-covered apartment blocks and glass-and-steel offices (Roche, Yves Saint-Laurent), gastronomic 'canteens' like Le Petit Poucet and Les Pieds dans l'Eau, and yet another stadium for upwardly mobile *sportifs*.

The impressionist place to lunch is La Guinguette de Neuilly, preferably on the terrace overlooking the river. Its coloured lights and check tablecloths go with the good, simple food.

For those minus a car, Ile de la Jatte is a short walk from **Métro Neuilly**.

4

LA BUTTE MONTMARTRE

The sign of a Montmartre bistro where van Gogh once painted.

A late nineteenth-century cartoon perfectly expresses the split personality of Montmartre: sacred and profane, above and below. On top of the hill, Sacré-Coeur basilica with an angel piously afloat; at the bottom, the Elysée-Montmartre dance-hall with a devil straddling a drum-kit and a laundress dancing provocatively with a toff.

No wonder. The eccentric miracle of its third-century patron Saint Denis, the bishop of Paris, could be said to be Montmartre's first act of popular entertainment. Legend has it that, after decapitation by the Romans with two other early Christian martyrs, the bishop promptly picked up his head from where it had fallen and walked with it until he dropped dead. At that spot, in celebration of his three-mile headless walk from the Montmartre hilltop, the Basilica of St-Denis was founded.

It was Saint Denis's two partners in death, Eleuthera and Rustique, who inspired the name of the famous pre-impressionist gathering-place, La Brasserie des Martyrs. Martyrdom was seldom in evidence in the smoke-filled, beer-swilling cellar where the experimentalists in the arts of the early 1860s brandished their egos like duelling pistols. Courbet, pipe in mouth, was chief pontificator, surrounded by his admirers, including Baudelaire and Alphonse Daudet, author of *Letters from My Windmill*. It was too downmarket for the radical chic Manet, who preferred the gossip of the glitterati at Café Tortoni on the Boulevard des Italiens. Monet and Pissarro, studying at the Académie Suisse, came there after work for a beer and to talk shop. Courbet was their god, a god of nature and all things natural; they worshipped like pagans at his shrine, treasuring the oracle's words.

La Butte (the hillock) seems like a natural habitat of the revolutionary young impressionists. Oddly, apart from Renoir who painted it frequently and lived there for much of his life, others, like Gauguin, Pissarro and Cézanne, were only temporary visitors.

Already Montmartre was changing. In the seventeenth century, thirty windmills graced the hilltop slopes. In an 1813 picture the hillock seen from the Left Bank has only nine. And, by the 1860s, these had been reduced to two, which together formed the famous dance-hall. The Moulin de la Galette was celebrated by so many painters – Renoir, van Gogh, Signac, Lautrec, Zandomeneghi, van Dongen, Picasso, Utrillo – that it became known as Le Moulin de la Palette.

Montmartre's nature was fragile. The outskirts of Paris seem to be encroaching on countryside in Sisley's 1869 *View of Montmartre*. A faraway windmill looks like an endangered species, as Sisley distances himself in Cité des Fleurs from what will soon become, to him, an alien Parisian playground.

Equally, Pissarro's early work in Montmartre reflects a yearning to preserve the warmth of a summery, tree-shaded sidestreet in the drawing *Rue St-Vincent* (1860). Harmony, tranquillity, a place for lovers to stroll. Even the dingy working-class back alley of his friend Guillaumin's more descriptive *Montmartre* (1865) is offset by a fine white house in sunshine, and the thin chimney of a workshop matches the slender trunks of young trees in little gardens with chickens. In light and shade, greenery and grime, decadence and innocence, Montmartre was Paris sacred and profane. Its appeal was independent and special.

The independence established itself early in the 1870s. An important name associated with impressionist Montmartre was not a painter at all but a politician: Georges Clemenceau. Later responsible for commissioning Monet's *Water Lilies* for the State, Clemenceau was Montmartre's 29-year-old mayor. It was his pleasant official job to give a hero's welcome to Victor Hugo, back from exile after Napoleon III's demise.

During the Prussian siege of 1870 Clemenceau organized a postal service of thirty balloons, overflying the Prussian lines to maintain contact with the rest of France. He was a member of the Montmartre Revolutionary Club, which was the brains of the Commune. Later, the Communards considered him a traitor for intervening to try to prevent them from shooting two Republican generals. The generals were executed. Clemenceau was forced to resign as mayor.

The short civil war caused much suffering – starvation during a bitterly cold winter, bloody massacres. The basilica of Sacré-Coeur was built to commemorate the victims of the Commune, while Clemenceau, back in favour as deputy of the 18th *arrondissement*, worked ceaselessly for an amnesty for former Communards. Among those pardoned was the distinguished Montmartre engraver, Auguste Delâtre, a close friend of Renoir.

Renoir forged the link between early 'country' impressionist images and the 'city' Montmartre of post-impressionist Toulouse-Lautrec, whose earthy expressionism owed much to Degas.

The Moulin de la Galette, for Renoir, was still a country dance-hall; he loved what he called the *bon enfant* side of young Parisians out for a good time, like a children's party where no one fights and the girls and boys have good, clean fun. 'Liberty without debauchery . . . abandon without coarseness . . . in a village not yet degenerated into the picturesque' was how Renoir described it to his son, Jean. Its clientele were locals – *petit bourgeois* attracted by low rents and good air, a few smallholders cultivating a patch of land, workers who descended the northern slopes to 'ruin their lungs' in the new factories of St-Ouen. And, of course, the shopgirls, seamstresses and laundresses from all over north Paris, out for weekend adventure with their errand-boys and clerks.

From Renoir's comparatively innocent hilltop, the Moulin de la Galette with its light-footed, summery waltzes and jolly polkas, it was a descent down slippery slopes to the sweaty, floor-stamping cancans of Toulouse-Lautrec's raunchier Moulin Rouge on the urban Boulevard de Clichy. Renoir, the family man of humble origins, and Lautrec, the crippled aristocratic batchelor, knew each other, liked each other, joked and ate together. Yet Lautrec, depicting Montmartre nightlife nearly fifteen years after Renoir, focused his more astringent vision through absinthe-coloured spectacles, heralding the go-for-it, rip-roaring decadence of the Nineties.

The new Montmartrois – Lautrec, van Gogh and, peripherally, Gauguin – were known as the 'painters of the *petit* boulevard' as opposed to the 'painters of the *grand* boulevard' (Monet, Renoir, Degas, Manet and Pissarro). Lautrec had met van Gogh, when they were both studying in Rue Coutance under the *pompier* Cormon. The mere mention of Seurat's pointillist experiments, much admired by the young painters for their revolutionary daring, caused risible explosions from their out-of-touch master, and van Gogh soon left.

It was in Montmartre that Vincent, as he always signed himself, began to find himself as a painter. Eager, bookish, hyper-active, he had already thrown himself unsuccessfully into art dealing, teaching, lay preaching and a stint as a missionary in a Belgian mining district. Solitude attracted him. Hikes into the desolate no man's land of La Plaine St-Denis behind Montmartre produced *The Outskirts of Paris* (1886), in which a single lamp-post in the foreground shows a boulevard petering out in scrubby fields. Isolated people wander listlessly along vague dirt tracks. Van Gogh was in transition from the relentlessly grim subject-matter and dark treatment of works like *The Return of the Miners*, taking tentative steps towards a lighter palette under impressionist influence.

Both van Gogh and Lautrec were also familiar with the Montmartre Maquis, that scrubby hillside where layabouts escaping from the police could hide in the low bushes and winding alleys of card-pack houses. Occupants cobbled these together with tar-covered board and carpenter's offcuts, and proudly referred to them as their cottage or chalet. Somehow they managed a ramshackle garden, and to keep rabbits or a couple of goats. Inhabitants ranged from Renoir's fishwife friend Josephine, who supplied his herrings, to the distinguished illustrator Steinlen.

Steinlen, Delâtre and their new technique of lithography coincided with

Montmartre's ascendancy as a place of popular entertainment, its creation and performance. Posters, song-sheets and theatre programmes were in demand.

Steinlen did posters for Rodolph Salis's Le Chat Noir, a literary cabaret where young journalists, politicians, singers, poets and painters such as Signac and Seurat could meet. Respectful silence came only at cabaret time, for which lithographer Henri Rivière produced forty-five 'shadow plays', with colour eventually added to the black projections, plus voices and music.

Unlike the standoffish Degas, the sociable Lautrec was involved with the cabaret artists he portrayed in his posters. Degas never even met the popular singer Thérésa, a frequent subject, whereas Lautrec was close friends with the more sophisticated Yvette Guilbert. A subjective intimacy informs *Mlle Eglantine's Troupe* – four girls performing a *quadrille* like friends at a party. Their names – Eglantine, Jane Avril, Cléopatre and Gazelle – sound almost suitable enough for them to be introduced to Lautrec's mother, the Countess. Other cancan dancers less so: La Goulue (Greedyguts), Nini Patte en-l'Air whose high kicks removed many a man's top hat, and La Môme Cri-Cri whose too-wide splits caused a memorable painful shriek.

Degas's cartoonist protégé, Forain, wittily shows *The Englishman at the Promenade* of the Moulin Rouge, the pickup bar that did particularly thriving business on the nights when women were allowed in free. The Englishman looks a bit lost, eyeing the girls furtively, as though he has just dropped in from a grouse moor, with his tweed cap and ulster, a game bag's strap just visible. He would be poaching on no one's preserves, as long as he stayed clear of the Prince of Wales. 'Wotcha, Wales!' is an approximate cockney translation of the dancer La Goulue's famous greeting to the Prince. 'Buy us a drink, luv!'

Lautrec also did the poster *Aristide Bruant at his Cabaret*. I have often envied the poet-performer's swashbuckling black hat and red scarf thrown insouciantly round the neck, and Bruant's ability to insult his audience without diminishing the Full House signs at Le Mirliton. Many of them were marginals like himself, misfits in a Paris full of bourgeois humbug, hypocrisy and *fin-de-siècle* angst, the Belle Epoque's dissenters.

It was a time of total theatre at Le Théâtre Libre, for which Lautrec designed programmes. Artistic cross-fertilization had Debussy setting a Verlaine poem, with sheet music illustrated by Willette. Debussy met Erik Satie, one of the first serious composers to use ragtime, at Le Chat Noir, where Satie was doing a gig as pianist. And the former tightrope-walker turned painter, Suzanne Valadon, did her *Portrait of Erik Satie* (1892), showing him in bright colours befitting a witty and highly complex composer.

With Valadon we come full circle. In 1909, herself a respected artist (and former model of Chavannes, Renoir, Degas and Lautrec), she came to live at 12 Rue Cortot, where Renoir had worked on *Dancing at the Moulin de la Galette* (O) more than three decades before. Also sharing her turret studio were her son Maurice Utrillo, between bouts of alcoholic depression, and her husband, painter André Utter. Always in trouble of some kind, the eccentric, sociable family was known as the Unholy Trinity. Paintings of Montmartre by mother and son are hard to categorize; Utrillo's snowscapes are reminiscent of Sisley or Pissarro, and could be called late impressionist.

In his old age Degas found comfort in visits to Valadon at Rue Cortot; she was one of the few friends whom he had not offended irretrievably.

Degas admired Valadon as a draughtswoman rather than as a model. When he was first introduced to her he looked at one of her drawings in a long, long silence, while she waited and waited for any response. 'You are one of us,' he said finally.

Valadon always denied sex between them. With typical, earthy humour, she tells us: 'Hell, no man has given me so many compliments on my skin, my hair, my muscles. He flattered me as though I'd been a horse or a dancer. I was never pretty, his admiration was totally practical, concentrated on a body trained for tightrope-walking.'

Hardly the makings of romance. But in his strange way Degas loved Suzanne Valadon, as he did Mary Cassatt, because she was a woman who had succeeded as an artist. She was a link with a rapidly receding past. While Monet and Renoir led full family lives to the end, Degas relied on his solitary peregrinations in the Montmartre streets, near-blind as he was, to keep even peripherally in touch before his death in 1917.

The poet Léo Larguier describes the well-known white-bearded octogenarian, spotted while tapping his white stick past the barkers and Barbary organs of the funfair on the Boulevard Rochechouart. 'We stopped to watch him. He went away slowly, with a stiff step, like an automaton. He was heading for his bleak home where only a tyrant of a servant waited for him, in the beautiful evening light of Montmartre when I was young . . .'

A Walk
ON
La Butte Montmartre

The Swing *by Renoir (1876) (O).*

INFORMATION

Walk on La Butte (full day)

Start: Métro Pigalle, Boulevard de Clichy. End: Métro Abbesses, Place des Abbesses.

Lunch: Moulin de la Galette area.

Short cut to avoid hill climb: Funicular Place St-Pierre to Sacré-Coeur.

Refreshment, Meals and Overnight

Restaurants and Bars

Le Métro (café-bar), Place des Abbesses.

Le Vrai Paris (brasserie), (**C**), 33 Rue des Abbesses.

Le Sancerre (late-night café-bar), (**C**), 35 Rue des Abbesses.

☆ Da Graziano (Italian), (**C**), 83 Rue Lepic. Tel. 01.46.06.84.77.

La Mère Catherine (bistro), (**B**), 6 Rue Norvins. Tel. 01.46.06.32.69.

L'Assommoir (bistro), (**C**), 12 Rue Girardon. Tel. 01.42.64.55.01.

Le Cépage (shellfish), (**B**), 65 Rue Caulaincourt. Tel. 01.46.06.95.15.

Les Copains d'Abord (restaurant), (**B**), 62 Rue Caulaincourt. Tel. 01.46.06.29.83.

☆ La Bonne Franquette (bistro with accordion), (**B**), 18 Rue St-Rustique. Tel. 01.42.52.02.42.

Hotels

Des Arts, (**B**), (no meals), 5 Rue Tholozé. Tel. 01.46.06.30.52.

Regyn's, (no meals), 18 Place des Abbesses. Tel. 01.42.54.45.21.

Terrass, (**A**), 12 Rue J. de Maistre. Tel. 01.46.06.72.85.

Nightlife

Bal Au Moulin Rouge, Place Blanche (Métro Pigalle or Blanche). Two shows (drinks only), 10pm (510F) and midnight (450F). With dinner (from 750F). Reservations: tel. 01.46.06.00.19.

Folies-Bergère, 32 Rue Richer (Métro Cadet or Rue Montmartre). Dinner-and-show daily (except Sun and Mon) 7pm (580–690F). Show only daily 9pm (except Sun and Mon), Sunday 5pm (150–320F). Reservations: tel. 01.44.79.98.98.

Au Lapin Agile, 22 Rue des Saules (Métro Lamarck-Caulaincourt). Open 9pm–2am. Show, with drink, (110F). Reservations: tel. 01.46.06.85.87.

Chez Madame Arthur (drag), 75bis Rue des Martyrs. Dinner-and-show 9pm (295F), show only 10.30pm (165F). Reservations: tel. 01.42.54.40.21.

Museums and Sites

Vieux Montmartre, 12 Rue Cortot. Open daily (except Mon), 11–6. Entry: 25F. Tel. 01.46.06.61.11.

Sacré-Coeur Basilica

Eglise St-Pierre

Place du Tertre

Tourist Office

Office du Tourisme, 21 Place du Tertre, 75018. Open daily Apr–Sep, 10–10; Oct–Mar, 10–7. Tel. 01.42.62.21.21.

A Walk on La Butte

whole day

During this up-and-down stroll I kept thinking of Renoir, 'commuting' on foot between his Rue St-Georges studio on the lower slopes and his hilltop studio in Rue Cortot, while engaged on *Dancing at the Moulin de la Galette* (O); and Toulouse-Lautrec, climbing and descending the winding streets and steep steps on his short legs in all weathers and states of hangover.

Cabbies refused to take fares beyond **Place des Abbesses**, the lower village centre; the climb was too much for their horses, the descent too much for their brakes. Nowadays visitors daunted by the steep climb on foot can be borne skywards by **Funicular** from **Place St-Pierre** to **Sacré-Coeur**; there's much jockeying for Camcorder position as the great panorama of Paris spreads out below. From the top it's an easy, flattish walk to many of the important sites of my Montmartre map.

Allowing a good day to make the most of the ups and downs without exhaustion, I started where we just left Degas, heading for home in **Boulevard de Clichy** from **Boulevard Rochechouart**. A narrow street, heading north, begins the gentle climb.

Rue des Martyrs. On the Boulevard Rochechouart corner once stood the **Cirque Fernando** (later called **Medrano** after a famous clown), very conveniently placed for Degas to study the tense muscles of the acrobat Miss Lala, perilously suspended on her wire.

The Medrano was a good halfway house for Renoir between his two studios. Even in rare moments of leisure his eyes and hands were seldom idle, and ever since his early *The Clown* (1868) (O) the circus had fascinated him. He saw, in the children's easy contact with clowns and rapt attention to high-wire feats, how the young could best appreciate art. 'Children should get used to seeing for themselves and not asking opinions.'

The Fernando was also the scene of Seurat's last unfinished masterpiece *The Circus* (1890) (O). Poignantly, for one so near premature death from meningitis, it is filled with life-affirming energy: full-blast musicians,

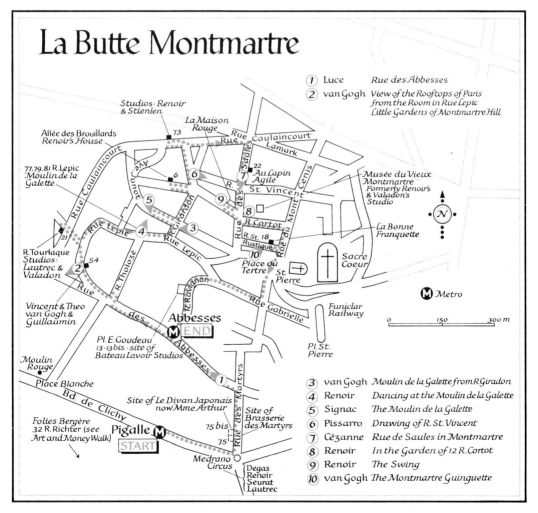

La Butte Montmartre

① Luce   *Rue des Abbesses*
② van Gogh   *View of the Rooftops of Paris from the Room in Rue Lepic*
     Little Gardens of Montmartre Hill

Studios: Renoir & Stienlen
La Maison Rouge
Allée des Brouillards
Renoir's House
73
Rue Caulaincourt
Rue Lamark
77,79,81 R.Lepic
Moulin de la Galette
22 Au Lapin Agile
7
R. St. Vincent
Musée du Vieux Montmartre Formerly Renoir's & Valadon's Studio
6
6
Ave. Junot
5
9
R. des Saules
8
R.Cortot
La Bonne Franquette
21
Rue Lepic
R.Girardon
3
R.St. 18
Rustique
La Bonne Franquette
R.Tourlaque
Studios:
Lautrec & Valadon
2
54
R.Tholoze
Rue Lepic
10
Place du Tertre
St. Pierre
Sacre Coeur
Vincent & Theo van Gogh & Guillaumin
Rue des Abbesses
R.Ravignan
Rue Gabrielle
Funiclar Railway
Ⓜ Metro
Abbesses
Ⓜ END
Pl.St. Pierre
Pl. E. Goudeau
13-13 bis: site of Bateau Lavoir Studios
①
0   150   300 m
Moulin Rouge
Place Blanche
Bd. de Clichy
Site of Le Divan Japonais now Mme Arthur
Site of Brasserie des Martyrs
Folies Bergère
32 R. Richter (see Art and Money Walk)
75 bis
Pigalle Ⓜ
START
75 bis
Medrano Circus
Degas
Renoir
Seurat
Lautrec

③ van Gogh   *Moulin de la Galette from R Girardon*
④ Renoir   *Dancing at the Moulin de la Galette*
⑤ Signac   *The Moulin de la Galette*
⑥ Pissarro   *Drawing of R. St. Vincent*
⑦ Cézanne   *Rue de Saules in Montmartre*
⑧ Renoir   *In the Garden of 12 R.Cortot*
⑨ Renoir   *The Swing*
⑩ van Gogh   *The Montmartre Guinguette*

Above: *Post-impressionist Toulouse-Lautrec, relishing Montmartre nightlife to the hilt, pioneered posters of cabaret performer friends like Jane Avril watching Yvette Guilbert at* Le Divan Japonais *(1892).*

Left: *Seurat's pointillist* The Circus *(1890) (O) shows the Cirque Medrano which also inspired a Renoir clown, a Degas acrobat and Lautrec trapeze artists.*

diabolic tumbling acrobat, posturing ringmaster, and graceful girl in yellow on her white horse.

Montmartre artists as different as Seurat and Picasso were attracted to the circus, but Lautrec's gratitude to it was special. His 1888 painting *At the Cirque Fernando* shows a raffish ringmaster with whip and a redhead in green on a strapping, sexy piebald. A year later, Lautrec's health collapsed through too much wild living. Confined to a Neuilly clinic for delirium tremens and loss of memory, he proved that he could remember perfectly by accurately conveying the circus in drawings like *The Flying Trapeze*. They secured his release.

At **No. 75** Rue des Martyrs, a modern entertainment hall Le Divan du Monde has long since replaced the **Brasserie des Martyrs**. Not a vestige remains of the illustrious beer-house, where some of the principles of pre-impressionist art were formulated.

To supplement his father's small allowance to him as an art student, Monet did lightning, on-the-spot cartoons of the colourful clientele. He considered it beneath him. And money easily earned disappeared no less easily on the tarts who frequented the dive at all hours. The cartoons at least got him noticed. Monet was pleased to discover that the starry Courbet had a soft spot for young talent, and flattered to receive Courbet's only too honest comments on his monumental *Déjeuner sur l'herbe*. 'Too ambitious,' warned Courbet. He was proved only partly right (Chapter One, p. 26).

Next door, at **No. 75bis**, is the site of **Le Divan Japonais**, where Lautrec always had too good a time to do many sketches on the spot. The Elysée-Montmartre and the Moulin Rouge were his sketching grounds; here, the acts were more *artistique* and the audience listened attentively to a singer's lyrics. In Lautrec's 1893 poster, dancer Jane Avril is a chic member of the audience with her elegant top-hatted escort, Edouard Dujardin, while willowy Yvette Guilbert, recognizable by her black gloves, sings on stage. Lautrec, influenced though he was by the impressionists, preferred footlights to sunlight, the often *risqué* songs ('The

Virgins' was banned by the censor) of Yvette Guilbert to riverside balls (he could not dance). From his many images of her in caricatural style, nobody could guess how good she looked in the flesh. 'For God's sake,' Guilbert once complained, 'don't make me so horribly ugly . . . not everyone sees just my artistic side.' It says much for Lautrec's charm that they remained friends.

One of Guilbert's most popular songs was 'Madame Arthur', and in 1945 Le Divan Japonais adopted the title as its name, which it has kept to this day. It is the venue for Paris's perennially most famous transvestite show. Cochinelle made his/her debut there. Montmartre cabarets like nothing more than a good literary plug, and Simone de Beauvoir pronounced, to the greater glory of **Madame Arthur**: 'One isn't born a woman. One becomes one.'

Rue des Abbesses. Montmartre's main street, where there are plenty of useful refreshment places. For *fin-de-siècle* ambience, best settle for brasseries like Le Métro and Le Vrai Paris rather than the inevitable tapas bars and *crêperies*. The regulars are not just there to provide local colour for tourists: Montmartre is still a working neighbourhood.

Degas would be happy about the main street's new modern dance school, currently in the process of construction, but probably was not happy about the redbrick Eglise St-Jean, completed in 1904, when his sight may, mercifully, have been just too bad to register 'Our Lady of the Bricks' in all its horror.

A modern street market, Hamon 4 Saisons, is reminiscent of the fruit and vegetable stalls in neo-impressionist Maximilien Luce's warm, glowing *La Rue des Abbesses* (1896). He managed to combine the non-realistic pointillism of Seurat and Signac with images from everyday life in the Paris streets. His friendship with Pissarro, whose anarchist sympathies he shared, is evident in the strong poetic realism of this underrated artist.

Passing **Rue Tholozé** on my right, I took in the classic view of **Le Moulin de la Galette**, the sails of its hilltop windmill in line with the tapering perspective of the rising street. It is almost too seductive, inviting one to take a short cut between picture-postcard houses, up camera-weary steps direct to the impressionist star turn. Sticking with the more gradual climb, I continued up Rue des Abbesses and took the right fork into **Rue Lepic** – van Gogh country.

Rue Lepic. Mutual help was one of the most attractive qualities of late nineteenth-century artists, collectors and dealers. Almost too well known is the legendary support of a younger to an older brother from Theo van Gogh. As manager of art dealers Goupil, Boussod & Valadon's Montmartre branch, he bravely handled Pissarro, Sisley, Monet and Renoir, whom his philistine bosses did not find sufficiently saleable; Theo persisted, later taking on Seurat, Signac, Gauguin and Cézanne. For a socially timid and retiring foreigner in Paris, to go consistently against his French employers was enough strain without having responsibility for a mad genius of a brother.

Imagine Theo's surprise – and secret misgivings – when he received a note in 1886 that Vincent had left Antwerp and was already in Paris to study with Cormon. It was a timely move. The impressionists as a group were breaking up, and he came into contact with the clash of stimulating new influences: the perennial gentle wisdom of Pissarro; the chill science of Seurat; the evangelical zeal of Signac; and the often foul-mouthed, over-the-top breakaway into pure colour of Gauguin. Pissarro, having seen Vincent's Paris work, became convinced he would 'either go mad or leave the impressionists far behind'. Cézanne thought his pictures were already those of a madman.

Theo's flat in Rue Victor-Massé was not big enough for the two of them. He rented a bigger apartment at **No. 54** Rue Lepic, where Vincent had his own room, bathed in southern light with a sumptuous view of Paris. 'I feel more like myself,' he declared, already under the impressionists' influence. 'I have made a series of colour studies . . . trying to render intense colour and not a grey harmony . . . I also did a dozen landscapes, frankly green, frankly

blue.' Visiting the Eighth (and last) Impressionist Show, organized by Berthe Morisot and her husband, Eugène Manet, Vincent was excited by the pointillists Seurat and Signac and adopted their technique for his *Little Gardens of Montmartre Hill* and *View of the Roofs of Paris from the Room in the Rue Lepic* (1887).

The view, through a gap between tall buildings as far as the towers of Notre-Dame, is not much changed. This bend in the street on the lower slopes of *La Butte* has been properly preserved from developers. The van Goghs lived on the third floor of the fine Louis-Philippe mansion (1886–8); Guillaumin occupied the first floor.

Vincent made friends with Gauguin, whose tempestuous nature matched his own. He observed sadly how Gauguin, jealous of the pointillists' success, refused to shake Signac's hand at the Nouvelle-Athènes; and the snubbing of Pissarro, who had encouraged Gauguin's early work and given him hospitality in the Oise valley (Chapter Five, p. 110). Vincent hated the squabbles among the impressionists. Yet with vivid slaps of colour to depict his pennants for *The Fourteenth of July, Paris*, he shows himself already influenced by Gauguin's bold colouring; they held a joint exhibition in a Montmartre restaurant that ended in a punch-up between Vincent and the owner.

More cooperative was Agostina Segatori, former Degas model and owner of Le Tambourin cabaret, a few minutes' walk down from Rue Lepic on the Boulevard de Clichy. For a joint exhibition there with Lautrec and Gauguin, his *Italian Woman* (O) allowed her beloved Vincent to decorate the place with fashionable Japanese prints that hardly went with her Italian décor of tambourines. Lautrec later painted her whitening her face with *Rice Powder* (1899), and Picasso caught her about to drink an *Apéritif* (1901). Vincent shows her in repose with cigarette and glass of wine. When she could stand his moods no longer, he had to break down her door to retrieve his Japanese prints.

These moods were becoming Montmartre legend. 'Vincent would get undressed,' Guillaumin recalled, 'go

In Dancing at the Moulin de la Galette *(1876) (O) Renoir captured the louche innocence of open-air dance halls where clerks and shopgirls, artists and models mingled on Sunday.*

down on his knees to help explain what he wanted to say, and nothing would calm him down.' Theo was glad to see him leave Paris for Arles in 1888, as suddenly as he had arrived. In two years Vincent had wrecked Theo's home life, turned his room into a pit, and made enemies of the mildest of people. He was nearly always forgiven.

Rue Tourlaque. A detour: turning left after the van Gogh house brought me down Rue Tourlaque to the crossroads with **Rue Caulaincourt**, where Lautrec lived from 1887 to 1897, on the corner of **Nos. 5–7** (studios with brick façade at **No. 21** Rue Caulaincourt).

Lautrec felt at home in Montmartre, where he was not the misfit he often seemed among the horsey, county crowd around his home in south-western France. A rare bone malady had caused fractures to fail to heal properly after two banal falls on parquet floors – not even from a horse, as his sporty father, the Count, would have preferred. Lautrec was a fine rider as a child, exemplary in country pursuits of all kinds. In his own family circle he became something of an embarrassment when his legs refused to grow; in Montmartre he was easily absorbed into a landscape with its share of eccentric figures. His stamina was incredible. Drink never seemed to affect his work, and anaesthetized the pain in his stunted legs. Nature had compensated him with parts of the body that were larger and stronger than normal, giving him a superhuman zest for work and play; owing to a particularly impressive profile when naked, he was known as 'Coffeepot' by the brothel girls.

Degas, whose brothel and cabaret paintings were much admired by Lautrec, respected his draughtsmanship but disapproved, as he always did of people who made a spectacle of themselves in public. Looking the way he looked, Lautrec could hardly do otherwise. Yet Degas continued to be his master. Once, showing his respect in typically flamboyant manner, Lautrec invited his puzzled dinner guests, after the cheese, to follow him to a certain Mademoiselle Dihau's nearby apartment. Lautrec pointed to the Degas portrait of her and said: 'There, my friends, is your dessert!'

Renoir's cousin-in-law, Gabrielle Renard, who both modelled for *le patron* and was Aline Renoir's indefatigable aide, had a soft spot for Lautrec. A winter freeze-up of fountains had Gabrielle fetching water from a supplier on the corner of Rues Lepic and Tholozé. Lautrec, on a similar mission, offered her a glass of mulled wine. She told Jean Renoir: 'Toulouse-Lautrec was polite. He always raised his hat to the woman at the shop. He was clean. White shirt well ironed, sometimes without a tie. When he wore one, it was black. A nice, kindly, funny man. At first people laughed at him and called him Short-Arse. He couldn't have cared less. You get used to it. You get used to anything. As *le patron* said: "You don't see yourself." '

Lautrec did two portraits of his neighbour Suzanne Valadon in the impressionist manner, around the time of his wonderful pastel of van Gogh (1887). Then he went a way very much his own, turning to expressionism in his posters. He was a better draughtsman than painter, above all interested in people, in their ambience, and had no use for the figureless landscapes of Monet and Sisley.

His studio was a jumble of artist's materials, exotic costumes for dressing up, cocktail ingredients and a rowing machine. Suzanne loved his lethal cocktails, always mixed with the very best liquor available to an artist of means; disdain of gut-rot may have secured a few much-needed years in his brief thirty-seven. Parties were often in fancydress, with Lautrec as a Japanese mikado, cooking gastronomic dishes such as *homard à l'armoricaine*. Once, Suzanne appeared naked to shock the particularly stuffy baby-sitter for her small son, Maurice. Daughter of a laundress, she took up modelling after an accident as a tightrope-walker. As a single parent, doing odd jobs to support her child, she hoped that Lautrec would be more than just a good lover and marry her. He encouraged her drawing, as Degas had done, but marriage was too hazardous a status for him – and her. She'd already fallen once from a tightrope, and once, Lautrec decided, was enough.

Lautrec, van Gogh and Gauguin were a wilder bunch than their predecessors. They were basking in the warm, louche climate of Montmartre, while Monet and Renoir were slowly becoming part of the very art establishment they had once despised. Thanks to Durand-Ruel's success with sales in America to a much less hostile public than in Paris and London (1886–7), Renoir said later: 'Perhaps it was due to the Americans we didn't starve to death.'

For Lautrec, van Gogh and Gauguin, the impressionists were a hard act to follow. Their own meteoric lives were brief and intense. They would catch fire, dazzle and burn out many years before the deaths of Degas, Renoir and Monet.

Rue Lepic (continued). Returning to the long, winding street from this detour, I climbed gently to Montmartre's most famous impressionist site, **Le Moulin de la Galette at Nos 77, 79, 81**.

The windmill, with its wooden sails and structure very much intact (though not the original), towers above ivy-clad banks amid the trees of its secret garden. Unfortunately, it is no longer visitable. As painted by the post-impressionist Bonnard, *Rue Tholozé* (1897), looking down from Le Moulin, over the rooftops on the left of the garden gateway, is unchanged.

The old entrance is on the corner of **Rue Girardon**, where van Gogh painted *The Moulin de la Galette, seen from Rue Girardon*, still in the impressionist manner. On the same corner is now an Italian restaurant, Da Graziano, with puffs from *le show biz*, including Lauren Bacall. I could endorse her *'Merci pour tout. Délicieux!'* after an inexpensive lunch menu, wine included. In a summer heatwave the Italianate back garden where I ate was cool, green and shady, with the second windmill, Le Radet, visible above the awning. It was as close as I could get to the old Moulin.

Moulins cabarets began in the eighteenth century. A family of Montmartre millers, the Debrays, owned two mills: Le Blute-fin and Le Radet. A hero of Napoleonic resistance,

Pierre-Charles Debray, defending Montmartre against the Allies in 1814, was speared by a Cossack and his remains were nailed to the sails of his windmill. Settling for a more peaceful life, his son – miller and wine merchant – opened the first Montmartre *guinguette*, Le Bal Debray, on the premises, providing hot *galettes* (pancakes) made from his own flour as refreshment.

In 1871 a large open-sided shed for the orchestra, rustic shelters round the dance-floor for the guests, and paper lanterns were added to the mills and gardens. By the time Renoir embarked on his masterpiece in 1876, its weekend dances were famous for the lively polka band, and all north Paris came to enjoy the 'Grand Jardin des Jeux' and 'Admirable Pointe de Vue'. Men and women were obliged to wear hats; a woman with loose hair was considered to have matching morals.

Unlike Lautrec, who took a sketchpad to the Moulin Rouge and did his main work in the studio, Renoir worked *in situ*, adding only finishing touches at the studio in Rue Cortot. During the week there were no dances and he could people the place with his own models. He was more interested in the effects of sunlight falling on them through the trees, speckling clothes and faces, and the strange green reflections, than in the people themselves. A critic claimed they looked like corpses.

Always in a hurry, 'quicker than quick-silver' as one of his models described him, Renoir made time to stop in the street any attractive Montmartroise seamstress or errand-girl who might be glad of a few extra sous. It embarrassed him to be taken for some old *satyr* (aged only forty!). He insisted on meeting the mothers, who were only too glad 'to put some butter on the spinach' by trusting their daughters to his care. In addition to his regulars Angèle, Jeanne and Estelle, he co-opted his former mistress *la petite* Margot. A wilder bird than his Montmartre pigeons, Margot's moonlight flits to other beds were tempered by a good humour and fresh beauty that made her hard not to forgive. Shortly after posing for *Dancing at the Moulin de la Galette*

Above: Toulouse-Lautrec shows La Goulue and Valentin-le-Désoggé Dancing at the Moulin Rouge *(1890) amid toffs on the prowl for a new mistress.*

Left: Fountains from Toulouse-Lautrec's time can still be seen on street corners.

Above: *Ornate old knockers adorn Montmartre's front doors.*

Right: *The archway at the entrance to the Museum of Old Montmartre.*

Below: *Manet's enigmatic swan song* A Bar at the Folies-Bergère *(1881–2) shows the pensive barmaid Suzon.*

she contracted smallpox and neither of the impressionist collectors. Doctors Gachet and de Bellio, could save her. She was Renoir's Mimi, and her death was more of a wrench than he might have imagined.

Margot is on the left of the picture, dancing in the arms of the dashing Cuban painter Pedro Vidal de Solarès y Cardenas, his bowler hat tilted over his eyes. The male models are all members of Renoir's close circle: Lamy, Rivière, Lhote, Lestringuez, Cordey, Goeneutte, Gervex, and his journalist brother, Edmond. The ensemble has an almost painful emanation of carefree weekends of long ago, waltzing on a summer Sunday, dappled sunlight falling on faces, the movement of bodies closely entwined, a dreamy conviviality among the foreground group at the table. It is Renoir at his most sensual and sensitive.

Rue Girardon/Avenue Junot. Soon after turning left into Rue Girardon from Da Graziano, I made a short detour into Avenue Junot at the top of the hill. This is Signac's view of *The Moulin de la Galette* from behind the windmill. Imposing old houses covered with Virginia creeper form an enclave of desirable residences and studios, heavily protected against sightseers. Further up Rue Girardon I reached the little plateau on top of *La Butte*.

Allée des Brouillards. At **No. 13** Rue Girardon a pedestrian alley goes off to the left. Renoir made his family home at **No. 6**, where Jean and his actor brother, Pierre, were born.

At the edge of the plateau, before *La Butte* plunges away down its northern slopes, a few ruins are all that are left of an eighteenth-century folly known pretentiously as Château des Brouillards. In fact, it was a dairy converted into a country house by a gentleman farmer called Marquis Lefranc de Pompignan. There was still the odd cow about when, in 1889, Renoir was attracted by the good air, clear light, low rent and rural tranquillity. His house had an attic studio. Lilac, roses and plum trees flourished in the little garden. Cherries, apricots and pears ripe from the trees, milk hot from the cow, and water from the fountain were among Jean Renoir's earliest memories.

The opium-smoking poet Gérard de Nerval had lived at Château des Brouillards, waxing lyrical about '. . . silent lanes bordered by cottages, granges and thickly wooded gardens, green shelves cut into cliffs with springs filtering through the clay. . . .' Renoir liked the mix of neighbours – from the owner of the orchard, Père Griès, and the alley's concierge, who was a genuine marquise, to writer Paul Alexis, Egyptologist Feuardent, local landowner Madame Brébant, and deputy for the 18th *arrondissement* Clovis Hugues.

By the late 1880s, the impressionists had gone their separate ways, and Renoir missed the comradeship. Compensation came with his own success as society portraitist and painter of nudes, and the luxuries that went with it: hot baths, log fires in every room and a bevy of pretty servants who, in Gabrielle Renard's charge, fetched the water from the fountain and saw to the sauces. Aline, who did not officially become Madame Renoir until 1890, grew large with pregnancies and an insatiable Burgundian appetite for red beans and bacon. But Aline no longer sweated over a hot stove for her husband. Under her supervision the maids prepared the grills and spit-roasts that Renoir loved, but sometimes a girl went missing. She would hurry in, hastily adjusting clothing, after nothing more home-breaking than a nude modelling session with *le patron*.

Inspired by classicism during visits to Italian art galleries, Renoir rendered the ancient art of the nude in modern undress. In *The Bathers* (1887) three recognizably Montmartre girls (Suzanne Valadon on the left) splash about in a pagan waterscape, their young flesh absorbing sunlight and water. Renoir found the canvas too big to be worked on in the attic and rented a separate studio in Rue Tourlaque. Maids went missing for even longer. Sauces may have been spoilt, but never *le patron*'s marriage: Aline trusted him implicitly. She once caught him in the street, laughing a little too familiarly with a loose-moralled model he sometimes used. As all models resembled Aline, the Renoir Nude prototype, the artist was able to get himself neatly out of it with: 'Funny, I thought she was you!'

Rue Girardon (continued). Opposite Allée des Brouillards, **Rue de l'Abreuvoir** was where the young Pissarro lived for a time during the Café Guerbois days pre-1870. Farther down the steps, on the right, is **Rue St-Vincent**, scene of the tranquil 1860 Pissarro drawing. He hardly worked in Paris again until old age, when he embarked on his great series of cityscapes (Chapter Six, p. 135).

Rue Caulaincourt. A moderately energetic step-climbing detour takes in one of Renoir's last Montmartre studios at **No. 73**. It is variously described as the Bavarian Pavilion, transported from the Paris World Fair of 1900, and, by Jean Renoir, as 'constructed in Old English style'. I penetrated the dull seven-storey apartment block (accessible on weekdays only) and was rewarded by a view of a half-timbered cottage with lattice-windows in a little garden at the back.

The Renoirs came to Paris less and less often when *le patron*'s worsening arthritis kept him at Cagnes in Riviera sunshine. He appreciated the ease of the Bavarian Pavilion's ground-floor studio and the horizontal walk home to **No. 43**, just up the street; the slopes of La Butte had become too much for his legs. As for his hands, deformed by arthritis, when a journalist asked how he still worked, Renoir answered: 'I paint with my prick.'

It was pleasant to have another Montmartrois artist, Steinlen, in the same building. Steinlen's fine etching, *Rue Caulaincourt*, shows two furtive night birds leaning forward as they walk against the buffeting wind of this grim gorge of a street. Renoir found its baker's wife most congenial and, after Gabrielle, Marie Dupuis was probably his most frequently used model: true to Renoir type, with retroussé nose, full lips, small hands and feet, voluptuous body, translucent skin and auburn hair tumbling in disarray.

Today the best reminders of Renoir are the pleasant ambience of Le Cépage oyster bar with its glass awning, and the art nouveau shop of Boucher Guay, who still displays his lamb cutlets with ruffs. Given Renoir's delight in having his friends around

him, the Restaurant Les Copains D'Abord (Friends First), named after the Brassens song, is well situated.

Rue des Saules. From the open space where **Rue Lamarck** joins Rue Caulaincourt, a flight of steps leads back up towards *La Butte*. Rue des Saules can also be reached directly from Rue St-Vincent for those who settle for skipping the Rue Caulaincourt detour.

The junction of Rue St-Vincent and Rue des Saules is one of the prettiest in Montmartre. The steep street inspired an early Cézanne, *Rue des Saules à Montmartre* (1867). It reflects a moment of solitary tranquillity, time out from playing the perverse young Provençal out to shock with soft-porn extravaganzas that he himself described as *couillard* (randy) (Chapter Seven, pp. 162–3).

The period cabaret, **Au Lapin Agile**, is a charming Montmartre landmark (**No. 22**), portrayed by Utrillo with late-impressionist panache in 1913. By day the terracotta house with green shutters tends to be overrun with sightseers madly snapping each other beneath the inn sign with its agile rabbit balancing a bottle in a frying pan. Visit by night for the ambience, described on p. 106.

The street also contains Paris's only vineyard. Viticulture was once the main peasant activity of *La Butte*, but is now reduced to this well-kept, north-facing patch, more for show than oenology. The red wine is known by the Italian word for small, *piccolo*, as if not worthy of a French name.

Rue Cortot. This cobble-stoned, country town street, surrounded by so much greenery, must have reminded Erik Satie at **No. 6** of his birthplace, Honfleur in Normandy. Maximilien Luce, who also lived in Rue Cortot, relished its peace and quiet, far from the noisy Paris inspiration of his vibrantly peopled works.

A left turn at the top of Rue des Saules took me to one of the best-loved impressionist and post-impressionist sites, painted by Valadon, Dufy, Utrillo and Renoir. Overlooking the vineyard, with an open view across the Plaine St-Denis, is the famous folly of the seventeenth-century actor Rosimond, now the **Museum of Old Montmartre**

(**No. 12**). An ivy-covered building with white shutters conceals an enchanted garden with 200-year-old trees where a friendly cat greeted me. The museum is housed discreetly in the small country house at the back. Lautrec and Steinlen share the walls with evocative lesser-known Montmartre artists too often lost among the stars – Willette, Warnod and the humorist Léandre.

Renoir had to have a base nearer to the Moulin de la Galette than Rue St-Georges to work on the painting. He was delighted to find this abandoned folly at a rent of 100 francs a month. The stables were big enough for the large canvas, which willing friends transported backwards and forwards between Rue Cortot and the Moulin. Among the nettles and brambles bloomed lilac and seringa, and *The Garden at 12 Rue Cortot* (1876) was, for Renoir, 'mysterious and noble'.

It was like a peaceful oasis where he could work on several paintings at once. 'You have to learn to put a painting on one side and let it rest.' Even with his sure touch, he never knew how it would turn out; it was an entity whose meaning only became clear bit by bit. 'The smallest section is composed of innumerable elements.' He would start with a few seemingly unformed strokes on a white canvas with a mixture of turpentine and linseed oil running down it. Thanks to what he called 'the juice', several bold strokes all over the canvas would establish the general tonality of the picture. Then he would leave it to dry for several days before continuing.

Working in tandem with *Dancing at the Moulin de la Galette* was *The Swing* (O). Altogether a more intimate study, it has the same tantalizing sunlight through trees dappling the girl standing on the swing. Renoir installed himself at what is now Restaurant La Maison Rouge, with its garden swing, on the corner of Rue des Saules. The garden became a closed terrace – to the fury of Jean Renoir. Tourist desecrations were anathema to him.

However, the rowdy gang has still not succeeded in chasing away the ghosts of the Angèles, Jeannes, and Estelles . . . you can meet their great granddaughters on the steps of La Butte . . . their smiles and the wicked twinkle in their eyes would be enough to have a Renoir's heart beating if we were lucky enough to have him back on La Butte. (From *Renoir, My Father*.)

Rue Mont-Cenis continues the walk from Rue Cortot, past **Rue St-Rustique** on the right. I took a quick detour down this touristy backstreet to **La Bonne Franquette (No. 18)**, a bistro known for its traditional Paris accordion music. It used to be called Les Billards de Paris, its charming arbour depicted by van Gogh in *The Montmartre Guinguette* (1886) (O).

Place du Tertre. Tourist paradise with quick-sketch artists, best visited early in the morning, late at night, and off season. Eat at La Mère Catherine (**No. 16**), which is surprisingly good value for money in the midst of the mayhem. Her bar earned its fame in 1814, when occupying Cossacks were forbidden to drink in French bars so ordered their drinks to be served '*bistro! bistro!*' ('quick, quick' in Russian). Hence one foreign word that not even the purest French Academician could refuse entry to the dictionary.

At **No. 3** is Poulbot House, a crèche where working women could leave their children during the day and keep them off the streets. It was founded by Poulbot, the famous drawer of Parisian urchins. Renoir had had the same idea fifty years before, and organized a costume charity ball at the Moulin de la Galette. Though a wild social success, it barely covered its costs. Later he persuaded his patroness, Madame Charpentier, to help him with the charity, and with her social connections it succeeded.

A leisurely descent down the steps of **Rue du Calvaire**, via **Rues Gabrielle** and **Ravignan**, leads to one of the most enchanting little squares of Montmartre.

Place Emile Goudeau. A fountain tinkles as *clochards* pass round the wine bottle on a bench beneath a spreading plane tree. The **Bateau-Lavoir** studios at **Nos 13–13bis**, which owed their 'Laundry-Boat' nickname to poet-artist Max Jacob, were the birthplace of the next great art revolution after impressionism: cubism. Van Dongen, Braque, Juan Gris and Picasso worked in what was originally called The Trapper's House because of its rickety wooden structure and dangerously primitive stoves. Fire destroyed it in 1970, and all that can now be seen from outside is the entrance to a modern block of studios.

Picasso came to Paris in 1900. His bleak Blue and gentle Pink periods have definite impressionist resonances. In exploring cubism, he and Braque both recognized their debt to Cézanne who, as a result of his early geometric experiments, had advised: 'Treat nature as cylinder, sphere and cone.' In Picasso's private collection is Cézanne's masterpiece, *Five Bathers* (Picasso Museum).

It was an appropriate place to end the Montmartre walk. From there a short walk took me back down to **Place des Abbesses**, a well-earned beer at Le Métro brasserie, and departure from what is one of the best-preserved art nouveau Métro stations in Paris.

Montmartre Nightlife

Le Bal du Moulin Rouge, Place Blanche. The best way to arrive at Le Moulin is on foot from Métro, Place Pigalle, with the last rays of the sun shining through the trees of the central promenade of the **Boulevard de Clichy**. The windmill's red neon-lit sails, perfectly post-impressionist, cannot fail to warm the heart of the most blasé Paris-lover.

Opened in 1889, Le Moulin is to entertainment what Notre-Dame is to religion, a permanent Paris fixture that began a chain of creative inspiration from Lautrec via Picasso to movie-makers Jean Renoir and John Huston, while widening its international appeal over the years with appearances from Mistinguett, Chevalier, Ginger Rogers, Jerry Lewis, Peter Ustinov, Charles Aznavour and Liza Minelli.

What would it be like now, I wondered? Tourist trap? Tawdry like the rest of the neighbourhood? I feared the worst, and got the best. Le Moulin may be corny but it is also a haven of taste in a sea of tat, quite the most

spectacular show south of the Northern Lights, and its total Frenchness of spirit gives enormous pleasure to an almost entirely foreign audience. At my floor-side table Japanese and Argentinian total strangers found they had a mutual business aquaintance in Hong Kong. On a steamy Sunday night in August a packed house was grateful for air-conditioning fit to freeze the frou-frou off a bare-breasted showgirl; smiling service from scurrying waiters was impeccable, whether you were dining with champagne or just drinking a beer like me.

The CanCan (a standard feature, inevitably introduced by 'T-L' himself to huge applause) has each soloist topping the last, climaxing with the last girl's definitive eight cartwheels and crotch-wincing splits. The seemingly endless permutations and combinations, the cries of pain and pleasure, make the CanCan the Kama Sutra of dance – seen at its best at Le Moulin. Lautrec never depicted it vulgarly: I was glad to find a small permanent exhibition of original T-L posters in the souvenir kiosk's red plush foyer: *La Goulue*, *Jane Avril*, *Aristide Bruant*, *Le Divan Japonais*.

Folies-Bergère, No. 32 Rue Richer. The outside of the music-hall can be visited on the Art and Money Walk described in Chapter Six (p. 151). Although not strictly in Montmartre, it is near enough to be included in this chapter as one of the only three places of entertainment in Paris retaining even the remotest vestiges of its past. Be warned: only the name is the same. Visiting the scene of Manet's key painting *A Bar at the Folies-Bergère* (1882, a year before his death from creeping paralysis) involves buying a ticket to the show, and the bar has greatly cleaned up its act since then.

Manet's approach is, as always, with the explorer's compass rather than Degas's clinical scalpel. Here he describes the louche netherworld of pickup bars, and specifically the notorious Folies-Bergère: 'The only place in Paris with the fragrant odour of painted, paid-for tenderness and extreme, jaded corruption.'

His picture is an enigma, even if his barmaid Suzon is not. At the time of

Zola's Nana, prostitution came gift-wrapped, with girls like Suzon, a typical product of the new *petit-bourgeois* class with her veneer of respectability, available after hours for the right customer. The choice was hers, unlike a brothel girl's. She had the illusion of liberty, unlike her wage-slave sisters; her dream was to become a fully-fledged *cocotte* with her own apartment near the Parc Monceau. All too often she ended life in a cheap whorehouse in Lille.

The enigma is about what exactly is going on. The feet of a trapeze artist, bottles of Bass and champagne on the marble-topped table, top-hatted toffs and begloved women whispering behind fans on the mezzanine, globe lamps and chandeliers clearly establish the Folies-Bergère. And, yes, it is reflected in a big mirror behind Suzon. What does Manet's purposely false perspective give us? Realistically, the couple in the mirror bear no spatial relationship to Suzon. Suzon's back view being parleyed by the gentleman looks like a different barmaid altogether – a hazier, more voluptuous, looser-haired version of the rather prim figure who confronts us. Suzon's front view does not appear to be talking to anyone, more lost in her thoughts, waiting for a client.

Theories are a million, so why not one more? Perhaps Manet is showing two distinct moments in Suzon's life: the first a flesh-and-blood Suzon at her bar, the second a Suzon-in-Suzon's-mind, the Nana-Suzon appearing in the 'distorted' mirror. The first waiting for her rich man – or thinking about a former candidate who may turn up again. The second the moment of his appearance – larger-than-life, intense eyes looking appealingly into hers, determined to get what he wants and willing to pay for it. And what he wants is Suzon. If Caillebotte could show us the same man at three different places on a Boulevard Haussmann traffic island in the same picture, why not Manet two different moments at *A Bar at the Folies-Bergère?*

Today's Folies is art deco. No relic of Suzon remains, not even a reproduction of Manet's painting. The management are right – it would seem thoroughly out of place among the kitchy glitz, juke-boxes and coral pink Fifties Renault Dauphine decorating the large foyer for *Les Années Twist*, the show playing when I visited. The tacky hit, celebrating the eternal Johnny Holliday, Eddie Mitchell and Sylvie Vartan, hardly did justice to the horseshoe-shaped, intimate auditorium and wide, red-carpeted *promenoir*. Still looking like a genuine Parisian music-hall, it gets nearer to impressionist times when the inventive Argentine director, Roberto Arias, puts on one of his dazzling tongue-in-cheek Belle Epoque spectaculars.

Au Lapin Agile, No. 22 Rue de Saules. The origin of 'The Agile Rabbit', the only genuine nineteenth-century bohemian cabaret in Montmartre, is an outrageous pun. An artist called A. Gill who painted there – *là peint A. Gill* – did the Lapin Agile's graphic inn sign for *le patron*, Frédé, a potter, singer, guitarist and fishmonger who dressed throughout his life as a Corsican bandit. Though strictly post-impressionist, it is worth a visit at night.

In spite of its popularity with the Camcorder set, the doll's house cabaret still preserves an Old Montmartre ambience – copper pans, faience, and graffiti on dingy walls. The main room has a cosy corner fireplace with log fire and Cambodian goddess carved on stone. My wooden table and chair looked old enough to have appeared in Picasso's *At the Lapin Agile, or Harlequin with Glass* (1905), a self-portrait dressed as Cézanne's Harlequin, accompanied by his own pouting mistress, Fernande Olivier. I was offered the traditional cherry brandy but settled for whisky (all drinks the same price). Entertainment was traditional, too: lusty local singers seated round a refectory table – youngish men, one older woman – giving us the old songs, accompanied by a hyper-active pianist. We could sing along, and occasionally, to make sure we were still awake, a singer would jump up and circulate among the tables for a chorus of 'Mamselle de Paris' or 'La Cornemuse' (with Breton bagpipe noises).

THE RIVER OISE

. . . .

Intricate ironwork protecting a Pontoise house.

Dr Paul Gachet of Auvers-sur-Oise was a man of many parts. Medical adviser to Northern French Railways, inspector of Paris Schools, on the board of numerous literary and historic societies, teacher of anatomical drawing, homeopath, palmist and neurologist, he was also a talented engraver and collector of works by his patients Daumier, Renoir, Cézanne, Pissarro and van Gogh. Every malady seemed within his scope – from the measles of Pissarro's eight children to the madness of van Gogh.

Himself suffering from the twitching condition known as St Vitus's dance, Gachet cut a most colourful figure among the young artists around Manet at the Café Guerbois (Chapter Two, pp. 46–7). In 1866 Pissarro, then living at 108 Boulevard de Rochechouart, was attracted by the doctor's suggestion of cheaper, country living for his growing family at Pontoise, a mere 22 miles from Paris.

Over sixteen years, from *The Jallais Hillside* (1867) to *The Road from Pontoise at Osny* (1883), Pissarro developed the serene, naturalistic landscape style that was to have Cézanne, Gauguin and Guillaumin hurrying to the Oise valley to paint with him.

Despite its closeness to Paris (reached via autoroutes A86 and A15 from La Défense in under an hour), the Oise retains much of the natural beauty that attracted Pissarro. Narrower than the Seine, which it joins at Conflans-Ste-Honorine south of Pontoise, it carries barge traffic from Belgium, the Netherlands and Germany between lush, leafy banks. Pleasure boats putter gently past thickly wooded slopes. Above the escarpment to the west, from which Pontoise and Auvers dominate the river, the Vexin plateau is the first open country beyond the western outskirts of Paris and still much as van Gogh painted it in *Wheat Fields* (1890), with their quilted golds and greens speckled with poppies.

As an early ecologist Pissarro noted with a beady eye industry proliferating along the riverbank. The peasant in his own beetroot field, Pissarro's anarchist principles told him, was less dehumanized than the worker in somebody else's beetroot alcohol distillery. Nowadays, when many French farmers dress American and drive Japanese trucks, the country people in his paintings look as quaint as Millet's. 'Millet was biblical,' he said. 'I am Hebrew.' There was a spirit of kibbutz community living about his home. He and Julie worked their land, feeding family and friends with fresh eggs from their own hens, fruit and vegetables from their own garden. 'Work,' Pissarro claimed, 'is a marvellous regulator of moral and physical health.'

With its ramparts and medieval town superbly situated on a spur jutting over the River Oise, Pontoise had only one factory and many fruit and vegetable gardens when Pissarro made his first, two-year stay in 1866. It was only 45 minutes from Paris by train, and an easy walk from the station to 1 Rue du Fond-de-l'Hermitage. Nearby, Pissarro had an inexhaustible variety of images: wheatfields, gently sloping hills, cliffs, streams, gardens, traditional villages, modern villas, barnyards, markets, towpaths.

In 1872 the Pissarro family (now four children strong) returned from Louveciennes for their second Pontoise stay. A year later, Cézanne followed. With Hortense Fiquet and their newborn baby, Paul, he installed himself at L'Hôtel du Grand Cerf (still there) at St-Ouen-l'Aumône across the river. This was better than Les Halles des Vins; the painter had been holed up near his friend Guillaumin, where the noisy barrel-rolling of a Paris wine market and a crying child were hardly conducive to tranquil creation. Cézanne was also terrified that his philistine father, who thought he should have been a lawyer, would find out about Hortense and Paul and cut off his allowance, already too small to support a family. Lying low in the Oise valley, Cézanne could keep his family a secret, live more cheaply, and work in countryside very different from his native Provence.

'Perhaps we all came from Pissarro,' Cézanne later said of his master, whose fatherly interest gave him much-needed confidence. In fact, the influence was mutual. When they worked together Pissarro began down to earth, Cézanne head in clouds. As they cross-fertilized each other, Pissarro became more poetic and bold in his colouring, while Cézanne's lighter palette and smaller brushstrokes, learned from Pissarro, imposed form and vigour upon what before had been dark, baroque shock tactics. By 1881 Cézanne's *The Couleuvre Watermill* and Pissarro's *Young Girl with a Stick* show the artists going very different ways in the same place.

Guillaumin's *Environs of Paris* was also painted in the Oise valley. 'Guillaumin has just spent several days at our house,' Pissarro wrote in a letter to a friend about this modest employee of the Paris municipality. 'He works at painting in the daytime and at his bridges and roads in the evening. What courage!'

The double life persuaded the perennially broke Pissarro to decorate blinds and fans in the fashionable Japanese manner for a little extra money; once, he even did murals for the Paris shop of Guillaumin's schoolfriend, the art-collecting pastry-cook Eugène Mürer. Mürer held a tombola for Pissarro at his *pâtisserie*, the prize being one of the artist's paintings. The woman who won was so disappointed in her prize that she exchanged it for a cake.

Mürer also had a village house at Auvers, where works acquired in exchange for meals to hungry artists included 25 Pissarros, 22 Guillaumins, 15 Renoirs,

10 Monets, 8 Cézannes, 2 van Goghs. The high score of Guillaumin shows the loyalty of his schoolfriend. 'Guillaumin's art remained always a bit violent, too explosive and often clumsy,' was Mürer's opinion. 'His tenacity, his genuine love of nature give him a certain command, a special, very personal treatment, but also a little brutal. . . .' This made him more adept at conveying the quaysides of eastern Paris than the gentle banks of the Oise.

Gauguin was another with two jobs when he first visited Pissarro in 1879. His resourceful guardian Gustave Arosa had pulled strings to get him gainfully employed in the money market after childhood in Peru (where his father, a French journalist, had met his mother, a Peruvian Creole) and a stint as a merchant seaman; Arosa also gave him an introduction to his friend Pissarro at the Nouvelle-Athènes. Gauguin, the golden boy, had lent three Pissarros from his private collection to the Fourth Impressionist Show in April, and bought another in July. No wonder he was a welcome guest at Pontoise.

Pissarro took Gauguin under his wing. He had already proved, with Cézanne, that he could take on awkward characters, and here was another. The *heimisch* nature of the Pissarro household defied rudeness and aggressive ego trips. During his weekend visits Gauguin humbly painted three versions of *Apple Trees in Flower* in the impressionist manner at L'Hermitage.

His confidence grew. After the Crash of 1882, when he lost his lucrative job, he threw caution to the trade winds and set out on the adventure that would lead to the South Seas (Chapter Seven, pp. 175, 178). Pissarro did not need to warn Gauguin of the hazards of a painter's life; he saw how precariously Pissarro lived. The following summer he spent three weeks at the nearby village of Osny, where Pissarro, fed up with paying the butcher and baker with paintings, had moved from Pontoise to escape the pestering of creditors.

Pissarro and he were very close. They drew sketches of each other. They dreamed up a plan, which came to nothing, to manufacture impressionist tapestries. They painted the same scenes, for example *The Road from Pontoise at Osny*. As with Cézanne, the guru encouraged his pupil to break out; Gauguin's own vision, his own feeling, his own travels, in the world and within himself, which were his originality, had their source in Osny. Just before their deaths in 1903 Gauguin wrote:

> If you examine the art of Pissarro as a whole, in spite of his frustrations, you find not only an exceptional artistic will which never lies, but also art which is essentially intuitive and of a high pedigree. . . . He was one of my masters, and I never rejected him.

Cézanne, meanwhile, had moved on to Auvers, to be nearer to Dr Gachet. His baby son Paul was none too strong, and the engraver-doctor, then a widower with two children of his own, kindly put up the family in his vast house. Later Cézanne rented a place of his own in nearby Rue Rémy and worked in Gachet's studio. Warned of Cézanne's hatred of being contradicted, the doctor let him express his views freely, however crazy and inarticulate they may have been at the time.

Auvers was, and still is, more rural than Pontoise. Four miles farther upstream, the straggly hillside village with its riverside cottages and *guinguettes* appealed to pre-impressionist Daubigny, pioneer of the painting-boat that inspired Monet to make his own. Just as Manet later painted Monet in his boat, so Corot had painted *Daubigny Working in his Botin near Auvers-sur-Oise* (1860); impressionists had no hesitation in reworking the ideas of others.

On Corot's recommendation the Morisot family rented a peasant cottage on the towpath between Auvers and Pontoise in 1863. The 22-year-old Berthe learnt much from Daubigny, pioneer of painting directly from nature, and added her own feminine touch to convey the mood of a moment. *The Old Road at Auvers* evokes a young girl's search for herself: a solitary figure reading under a tree, a pet nearby, the red roof of a modern white villa on the horizon, a village beginning on the edge of woods.

Between the early Auvers painters and van Gogh's arrival nearly thirty years elapsed. After his release from the St-Rémy-en-Provence asylum in 1890, Vincent was in good shape physically when brother Theo arranged for him to be under the care of Dr Gachet.

Recently married and with a child, Theo also had fragile health, aggravated by years of feeling trapped by the Goupil, Boussod & Valadon gallery. He wanted to strike out on his own as a dealer, and give his family life a chance. The presence of Vincent in Paris again would surely sabotage such bourgeois ambitions – and Vincent knew it. Although he saw Theo's family as a threat to their relationship, Vincent felt he'd been enough of a burden to his brother and readily accepted the Auvers idea.

Until he met Dr Gachet. Gachet, like Julie Pissarro, was unwilling to have a former inmate of an asylum for the insane, who had cut off his ear lobe with a razor, stay in a family house. Vincent found the very basic lodgings Gachet had arranged for him too expensive. He preferred the inn of the Ravoux family, who fed him and kept him company for a pittance. Gachet remained friendly, invited him to dinner, and let him paint his daughter in the garden. Yet Vincent wrote to Theo: 'We cannot count on Dr Gachet *at all*.' He saw through the neurologist's over-simplistic therapy: the idea that painting in the wheatfields and village lanes – the hard work Vincent loved – would establish his mental equilibrium. The doctor was not taking into account the gaps between the work, the loneliness of sleepless nights, of country walks when the mind is not silent. Vincent was not a mere hard-drinking melancholic embittered by lack of recognition and guilt at being a burden to a struggling younger brother: his manic-depressive mood-swings had been aggravated by epilepsy, persecution complex, hallucinations, identification with Christ, self-mutilation, and suicide attempts.

His painting was at its height when once again his morale sank to a new low. The consolation of achievement was not enough. While painting crows in a field, Vincent was overcome with a sense of isolation. He shot himself near to the heart – not, as is often claimed, in the groin – with the revolver he had begun secretly to carry. Somehow managing to get back to the Auberge Ravoux, he was found later by the family, bleeding to death in his room. Dr Gachet was in Paris, so a local doctor was called. When Gachet arrived, it was too late. Vincent was too sick to be moved without excruciating pain. All Gachet could do was contact Theo, who came immediately. Vincent, strong enough to smoke a last pipe, died in his brother's arms with the words: 'Sadness will last a lifetime.'

In fact, the sadness of Theo van Gogh had lasted only six months when he himself died at 34 – three years younger than Vincent. They were like twins, the inseparable mirror image even unto death, each one feeling his life to be a failure, however mistakenly; each one agonizing with the introspection of a Dutch puritan upbringing that had equipped neither of them for the materialistic cruelty of the Paris art world; loving and hating each other with equal passion, totally unable and unwilling to break the fraternal tie.

With the cosmic vision of a mind that saw the heavens as swirling suns and intensely bright stars, Vincent reached beyond earthly suffering to the intense beauty of the universe. Death was a natural part of it. 'If we can take a train to Tarascon or Rouen,' he once wrote to Theo, 'we take death to reach a star.'

Walks and Drives
by
The River Oise

The Church at Auvers *by van Gogh (1890).*

Information

Itinerary

2 full days, either making day trips from Paris or staying overnight. Allow a little over 1 hour for the drive.

Day 1

Paris–Pontoise via autoroutes A86 and A15 from Paris La Défense to Exit 7. Follow signs to Pontoise Centre Ville (not Cergy-Pontoise).

L'Hermitage Walk. Start: Rue de Gisors. End: Boulevard Jean-Jaurès.

Lunch

Visit Pissarro Museum, Pontoise.

Circular drive Pontoise–Osny–Ennery:

Pontoise–Osny by D92. Visit Osny. Osny–Ennery by D27 and D927. Visit Ennery. Continue to Pontoise on N327.

Return Paris or stay overnight.

Day 2

Paris–Pontoise by autoroutes A86 and A15 to Exit 7. N184 to Méry-sur-Oise, left on N328 to Auvers-sur-Oise. If coming from Pontoise town, riverside D4 to Auvers (4–5 miles).

Auvers Walk. Start: Hôtel de Ville. End: Auberge Ravoux.

Lunch: Auberge Ravoux (second sitting at 2pm) and visit the House of Van Gogh.

Audio-visual show 'Voyage in the Days of the Impressionists' at Château d'Auvers.

Return Paris by same route.

Public Transport

Best: RER (Line A) to Cergy-Pontoise, frequent buses or taxi to Pontoise and Auvers. Worst: SNCF train from Gare St-Lazare to Pontoise, with connection to Auvers. Latter rewarded by instant van Gogh reproduction on panel outside station that might be missed by other routes.

Refreshment, Meals and Overnight

Pontoise

Au Péché Mignon (restaurant), (C),19 Boulevard Jean-Jaurès. Tel. 01.30.38.48.28.

Auberge du Cheval Blanc (hotel), (C), 47 Rue de Gisors. Tel. 01.30.32.25.05.

Campanile (hotel), (C), 8 Rue Pierre-de-Coubertin. Tel. 01.30.38.55.44.

St-Ouen-l'Aumône

☆ Le Grand Cerf (hotel) (C), 59 Rue du Général-Leclerc. Tel. 01.30.37.51.08.

Osny

Moulin de la Renardière (restaurant), (B), Rue Grand Moulin. Tel. 01.30.30.21.13.

Auvers-sur-Oise

☆ Auberge Ravoux (restaurant), (B), 8 Rue de la Sansonne. Tel. 01.34.48.05.47. Two lunch sittings 12pm and 2pm. Because of its van Gogh fame, reserve well ahead. If that fails, try the guinguette annexe.

Café de la Paix (restaurant), (C), 11 Rue du Général-de-Gaulle. Tel. 01.30.36.73.23.

Madame Amaniera (b & b), (C), Chemin des Vallées. Tel. 01.30.36.79.32.

L'Isle-Adam

Le Cabouillet (hotel), (C), 5 Quai de l'Oise. Tel. 01.34.69.00.90.

Le Troubadour (restaurant), (B), 23 Quai de l'Oise. Tel. 01.34.08.10.34.

Museums and Sites

Pissarro Museum, 17 Rue du Château, Pontoise. Open Wed–Sun, 2–6. Entry: free. Tel. 01.30.38.02.40.

Medieval Town, Cathedral and Market, Pontoise.

Daubigny Museum, Manoir des Colombières, Rue de la Sansonne, Auvers. Open daily summer 2.30–6.30, winter 2–5.30. Tel. 01.30.36.80.30.

Daubigny's House, 61 Rue Daubigny, Auvers. Open daily (except Mon) from Easter to All Saints' Day, 2–6.30. Entry: 20F. Tel. 01.34.48.03.03.

Absinthe Museum, 44 Rue Callé, Auvers. Open June–Sep, Wed–Sun, 11–6; Oct–May, Sat–Sun, 11–6. Entry: 25F. Tel. 01.30.36.83.26.

House of van Gogh (Auberge Ravoux), Place de la Mairie (entrance Rue de la Sansonne), Auvers. House open daily (except Mon), 10–6; restaurant 12–12 (closed Sun evening and Mon). Entry (house only): 30F. Tel. 01.34.48.05.47.

Château d'Auvers, Rue de Léry. Audio-visual show 'Voyage in the Days of the Impressionists'. Continuous daily (except Mon) 10–6.30. Entry: 40–55F. Tel. 01.34.48.48.48.

Tourist Offices

Office du Tourisme, 6 Rue de Martroy, Pontoise. Tel. 01.30.38.24.25.

Office du Tourisme, Manoir des Colombières, Rue de la Sansonne, Auvers. Tel. 01.30.36.10.06.

Pontoise

The square of the **Hôtel de Ville** seems to belong to somewhere much further from Paris – a pleasant, medieval town in central France. Besides the classy Parisian boutiques of its sleepy main street (**Rue de l'Hôtel de Ville**), 'La Ferme du Vexin' sells cheese, game and poultry fresh from the rural western plateau. Farmers head for little country bars on market day.

The **tourist office** at the end of the street is in **Place du Grand Martroy**, near the flamboyant Gothic cathedral of **St-Maclou**. There are two options for walking the Pissarros and Cézannes: a solo trek with the aid of an essential map; or in a group with a guide, which has to be set up in advance by telephone. As there are no panels displaying paintings (as on the Seine and Auvers walks), it might be wiser to take the second option. I met one of the guides, who combined erudition, charm and a relaxed manner while accompanying a small group of three. As I had not telephoned first, I did the walk unaccompanied.

Walking the Pissarros and Cézannes

half-day

Free parking near **Boulevard Jean-Jaurès**, where the walk ends, was followed by a short, gentle climb to the top of the town, where it begins.

Rue de Gisors. A left turn took me on a brief detour to **No. 16 Rue Revert**, Pissarro's first of many Pontoise addresses after his return there in 1872. He found it conveniently placed for easy walking to the Vexin plateau and the valleys of L'Hermitage and the Viosne on either side of town.

Looking back towards town on Rue de Gisors, the downward slope curves to the left, still recognizable though snowy in *The Gisors Road*. Pissarro did another on this road, from the fields of the Vexin plateau looking towards Pontoise: modern life represented by a new white villa with bright red roof on the left of the picture and, in contrast, an old farm on the right.

Suburbs (**Rue de la Citadelle, Rue Pasteur**) of turn-of-the-century

redbrick houses with viciously barking guard dogs are soon followed by a more countrified scene. Down a lane (**Route des Fortes Terres**) the barking dogs give way to crowing cocks, and smug *parcs* turn into shambly, half-tended patches of Brussels sprouts and lettuces and primroses growing wild. More white villas with red roofs signify Pissarro country proper.

The **Jallais Hill**. One of the most famous Pissarro painting sites is best viewed from a junction of lanes (**Rue Le Charpentier, Sente des Grivières** and **Chemin des Bottes**). Not much changed, *The Jallais Hill, Pontoise* (1867) shows houses, barns, orchards and fields, the slope up to the skyline on the opposite side of the valley of **L'Hermitage**, and the road that I was now about to take down into it. Most of the walk covers this valley where Pissarro did so much of his work. Not more than half a mile or so from home, two hillsides, a stream leading down to the Oise, a country village, a few farms . . . that was about it.

This key picture was painted on Pissarro's first Pontoise visit (1866–9), when he lived at **No. 1 Rue du Fond-de-l'Hermitage**. The deep greens against a vivid blue sky show the influence of Courbet and Corot. His colours were still subdued, plenty of brown and grey to replace the bitumen. Pre-impressionist, yes, but the people have no faces, landscape is patterned, bushes are imprecise. Broad brushstrokes add to its blend of tradition and avant-garde.

The **Ennery Road**. A steep hill leads down to the bottom of the valley. The outskirts of Pontoise cannot be said to be *la belle France*, and nobody but locals would dream of walking them, if it weren't for Pissarro and Cézanne. Sleuthing for picture sites can be fun, given time, patience and a good local map. Mine had one mistake, showing a path I wanted to take, Sente des Toits Rouges, that has disappeared.

The Ennery Road leads from the village of that name, five miles to the north-west on the plateau, and winds down to become the main street of Pissarro's village, **Rue de l'Hermitage**. The road was also confusingly known as *The Saint-Antoine Road at*

Left: *Pissarro was often specific in his titles, stating colour, place, and time. Red Roofs, A Corner of the Village in Winter (1877) (O) shows the Hillside of the Oxen not far from his house at L'Hermitage, now a suburb of Pontoise.*

Below left: *The island at Pontoise.*

Below: *After working with Pissarro, Cézanne's The House of the Hanged Man (1873) (O) is an early Auvers landscape with limited palette like his master's, illuminated by the harsh, clear light of Ile-de-France.*

l'Hermitage (1875), and on the left, going south, I spotted the convent buildings in the painting.

Couvent des Mathurins. A lane to the left off Rue de l'Hermitage leads to the former convent, under an arch with a No Entry sign. The school presently occupying it will hardly object to anyone taking a quick look at the house and surroundings of *The Garden of Les Mathurins* (1876). A child plays with a balloon, and the woman in the doorway is Maria Deraismes, Pissarro's friend and neighbour, an early militant who campaigned for oppressed women and children.

Maison Bourgeoise. No. 58 Rue de l'Hermitage is the handsome Louis-Philippe merchant's house, Villa Davenport, to which Pissarro added his anarchist's social comment by including the word *bourgeoise* in the title of his 1873 painting. Beyond a spooky red wall, the grand white mansion with *oeil-de-boeuf* windows stands in its own fine garden. Hardly the unacceptable face of capitalism.

La Côte des Boeufs. To the right of Rue de l'Hermitage as it descends towards the Oise is the other much-painted slope of the valley. Its still existent eighteenth-century farm buildings among the trees (best to walk the paintings at a not-too-leafy time of year, otherwise sleuthing is impossible) can be approached by **Rue Vieille de l'Hermitage**.

Climbing a Path at L'Hermitage shows a steep footpath with a traditional Vexin farmhouse of rough stone and thatched cottages. *The Hillside of the Oxen* is best seen, however, by making the short climb up the opposite slope via **Rue Maria-Deraismes** (where Pissarro once lived at **No. 1**) and **Rue du Château Belger** to **Rue Adrien-Lemoine**. From this vantage-point I looked across the valley to the scene of *Red Roofs, a Corner of the Village in Winter* (1877) (O). Pissarro is precise about place and season. He also painted it in early spring, with trees about to burst into flower. This shows the smaller brushstrokes and brighter harmony learnt over the ten years since *The Jallais Hillside*. 'I felt the freeing of my consciousness as soon as I freed my eyes,' he said, advising Cézanne to

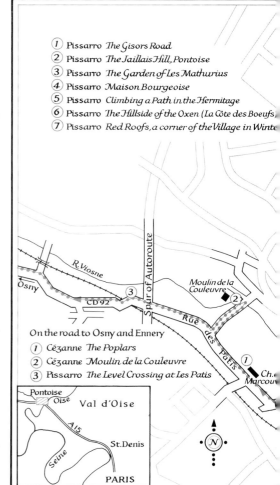

① Pissarro *The Gisors Road*
② Pissarro *The Jaillais Hill, Pontoise*
③ Pissarro *The Garden of Les Mathurius*
④ Pissarro *Maison Bourgeoise*
⑤ Pissarro *Climbing a Path in the Hermitage*
⑥ Pissarro *The Hillside of the Oxen (La Côte des Boeufs,*
⑦ Pissarro *Red Roofs, a corner of the Village in Winte*

On the road to Osny and Ennery
① Cézanne *The Poplars*
② Cézanne *Moulin de la Couleuvre*
③ Pissarro *The Level Crossing at Les Patis*

paint with only the three primary colours (red, blue, yellow) and their immediate derivatives. Red roof tiles and the white or cream stucco of new houses made geometric shapes and floating planes that Cézanne described as 'playing cards'.

Rue Adrien-Lemoine. Continuing downhill on this lane, a glance to the left reveals the scene of Cézanne's work with Pissarro. Little changed is the expanse of vegetation between hill and river, where Cézanne and Pissarro used the same title, *Orchard in Pontoise, Quai de Pothuis*, in 1877.

During this joint work, begun in 1873, Cézanne abandoned the influence of heavy contemporary Provençal painting with its lurid expressionism (*The Murder, The Rape*), and modestly adopted the lighter palette of his *pleinairiste* mentor. He began painting outdoors. Pissarro wrote to his artist son, Lucien, in 1895: 'We were always together; but one has to admit that each kept for himself the one thing that counts – a

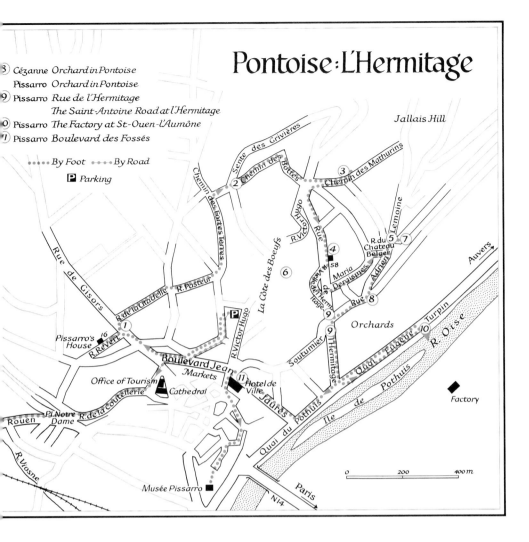

Pontoise·L'Hermitage

③ Cézanne *Orchard in Pontoise*
　 Pissarro *Orchard in Pontoise*
⑨ Pissarro *Rue de l'Hermitage*
　 The Saint-Antoine Road at l'Hermitage
⑩ Pissarro *The Factory at St-Ouen-l'Aumône*
⑪ Pissarro *Boulevard des Fossés*

●●●● *By Foot* ●●●● *By Road*
P *Parking*

Jallais Hill

---

sensation unique to him.'

Cézanne called it 'the little
sensation' that began each painting.
The eighteen pictures, some resulting
from his Oise work, exhibited at the
Third Impressionist Show (1877),
marked the start of his distancing
himself from the group. Greater
intensity of touch made his objects,
placed in no traditional perspective,
take on the aspect of unconnected
geometric shapes on different planes.
Paying homage to Pissarro in *Still Life
with Basket and Soup Tureen*, he
reproduces two of his master's Pontoise
paintings on the wall behind.

Rue de l'Hermitage. Rue Adrien-
Lemoine leads back down to the main
street at the bottom of the valley and
the village centre, such as it is, at the
crossroads with **Rue Jean-Paul
Soutumier**. Just a newspaper shop,
baker, bus stop and Bar de
l'Hermitage. Pissarro did several
paintings of the street and crossroads
when at his various nearby homes,
each 'barracks' rented more for size

than beauty as his family expanded
(**Nos 10, 26, and 18bis**).

Even Pissarro's celebrated patience
must have been tried by the demands
and noise of Lucien, Jeanne-Rachel
(Minette), Adèle-Emma and Georges,
not to mention later additions Félix,
Ludovic-Rudolph, Jeanne and Paul-
Emile. The Pissarro tribe, however,
provided solidarity in a life of
fluctuating fortune.

In 1873 things looked brighter. At
the Durand-Ruel sale one Pissarro
reached a record 950 francs, and the
total was 2750 francs. It was short-
lived. The following year Durand-Ruel,
strapped by the sudden recession,
stopped buying. And, much worse, the
death of his daughter Minette, aged
nine, made Pissarro despair. 'Worry,
indeed even misery, is running rife
through the home,' he wrote to Mürer,
'and threatens our household at every
moment. When will I get out of this
gloom and calmly find my zest for life
again? My work is done with no
lightness of touch, because I keep

thinking I should give up art and try something else. . . . '

Happily, the visits of Cézanne, Guillaumin and, later, Gauguin did much to restore his faith in himself, and he was quick to rally in their stimulating presence.

Quai de Pothuis. Cézanne flitted backwards and forwards between Aix-en-Provence and the Oise valley, with a short stay in 1877 and a year (1881) at **No. 31** Quai de Pothuis. Rue de l'Hermitage reaches the river at the quay with the strange name, a medieval contraction of *poterne* (entry gate) and *pont-levis* (drawbridge). The numbers do not now go up to **No. 85**, to which Pissarro moved in 1881, but the house was probably one of the romantic old houses with fine gardens like **No. 53 Quai Eugène-Turpin**, which extends upstream in the Auvers direction.

Now juggernauts hurtle along the quayside. A more peaceful walk along the fishermen's path took me past **Ile de Pothuis**, a narrow strip of land in mid-Oise where tall poplars are heavy with mistletoe bunches and rooks caw. Beyond the tip of the island, *The Factory at St-Ouen-l'Aumône* (1873) is still very much in evidence on the opposite bank. Now a wood-waxing factory, it still has old chimneys and buildings on its countrified riverside, but those looking for Pissarro's Friesian cows in front of it will be disappointed.

Boulevard Jean-Jaurès. Returning in the direction of town, a right turn took me into the wide, tree-lined boulevard that leads up to the old town. The markets Pissarro loved are now held here. The view he painted of it, under its old name *Boulevard des Fossés*, looks down towards the river. His view over to the forest of Montmorency, where his parents once lived, takes in more red-roofed, white and cream houses. Strangely, they seem to belong to our own time, whereas they actually predated more elaborate *fin-de-siècle* Ile-de-France architecture – turreted riverside Gothic, gingerbread colonial, and bourgeois redbrick. Pissarro's taste was for simplicity.

Pissarro Museum (half-hour after lunch). A ten-minute walk took me through the old town to **Place du**

Château where, disappointingly, the castle no longer tops the ramparts, and the public gardens have a downbeat view across the river to the urban mishmash of Cergy, St-Ouen-l'Aumône and the autoroute. No matter. Housed in one of those bourgeois redbrick residences, the **Pissarro Museum** brought me quickly back to his own century.

Fresh flowers, creaking floorboards and a smell of beeswax provide an intimate, homely ambience for Monet's atmospheric *Argenteuil Railway Station*; Signac's fan-shaped *The Seine at Herblay*, showing the church on its hill; and Caillebotte's *Boat at Anchor, Argenteuil*, which he may well have constructed himself.

Two etchings by Pissarro show the vegetable market at Pontoise and a woman working in her kitchen garden, both with his dogged resistance to prettification. But it is a friend, Ludovic Piette, who ultimately steals the show with a touching portrait of Pissarro – now old, in shadow, with just a small beam of light in the background, a Rembrandt-style patriarch whose generosity of spirit infuses the whole picture. In the words of Mary Cassatt: 'Pissarro was such a good teacher he could have taught a stone to draw.'

Pontoise–Osny–Ennery

circular drive: 2–3 hours

The D92, reached from **Rue de Rouen**, follows the **Viosne valley** through the northern outskirts of Pontoise where Pissarro first lived on his return to the town in 1872, and where Cézanne first painted with him. Sites are conveniently placed on the road to **Osny**.

Château de Marcouville. To the right of the roadside by the **Jardin des Lavandières**, a park where Pissarro and Cézanne painted, the white mansion is now the chamber of commerce. No problem about visiting the park. A pungent smell of box wafted from the romantic, overgrown garden with its dilapidated urns. Beeches and chestnut trees have now replaced *The Poplars* of Cézanne.

Le Moulin de la Couleuvre. At the

end of the park on the Osny road, a drive to the right leads to a modern estate, Cité des Artistes. On the left of this drive, a watermill surrounded by weeping willows, its wheel turning in the Viosne, is Cézanne's *The Couleuvre Watermill* (1881). Its superb restoration makes the buildings look somewhat different, but the open space around it is much the same, with the outskirts of Pontoise on the rising ground behind it.

Les Patis. Near this hamlet the valley becomes more countrified, and Pissarro painted the lush landscape around it in 1868. The road crosses the railway, and not many trains can have disturbed the tranquillity of the people who were in charge of *The Level Crossing at Les Patis*.

Osny (pronounced Owny). Like many villages in the Ile-de-France, a haphazard mix of ancient and modern.

From the roundabout at the entry of the village, as painted by Pissarro and Gauguin in 1883, look one way and it's their rural view, while in the other direction you could be looking at the scene of Hockney's new town *French Shop* (1971). Beyond the railway bridge is the long, unspoilt main street. Gauguin's narrow *Street in Osny* appealed to him for its peaceful, primitive beauty, a place in which to begin reaching for 'the invisible, underlying verities of life'. The church was painted by a British impressionist, William Thornley, during his fifty years of residence, which began at **Le Moulin de la Renardière**, an old watermill that is now a restaurant of repute. I needed a cold beer, and found it at the **Bar de la Mairie**, a village inn with genuine old beams, oil lamps, brass fittings and tankards.

Nobody seemed to know the house where Pissarro entertained Gauguin, but all reckoned it had long gone. It meant much to Pissarro, as an anarchist, that the former golden boy was a grandson of the feminist Flora Tristan. And Gauguin, under his mentor's influence, renounced bourgeois conventions for dedication to being 'an impressionist artist, that is to say a rebel'.

The influence went the other way with Seurat, who also worked with Pissarro. At Osny he produced *House with Red Roof* – Pissarro-like in its title but freer in its execution, the use of paint spots heralding pointillism. *Peasant Women at Work* (1882) intrigued Pissarro, who was always ready to learn. So much so that he went along with Seurat's outspoken opinion of Monet, Renoir and Sisley as unprogressive. It caused the fatal rift and break-up of the impressionists in 1886. For a time Pissarro was hooked on neo-impressionist experiments, but the dry, intellectual style of dots with no lines did not suit his temperament and he soon returned to his own warm naturalism.

Typical is *The Bridge at Osny*, which I drove across in **Rue Pasteur**. By the two-arched bridge over the Viosne, not much more than a bubbling brook, a fisherman moved testily on, disturbed by two freezing, but giggly, girls having a chilly evening picnic.

From here the road to **Ennery** climbs out of the valley to the undulating **Vexin** plateau – rolling prairie with few hedges, isolated clumps of trees, heavily wooded properties with high stone walls, pylons on the march across the countryside with the colonizing determination of Ancient Romans. These legions are all that separates us from van Gogh's wheatfields.

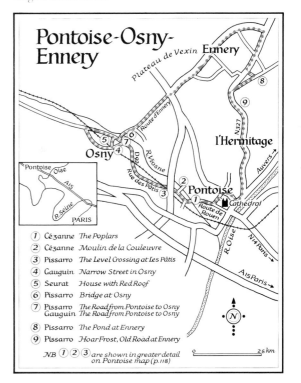

Pontoise-Osny-Ennery

① Cézanne *The Poplars*
② Cézanne *Moulin de la Couleuvre*
③ Pissarro *The Level Crossing at Les Pâtis*
④ Gauguin *Narrow Street in Osny*
⑤ Seurat *House with Red Roof*
⑥ Pissarro *Bridge at Osny*
⑦ Pissarro *The Road from Pontoise to Osny*
  Gauguin *The Road from Pontoise to Osny*
⑧ Pissarro *The Pond at Ennery*
⑨ Pissarro *Hoar Frost, Old Road at Ennery*

NB ①②③ *are shown in greater detail on Pontoise map (p.118)*

Ennery. A truly rural village, and well worth a detour off the Pontoise road, turning left after a big barn with massive door, down **Rue de l'Herbette**. Time has scarcely altered the sturdy stone buildings of **Place de la Mare** and **Rue de la Croix**, from which Pissarro painted *The Pond at Ennery*. It has a feeling of deepest France, yet it is barely an hour's drive from Paris.

On the descent back to the already familiar scenes of L'Hermitage I was reminded of two final Pissarros. In *Hoar Frost, Old Road to Ennery* (1873) (O), a peasant carries a heavy burden of firewood. An 1874 painting shows the same road in a greeny blue springtime, with a horse and buggy crossing a bridge, and a peasant following the S-bend between fields. My day at Pontoise had been taken at the same slowed-down tempo.

Auvers-sur-Oise

The train journey to Auvers took me 90 minutes from the Gare St-Lazare, 45 minutes longer than it took Dr Gachet in 1890. It is the Misery Line, apparently. Better to take the RER (Express Métro) to Cergy-Pontoise, and the excellent bus connections that will whisk you along the Oise valley to both Pontoise and Auvers in a matter of minutes.

Even Paris commuter trains have their rewards: in this case crossing the peaceful Oise at a leisurely pace, watching the straggle of Auvers unfold along its hillside. Immediately outside the **Station**, two Auvers artists (pre- and post-impressionist) are celebrated in one reproduction panel: *Daubigny's Garden* by van Gogh. It is a country house garden, little changed. All I missed was the prowling cat startling what looks like a flurry of white poultry. It was one of sixty paintings done in seventy days.

'And to anyone who tells you I did them too quickly,' Vincent wrote to Theo, 'reply that they looked at them too quickly.' Hardly off the train, eagerly exploring the banks of the river that he had first noticed from that same railway bridge, he dashed off 'one study of old thatched roofs with a field of peas in flower in the foreground and some wheat, with a background of hills'.

Clouds swirl, trees are buffeted by the wind, and one of the thatched roofs seems as fragile as Vincent himself. Painting from nature had travelled a long way from Daubigny's direct experiments with light and shade to the terrible beauty of van Gogh's complex vision.

Walking the van Goghs and Cézannes

half-day

The town centre is quickly reached by the Pontoise road, **Rue Général-de-Gaulle**. For drivers there is easy parking near two instantly recognizable van Gogh sites – **The Hôtel de Ville** and the **Auberge Ravoux**.

The Town Hall of Auvers, a Louis-Philippe doll's house in the main square, is shown on the Fourteenth of July, ironically festive a mere two weeks before Vincent's death at the inn opposite. Auberge Ravoux is where the walk ends. Owing to its popularity and limited space (forty places), two

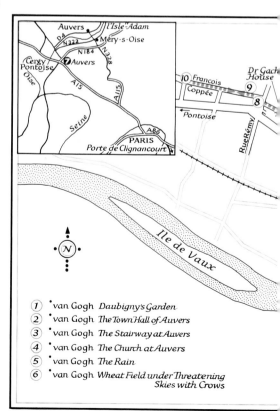

1. van Gogh *Daubigny's Garden*
2. van Gogh *The Town Hall of Auvers*
3. van Gogh *The Stairway at Auvers*
4. van Gogh *The Church at Auvers*
5. van Gogh *The Rain*
6. van Gogh *Wheat Field under Threatening Skies with Crows*

sittings of lunch (at 12pm and 2pm) are served at a moderate price. To give myself a good long morning for the walk, I reserved my place for the second sitting, a month ahead.

Rue de la Sansonne. First right after the inn brought me into a short, narrow street and the **Daubigny Museum**. Situated in the seigneurial Manoir des Colombières, it celebrates the many artists who worked at Auvers: Daubigny drawings of Oise fishermen; a garish pastel by Guillaumin of a forest scene, all bright greens, mauves and yellows; a drawing by Cézanne of Guillaumin sporting a jaunty hat; red roofs by Mürer; and other works by Dr Gachet, Marcellin Desboutin (who modelled the man in Degas's *Absinthe Drinker*), Schuffenecker (long-suffering host of Gauguin), Goeneutte (a dancer in Renoir's *Dancing at the Moulin de la Galette*), Daumier and Millet.

On the ground floor the **tourist office** proved to be the most helpful of my whole trip. Auvers does its painters proud.

Rue Daubigny. At the T-junction with this street I took a right towards the church. A reproduction panel of van Gogh's *The Stairway at Auvers*

shows two peasant women and two little girls, in identical white with straw hats, approaching the steps that are still there.

The **Church**. Van Gogh's painting made *The Church at Auvers* (O) one of the best-known village churches in France. His angle, from slightly to the west, profits from the many-roofed jumble of Gothic and Romanesque, sombre against a mauve sky full of foreboding while sunlight shines on the woman walking beside daisy-covered grass down Rue Daubigny.

The devout van Gogh, a descendant of two pastors and himself once destined for the church, was refused a funeral service by the local Abbé. A hearse had to be lent by the parish priest of the neighbouring village, Méry-sur-Oise. The mortal sin of suicide cannot be absolved, even for immortals.

Rue Emile-Bernard. The street suddenly becomes a country road as the village abruptly ends in a vast, hedgeless prairie on the Vexin plateau. Van Gogh recorded, after painting *The Rain* from this road: 'Yesterday, in the rain, I painted a large landscape from a place where sometimes the fields stretch as far as the eye can see, and

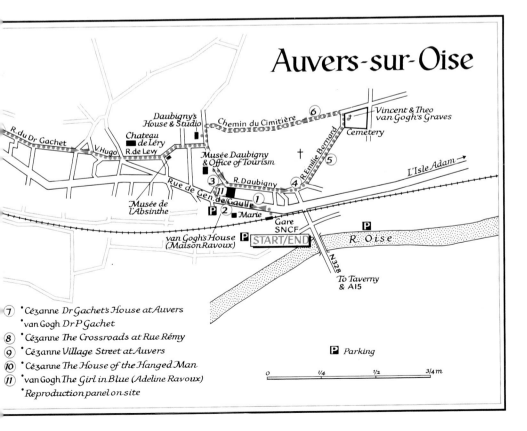

(7) • *Cézanne Dr Gachet's House at Auvers*
• *van Gogh Dr P Gachet*

(8) • *Cézanne The Crossroads at Rue Rémy*

(9) • *Cézanne Village Street at Auvers*

(10) • *Cézanne The House of the Hanged Man*

(11) • *van Gogh The Girl in Blue (Adeline Ravoux)*
• *Reproduction panel on site*

P *Parking*

*In Doctor Gachet at at Table with a Foxglove in his Hand (1890) (O),
van Gogh depicted the impressionist collector in melancholy mood.
Gachet entertained Cézanne at his Auvers home, but van Gogh
mistrusted him.*

Van Gogh's grave in Auvers cemetery.

fine rain striped the whole with blue or grey lines.'

The **Cemetery**. Surrounded by the wheatfields van Gogh loved, Auvers cemetery is an appropriate burial place. Half in love with easeful death, he often painted in its vicinity as though aware that it would soon give him peace. He is buried in a simple grave covered with ivy, spreading fraternally to the next grave where Theo's ashes were brought from Holland to rest by his side.

Theo and Vincent were reconciled in death. Theo felt as guilty about neglecting Vincent as Vincent felt about overloading him with pressures. Vincent's suicide was not, as suicide often is, committed in a spirit of revenge; it was, in its way, the repayment of a debt, and its generous courage can only be admired.

Chemin du Cimetière. Just beyond the cemetery a path to the left leads back to the village across an open field. From here the last canvas, *Wheat Field under Threatening Skies with Crows* was painted. Black crows are silhouetted against the rich gold of the wheat and the blue-grey darkness of the skies, as though swooping uncertainly between life and death. It has 'the sadness of extreme solitude'.

Rue de Léry. On the corner, still standing at the junction with Rue Daubigny, is **Daubigny's Studio**. As an early *pleinairiste*, Daubigny did not spend nearly as much time in his studio as his contemporaries Millet and Rousseau did in theirs. Its wood panelling, carved oak fireplace and dark, heavy paintings seemed fustian after the fields.

More interesting was the replica of Monet's painting-boat, lent temporarily by Argenteuil to Auvers, and displayed in the garden. Adapted from a Seine transport boat, with a little cabin added, it could be easily manoeuvred with only two oars. By contrast, Daubigny's *Le Botin* was a Oise fishing boat, much bigger, with a sail and room for six oarsmen. Sleeping on the bench of his cabin, Daubigny would go off painting for a month at a time in it, whereas Monet used his boat for day trips and only once took the family down to Rouen, returning under tow from a barge.

Next stop down Rue de Léry is the tiny **Absinthe Museum**, which tells you all you need to know about the lethal 'green fairy' that helped unhinge van Gogh. The drink was eventually banned in 1915.

Rue du Dr Gachet. Crossing the main road I caught a glimpse of the **Château de Léry**: in the grounds behind it is where van Gogh is reckoned to have shot himself. On the return walk to the Auberge Ravoux I realized with astonishment that he had managed to drag himself nearly three-quarters of a mile with two bullets lodged near the heart.

Those with cars or bikes may prefer to ride along this long, flattish road in the upper village, where parking is easy. Dr Gachet's house, **No. 78**, has a reproduction panel of van Gogh's portrait of him (O) 'with the heartbroken expression of our times'. The front gate bears a brusque, but no doubt wise, warning: *'Ne reçoit pas'* (no visitors). The house is still a landmark, its tall tower visible on the left of Cézanne's *Auvers, Panoramic View* (1873–5). The closer view, *Doctor Gachet's House at Auvers-sur-Oise* (1873–4) (O), shows the Pissarro influence of greys, dark greens and browns – with the startling innovation of a single pair of bright red shutters, a focal point of attention.

Cézanne learnt engraving from Gachet. He also learnt to take criticism. And Gachet helped him through a bad period financially by buying pictures. The generous Gachet, like a lion-tamer jumping fearless into the cage, said things even Pissarro would not have dared. With the result that, encouraged by Gachet, Cézanne made new strides. Even a continuation of his out-to-shock erotic mode in *A Modern Olympia* (1873–4) (O) – a flamboyant parody of Manet with Cézanne self-portrayed as a brothel client inspecting a buxom *pute* – has a less heavy palette than his earlier sex-and-violence fantasies; an impressionist experiment, it is an oil painting with the lightness of a watercolour. Gachet bought it for his collection.

Rue François-Coppée. On this long village street Cézanne loved to paint without being watched, going deeper and deeper into the secrets of nature, spending hours on one canvas that eventually produced a feeling of spontaneity and fresh vigour.

The Crossroads at Rue Rémy (O), near where he lived, may not have much that is recognizable from the reproduction panel, but it provoked a memorable comment from a peasant watching two impressionists' different methods of putting paint on the canvas. He is believed to have said 'Monsieur Pissarro pricks; Monsieur Cézanne plasters.'

Farther on, *Village Street at Auvers* has houses completely recognizable, albeit in a more rural setting. 'I cannot convey my sensation at the first attempt,' Cézanne said. 'So I redo some colouring, I redo it as best I can. But when I begin, I always try to lay the paint on thickly, giving it shape with the brush.'

Walking the paintings in such peaceful surroundings, I found it hard to relate to the creative agonizing of genius at work, the search for truth and perfection. At the end of the road a wonderful view of *The House of the Hanged Man* (O) is exactly the same but for one tree cut down. As for the house itself, prettification with beams over the windows suggests a Parisian's chic weekend retreat. Does the ghost of the hanged man haunt it, I wondered? Who was he? And who hanged him? Himself or another? It remained a mystery, until later I learnt the truth of what had been a black joke on Cézanne's part: *la Maison du Pendu* was inhabited at the time by a man with the unusual Breton name of Penn'du.

Thanks to Pissarro and Gachet, the loner Cézanne had begun to find where his strength lay as a painter: not in romantic narratives but in lyrical landscapes and still lifes. He was to become the impressionists' greatest innovator. 'I have always worked,' he said later, 'not to arrive at a result which fools will admire: I only have to try to complete something for the sheer pleasure of making it fuller of truth and skill.'

The Auvers–Pontoise room at a recent retrospective of Cézanne's work was suffused with green, blue and violet translucence.

La Maison de van Gogh

2 hours, including lunch

It was a good fifteen minutes' walk along the same road, via Rue Daubigny, back to the **Auberge Ravoux** (also known as **The House of van Gogh**), reached by the side entrance at **No. 8 Rue de la Sansonne**. Hungry and tired by 1.45pm, I would have been glad of the car for the return journey.

The 'Friends of van Gogh' insist rightly that it is a memorial rather than a museum. The Auberge Ravoux commemorates Vincent's zest for living, the fleeting happiness he found at the inn and his relish of the countryside, as well as his tragic end there.

Arthur Ravoux took to Vincent, as he did to other artists in search of full *pension* at 3.50 francs a day, including two meals of meat, vegetables, salad and bread. He and his wife, Louise (described as 'sultry'), had no hesitation in letting their 13-year-old daughter, Adeline, pose for Vincent as *The Girl in Blue*, the famous portrait now reproduced on a panel outside today's inn.

In the midst of death we are in life: the present wooden tables covered with dish cloths, the rush-seated chairs, the zinc-topped counter and the flagstones form a loving reproduction of the original dining room where Vincent took his meals. Wine-racks, with bottles of Burgundy and Bordeaux for sale, are reminders that Ravoux was also the local wine merchant; outside, the Auberge Ravoux declares itself to be a *Commerce de Vins Restaurant*, and two rings were provided for tethering one's horse and cart when stocking up. A pub piano and 1890s telephone complete the ambience.

Country pâtés with knives stuck in are invitingly displayed on the bar top. The house speciality, *le gigot à sept heures*, is lamb cooked slowly for seven hours, falling apart in its rich sauce, served with wheaty brown bread and butter, and Bordeaux Cru Bourgeois. If there is no room at the restaurant, highly recommended is the *guinguette* in the courtyard, which serves the same good, moderately priced country food, and has an open terrace modelled on

Turner's influence on Pissarro is evident in Hoar Frost, Old Road to Ennery *(1873) with its effect of vibrating haze.*

van Gogh's *Restaurant La Sirène at Asnières* (1887) (O).

Afterwards I visited Vincent's attic room on the second floor, its cracked plaster walls dimly lit by a tiny skylight. The simple bed and chair that furnished it have been removed, and the bare, empty look brings one nearer to his loneliness. Another Dutch artist, Anton Hirschig, who had the next room and had watched over the dying Vincent, was sent by Gachet to the Goupil, Boussod & Valadon gallery, Paris, in search of Theo. Hirschig's room is still furnished as sparsely as Vincent's must have been. A third room shows an informative short film about the artist's seventy days at Auvers.

After Vincent's death Theo made presents of paintings to Ravoux and to Gachet. The doctor never bought from van Gogh, as he did from Cézanne. In his whole life van Gogh sold only one painting, *The Red Vineyard*, to Anna Boch for 400 francs; in the 1987 Christie's auction his *Sunflowers* was sold for the highest price ever paid for a painting, £24,750,000.

Château d'Auvers

1½ hours

The seventeenth-century Château de Léry houses an enterprising audio-visual show entitled 'Voyage in the Days of the Impressionists'.

Purists may sniff at such a theme-park evocation of the masters, but the French really get these things right when someone as erudite as Sophie Moneret advises Jean Saint-Bris's team of creators.

Wearing headsets for the sound effects, visitors progress through various rooms and spaces that evoke the period and the people who made impressionism. The lips move on a projected Monet portrait. An animated Drouot auction is accompanied by critical insults, public jeers and low prices. An upper-middle-class Paris drawing room shows Caillebotte's top-hatted man on the balcony, looking out on to the street. By contrast, laundresses discuss their lot as Degas paintings are projected; scarifying statistics about prostitution accompany Lautrec brothel paintings.

There is a café-concert with Yvette Guilbert and Aristide Bruant singing; a railway journey through Pissarro and Sisley countryside; an eye-dazzling, six-screen projection of country pictures such as Monet's *Women in a Garden*; details of dresses, sunlight through trees; and rivers and absinthe bars and seaside and big stores, country people in Paris, Paris people in the country conjuring the whole change in society that the impressionists so brilliantly recorded.

I did Pontoise and Auvers in two long days, on day trips from Paris. It is possible but heavy. Better perhaps to come by car and stay a couple of nights either at an Auvers bed and breakfast (details provided by the Auvers tourist office) or at a Pontoise hotel (there is not a great deal of choice: L'Auberge du Cheval Blanc and Le Campanile). More fun might be Le Cabouillet, a hotel in **L'Isle-Adam** on the river. L'Isle-Adam is eight miles from Pontoise and five miles from Auvers, making it a convenient stop-over. For dinner there's Le Troubadour, an eclectic *guinguette* presided over by an Auvergnat serving Provençal food in an Ile-de-France village.

6

RIGHT BANK

· · · · · · · · · · · · · · · · · ·

The Tuileries.

'Let us cry "Long Live the Sun" which gives us such beautiful light,' wrote Cézanne to Zola from Aix-en-Provence. Yet it was not solely the privilege of Provence. Paris had its own equally beautiful light suffusing the new open spaces where, for centuries, a medieval warren of tortuous alleys had kept it out.

Manet, Monet, Renoir, Pissarro and others celebrated the changing Paris in all weathers and seasons and times of day; to them, Baron Haussmann's laying out of the city, much as we now enjoy it with its wide, tree-lined boulevards, plunging perspectives, avenues leading to well-known monuments, streets radiating from roundabouts, aesthetic street-lighting and pleasingly airy vistas, was the height of modernity. It earned Paris the title 'City of Light', timed well for the impressionists' experimentation with the multiple effects of light in art.

For this, the paradoxical figure of Emperor Napoleon III (1852–71) can take much credit. His portrait is on view at the Carnavalet Museum of Paris History: an unprepossessing figure as short as his illustrious uncle, Napoleon Bonaparte, but with none of the saturnine charisma; out of uniform, he could have been mistaken for one of his *nouveaux riches* property developers.

An hour or so in the Carnavalet provides a good background to the period. The museum is housed in one of the Marais's most sumptuous Renaissance mansions, once the home of the Marquise de Sévigné. Besides portraits of the Emperor, others of his Empress Eugénie, Baron Haussmann (Prefect of the Seine and town-planner extraordinary) and the ostentatious court set the high-life scene.

Napoleon III was a despot. He came to power with a military *coup d'état*, ruled at first with repressive measures, and insisted on strict political censorship (you could be arrested for singing the 'Marseillaise' in public). Capitalism and imperialism flourished. Yet the Emperor, imbued with a leftish idealism rare among French oligarchs, was sensitive to appalling conditions of work, even for many of the new *petite bourgeoisie*, and instituted the right to strike. His paternalistic, bread-and-circuses policy in the reshaping of Paris was much like Stalin's for Moscow (the world's biggest swimming pool, chandeliers in the Métro). It was to be a spectacular city, both for the people's pleasure and to arouse patriotic fervour, a city that would be the envy of the world. If his foreign policy led to his downfall in the Franco-Prussian War, his home policy was visionary for the times. France moved into the nineteenth century from almost medieval instability.

Visually, the Carnavalet charts this change in the capital and its continuation under the Third Republic. Not great art, but good journalism.

Among the best are Guillaumin's impressionist *The Seine Entering Paris* (1875); Signac's neo-impressionist *Le Moulin de la Galette* (1884); and Luce's *First Arch of the Pont St-Michel* (1903), showing old houses being knocked down to enlarge the Palais de Justice.

Renoir, more than the other impressionists, had experienced the change from below stairs. Son of a tailor who moved to Paris from Limoges when Pierre-Auguste was four, he started Parisian life in a rundown block of lower-class housing that had once been the apartments of courtiers near the Louvre Palace. After President Napoleon's promotion to Emperor after the coup of 1851 the Renoirs were victims of his cultural cleansing, kicked out of their home to make way for an extension of the Louvre Museum. They moved to one of the last bastions of medieval and Renaissance Paris, the Marais.

As a young man Renoir was thoroughly modern, going along with the Haussmann novelties. When he walked the widened, bustling Seine quays 'the air was charged with emanations of the city, the odour of the markets, the strong smell of leeks melding with the discreet yet persistent smell of lilac, borne upon a slightly acidic breeze – typical Paris air.'

Only later, shocked by the building over green fields and chopping down of trees in the Plaine Monceau by property sharks, did Renoir turn against the movement. 'You've no idea what fun and how beautiful Paris used to be! And whatever Haussmann and the other demolishers may think, much healthier than now. The streets were narrow; their central gutter didn't always smell too good, but behind each building there was a garden. Many people experienced the pleasure of picking a lettuce just before eating it.'

Whatever their objections, the artists who eventually made up the impressionist group found *plein-air* subjects to inspire them at every turn of the new Paris. At Manet's *Concert in the Tuileries Gardens*, the music is less important than the social event, a gathering of his peer group with their formal manners, elegant dress and doll-like children. Not a prole in sight. Manet has worked useful supporters into the canvas: Baudelaire in profile, his military friend Commandant Lejosne, art critic Champfleury, sculptor Astruc, writer Gautier, painter Fantin-Latour. Manet himself is in dashing, top-hatted evidence, as though giving a private party in a public place.

Manet met Degas when both were copying in the Louvre. As a young man-about-town Degas went racing at Longchamp as part of his social round, and Manet went with him. Degas was fascinated by the movement of jockeys and horses. *At the Races – Before the Start* (1862) shows a race meeting with its contradictory elements of grace and tension. Nervous jockeys and horses are captured as if in a freeze-frame of action. Spectators, too: *Edouard Manet at the Races* (1864) and *Two Ladies at the Races* (1879) are people caught at a specific moment in a specific place, the essence of impressionism. Another element was courageous colouring. Manet's *Ladies at the Races* (1865) are depicted in bold primary colours – green umbrella, blue dress, yellow and red carriage wheels.

An early Renoir view of *The Champs-Elysées during the Paris Fair* (1867), looking west, shows the Palais de l'Industrie suitably distanced – it housed the Salon, which refused so many of his youthful efforts – and nearer, on the right of the picture, the Café des Ambassadeurs, where Degas did his memorable paintings of the popular singer, Thérésa, belting out her 'Dog Song' beneath the trees and glare of white globe lamps.

Manet immortalized the Paris Fair, too, from his perch on the Trocadéro hill, looking across the river to the festive pavilions on the Champ-de-Mars. His friend and model, Berthe Morisot, who lived nearby in the Passy opulence of Rue Scheffer, had painted *Paris seen from the Trocadéro* (1866), a similar view, the year before; Manet was encouraged to follow suit. Thanks partly to her, the older artist began experimenting with impressionistic, outdoor subjects and a lighter palette. Outdoor Paris was a place of new optimism. Who could guess then that four years later Manet, an entrenched studio painter, would be depicting the grim facts of *Civil War* like today's photo-journalist or television reporter?

Despite Manet's courageous 'journalism', his politics were never very serious. Although he and Degas had done token military service as befitted their class, none of the impressionists can be said to have pursued *la gloire* in either the Franco-Prussian or Civil War. Even Bazille's death at Beaune-la-Rolande in Burgundy was a tragic farce; totally untrained for service with a crack Zouave regiment, and unusually tall, he failed to duck sufficiently to hide from a Prussian sniper.

As a group they cared little for active politics or flag-waving nationalism. Revolutionary energies were preserved for the cause of their art, subversive tactics directed against the Salon. Pissarro was an armchair anarchist. Renoir believed all men were born equal. Monet was his own underdog. Sisley and Cassatt were foreigners. Cézanne was Provençal – much the same thing in those days. Morisot was a woman and therefore, politically, a female eunuch.

Monet returned from self-imposed wartime exile in London and continued where he had left off, painting with Renoir. In 1872 they both did *Pont Neuf*, the oldest bridge in Paris, given a new look with horse-drawn buses and pleasure boats. Renoir's view shows the buildings of the Quai de l'Horloge on the Ile de La Cité and the Quai des Grands Augustins on the Left Bank, revived and thriving after the degradation of defeat by the Prussians. Monet's bridge has a more everyday look, people hurrying by with Parisian energy, umbrellas open beneath a rainy sky.

Guillaumin, during the early 1870s, was recording the workaday Seine from a less glamorous vantage-point, near his office at the Department of Bridges and Highways. *Pont de Charenton* (1878) (O) and *Sunset at Ivry* (1873) (O) are stunning evocations of the river's eastern entry to the industrial outskirts of Paris, near its confluence with the Marne. In the Sixth Impressionist Show (1881) he had paintings of several quays: Célestins, Austerlitz, Rapée, Henri IV and Sully.

Guillaumin later shared Daubigny's old studio with Cézanne on the Ile St-Louis. A more residential image is *Pont Louis-Philippe* (1875), looking west from the Quai de Bourbon, with the two theatres of Place du Châtelet beyond the new bridge's light arches, a busy laundry boat, and children playing on the Quai d'Anjou.

Not far away were the popular new stores La Samaritaine, Bon Marché and the Bazar de L'Hôtel de Ville, attracting *petit-bourgeois* Parisians who had a little money for the first time. It was an age of ostentation among all but the scavengers of the Paris outskirts. Look how prettily the poorly paid shopgirls in Renoir's paintings dressed, how stylishly the clerks and errand-boys at a Sunday ball.

In his sixties, at last enjoying modest financial success, Pissarro deserted the countryside to become *the* Paris painter of the *grands* boulevards. He changed hotels as Paris society women changed hats. Encouraged by his dealer, Durand-Ruel, to blow money on a well-placed suite with a good balcony, Pissarro captured the Mardi Gras parade on Boulevard Montmartre from the Grand Hôtel de Russie (1897); the Avenue de l'Opéra in sunshine on a winter's morning from the Grand Hôtel du Louvre (1898); and the Place du Havre from the Hôtel Garnier (1893) near the Gare St-Lazare, vibrant with sunny façades, traffic, and crowds hurrying to and from the station.

Pissarro's most generous early collector was Caillebotte (22 works), who had never known a day's financial hardship. Paradoxically, it was Caillebotte who showed the opulent novelty of Haussmann's Paris with the coldest, most critical eye. As a rich bourgeois of great intelligence, he sensed the malaise of his own circle. Questions occur. That *Young Man at the Window* (1876), his back to us as he looks out on the dazzling new residential buildings: does he really enjoy living in such sterile urbanity? That ship's prow of a building in *Paris Street; Rain* (1877): don't the dwarfed Parisians with umbrellas feel its menace, the rainy cobble-stones like a popply sea, the fashionably dressed couple in the foreground glancing apprehensively 'off-screen' at another 'steamship' bearing down on them? What amorous plot is unfolding in the carriage seen through the detailed wrought-iron balustrade in *View Beyond a Balcony* (1880)? The almost photographic angle of *Traffic Island, Boulevard Haussmann* shows three top-hatted men at different places; in fact, they are the same man at different times, giving a hallucinatory effect, prefiguring the work of Magritte.

Renoir disliked the uniform six- and seven-storey blocks with their cupolas and wrought-iron balconies, 'cold and lined up like soldiers at a review'. His own *Grands Boulevards* (1872) is much more animated than Caillebotte's bleak and sparsely peopled images. A nun, a mother and children cross in front of a carriage. The Grand Hôtel commands the right-hand corner of Boulevard des Capucines; on the left, a man reading by a newspaper kiosk, and top-hatted gentlemen gossiping. Though nothing special is happening, Paris is putting on its non-stop show.

Strolling musicians, one-man bands, acrobats, clowns and jugglers were not just confined to Shrove Tuesday, the Fourteenth of July and the popular Foire aux Pains d'Epices in the Place du Trône. Street theatre could be anywhere, any time. Barbary organs, banned by Napoleon III because they accompanied subversive songs, returned under the Third Republic. Characters like Manet's *The Old Musician* and *The Street Singer* were eternal, and though Manet sympathized with the plight of the poor, he was careful not to make either the itinerant violinist or the barefooted children look *too* poor or the Salon might have found him guilty of serious social conscience.

Outdoor Paris attracted the impressionists because it was the here-and-now, alive, modern. Most Parisians lived then and still live today in cramped, dark apartments, so they need to get out and about. The very light that Cézanne found so important nurtures the spirit, revives the body and stimulates the mind. *'Parisiens, sortez de vos trous!'* ('Parisians, leave your holes!') goes the saying. Now Haussmann's Paris has aged and weathered, the trees have grown, and some of those pristine Caillebotte buildings are looking comfortably worn. And whatever your opinion of the Beaubourg, the Pei Pyramid, the Arche de la Défense and other post-Haussmann additions to the City of Light, Paris is still the pleasantest, safest city in the world to walk. In many respects, thanks to Napoleon III.

Walks and Drives
ON
The Right Bank

The Dancing Class *by Degas (1873–6) (O).*

Information

Itineraries

Right Bank Walk (full day). Start: Métro Sully-Morland (for Ile St-Louis). End: Métro Trocadéro (Palais de Chaillot).

Lunch: Tuileries Gardens area.

Art and Money Walk (half-day). Start: Métro Madeleine. End: Métro Richelieu-Drouot. **Lunch:** Drouot auction rooms area.

Haussmann Bus Ride (1 hour). Round trip on 81 bus from Place du Châtelet to Place de Clichy.

Bois de Boulogne (2 hours, 4 hours with lunch). 63 bus to Porte de la Muette. Walk to Lac Inférieur. Rowing-boat trip. Visit Pré Catelan gardens. Lunch Pré Catelan restaurant – an expensive optional.

Longchamp Races. Main meetings Arc de Triomphe Grand Prix first Sunday in October, Paris Grand Prix last Sunday in June. No close public transport.

Refreshment, Meals and Overnight

Right Bank Walk
Restaurants, Cafés and Bars

Brasserie de l'Ile St-Louis, (**B**), 55 Quai Bourbon. Tel. 01.43.54.02.59.

Berthillon (the best ice-creams in town), Ile St. Louis.

Café du Louvre (refreshments), (**C**), Louvre Pyramid.

Café Marly (restaurant), (**B**), 93 Rue de Rivoli. Tel. 01.49.26.06.60.

Le Soufflé (restaurant), (**B**), 36 Rue Mont Thabor. Tel. 01.42.60.27.19.

Lescure (bistro), (**C**), 7 Rue Mondovi. Tel. 01.42.60.18.91.

La Table du Gouverneur (restaurant), (**B**), 10 Avenue des Champs-Elysées. Tel. 01.42.65.85.10.

La Butte Chaillot (restaurant), (**B**), 110bis Avenue Kléber. Tel. 01.47.27.88.88.

Café Kléber (refreshments), Place du Trocadéro.

Hotels

Saint-Louis, (**B**), (no meals), 75 Rue St-Louis-en-Ile. Tel. 01.46.34.04.80.

Les Deux Iles, (**B**), (no meals), 59 Rue St-Louis-en-Ile. Tel. 01.43.26.13.35.

Du Jeu de Paume, (**A**), (no meals), 5 Rue St-Louis-en-Ile. Tel. 01.43.26.14.18.

☆ Du Louvre, (**A**), Place André-Malraux. Tel. 01.44.58.38.38.

Montana Tuileries, (**B**), (no meals), 12 Rue St-Roch. Tel. 01.42.60.35.10.

Des Jardins du Trocadéro, (**A**), (snacks only), 35 Rue Franklyn. Tel. 01.53.70.17.70.

Art and Money Walk
Restaurants, Cafés and Bars

☆ Café de la Paix (refreshments/meals), (**B**), Boulevard des Capucines.

Hard Rock Café, (**C**), (with children), 14 Boulevard Montmartre.

☆ Au Petit Riche (restaurant), (**B**), 25 Rue Le Peletier. Tel. 01.47.70.68.68.

Beaujolais-Drouot (restaurant), (**B**), 7 Rue Rossini. Tel. 01.42.46.09.20.

☆ Chartier-Montmartre (brasserie), (**C**), 7 Rue du Fauberg Montmartre. Tel. 01.47.70.86.29.

Hotels

☆ Le Grand Hôtel Inter-Continental, (**A**), 2 Rue Scribe. Tel. 01.40.07.32.32.

☆ Lautrec Opéra, (**B**), (no meals), 8 Rue Amboise. Tel. 01.42.96.67.90.

Chopin, (**C**), (no meals), 46 Passage Jouffroy. Tel. 01.47.70.58.10.

Bois de Boulogne
Restaurant

☆ Pré Catelan (gastronomic), (**A**), Bois de Boulogne. Tel. 01.45.24.55.58.

Visits

Opera House

Palais Garnier, Place de l'Opéra (Métro Opéra). Open daily 10–4.30. Guided tours daily (except Mon) 2.30. Entry: 30F. Ballet performances: 60–370F. Tel. 01.44.73.13.00.

Museums

Louvre. Rue de Rivoli (Métro Palais Royal-Louvre). Open daily (except Tues) 9–6 (until 9.45pm Wed). Entry: 45F before 3pm, 26F after 3pm and all day Sun. Tel. 01.40.20.51.51.

Carnavalet (History of Paris), 23 Rue de Sévigné (Métro Saint-Paul). Open daily (except Mon and hols) 10–5.40. Entry: 27F. Tel. 01.42.72.21.13.

Tourist Office

Office du Tourisme, 127 Avenue des Champs-Elysées, 75008. Open daily 9–8. Tel. 01.49.52.53.54.

Right Bank Walk

whole day

Zola has Claude Lantier, his impressionist painter in *L'Oeuvre*, respond to the city's wide open spaces: 'When he crossed Paris, he discovered pictures everywhere, the whole town, with its streets, crossroads, bridges, vivid horizons, unfolded like immense frescoes. . . .'

Quais d'Anjou and de Bourbon. Reached by crossing **Pont Sully** to the **Ile St-Louis** from **Métro Sully-Morland**, the quays are now among the most highly priced residential enclaves of Paris. Once, artists occupied the opulent seventeenth-century mansions: on Quai d'Anjou cartoonist Daumier at **No. 9**; pre-impressionist Daubigny at **No. 27**, with a convenient studio-away-from-home down the road at **No. 13** Quai de Bourbon as well.

Beyond **Pont Marie**, at **No. 15** Quai de Bourbon lived symbolist Emile Bernard, a prime mover of the Pont-Aven Group, which had Gauguin as its most radical experimenter. Sculptress Camille Claudel, Rodin's mistress, worked in a ground-floor courtyard of **No. 19**.

Cézanne and Zola were to fall out over the hero of *L'Oeuvre*. Zola sited Lantier's first studio on Quai de Bourbon, where Cézanne was working with Guillaumin at **No. 13** in 1875, but apart from Lantier's bunch of carrots matching Cézanne's apples, the monumental nude, and the studio on Quai de Bourbon, the similarities are tenuous. The narrative has as many echoes of Manet and Monet as of Cézanne. Lantier's *Plein Air* painting is a parody of Manet's *Déjeuner sur l'herbe*, and Zola has him spend his idyll with Christine at Bennecourt, a Seine valley village where Monet had painted soon after meeting Camille. Also like Lantier, Monet made a suicide attempt.

By the time *L'Oeuvre* appeared in 1886 Manet was dead and respected, Monet already making good money. Sensitive to his own lack of recognition, Cézanne saw only himself in it: understandably, he over-reacted to the failed genius Lantier hanging himself in front of the erotic nude he cannot complete: the theme of the nude never quite perfected haunted Cézanne with his eternal *Bathers*. He took it as an invasion of privacy at its most hurtful. Thanking Zola for his copy of the book, he wrote briefly and coolly: '. . . and let me shake your hand, thinking of years gone by. Encouraged by vanished memories, I wish you my best. . . .' They never met again. Outliving Zola by four years, a very different Cézanne, himself respected and honoured, attended the 1902 unveiling of a memorial to his childhood friend. He wept tears of reconciliation.

The **Quais**. After crossing **Pont Louis-Philippe** back to mainland Paris, I continued west along the Right Bank. The **Quai de l'Hôtel de Ville** passes Haussmann's town hall, dripping with civic pomp. Manet offered his services to decorate the interior with murals extolling the virtues of the new city, even the sewers. The powers that be considered him too radical for civic employment in a town hall; his *Execution of Emperor Maximilian* had, after all, been banned by Emperor Napoleon from public exhibition.

The **Quai de Gesvres** leads to **Place du Châtelet**, where the actress Sarah Bernhardt owned a theatre. Her art nouveau friend Alphonse Mucha did posters for *Médéa*, *La Dame aux Camélias* and her female *Hamlet*.

Along the **Quai da la Mégisserie** the lovers Claude and Christine in *L'Oeuvre* would pass on their long, amorous walks by the Seine.

Pont Neuf. My eclectic view took in the distant nineteenth-century Eiffel Tower, the seventeenth-century Institute of France across the river, the sixteenth-century Pont Neuf and the fairytale fifteenth-century towers of the Ile de la Cité's Conciergerie, where Marie Antoinette spent her last days.

Renoir's and Monet's 1872 views of the bridge were done from the second floor of a corner café where the La Samaritaine store now stands. Renoir's resourceful journalist brother, Edmond, persuaded passers-by to pose for them. In both artists' versions the bronze equestrian statue of King Henri IV, known as Le Vert-Galant (Bright Old Spark), is clearly visible.

Square du Vert-Galant, a little garden at the downstream tip of the Ile de la Cité, was a favourite painting place of Pissarro. His 1902 bird's-eye view shows river and square on a sunny morning.

Louvre. 'Monsieur le Superintendent,' wrote the 26-year-old Monet to the art gauleiter Count Nieuwerkerke, Director-General of National Museums, 'I have the honour to ask you to grant me, most kindly, special authorization to do views from the windows of the Louvre and notably from the outside balcony a view of St-Germain-l'Auxerrois.'

Monet's characteristic chutzpah was rewarded, and in 1866 he produced three cityscapes in his clear, confident early style. From the Napoleon Gate in the museum's eastern façade at **Place du Louvre**, the church of *St-Germain-l'Auxerrois* is much as Monet saw it.

Returning towards the river, two views look across it: *The Garden of the Princess* (at the south-east corner of the museum, recently restored) and *Quai du Louvre*. The imperial lawn is empty for princesses to disport themselves; beyond the railings Parisians out for a good time are in close proximity to their rulers. The Panthéon rises majestically in the distance, to remind them that they are safe in the lap of benevolent gods.

The **Louvre Museum** is not our period, though the French painting on the second floor includes pre-impressionist influences: Barbizon works such as Rousseau's *Sunset in the Forest* (1867), Corot's lost, nostalgic landscapes, the bold colouring of Delacroix, the nudes of Ingres.

You can either walk the length of the museum along the **Quai du Louvre**, or go through the courtyards of the palace from the Napoleon Gate to the **Carrousel Arch**, passing the much-contested Pei Pyramid.

The **Tuileries Gardens**. Pissarro painted *The Carrousel* on a grey, autumn morning. How he would have rejoiced in its joyous restoration, all gilded horses and pink columns. In triumphal gaiety, it matches his *Tuileries Gardens, Afternoon Sun* (1899). President Mitterrand completed the work Napoleon III had begun – a straight line linking the Carrousel, the Luxor Obelisk, the Arc de Triomphe and the new Arche de la Défense. The Opéra-Bastille, the National Library, the Finance Ministry and the Arab Cultural Centre are other legacies of his presidency; he may well be remembered as Monument Mitterrand.

Monet's *Les Tuileries* (1875) (O) shows a haven of calm in central Paris, a place for people to relax in or, as at Manet's *Concert in the Tuileries Gardens*, to sit in the shade of chestnut trees listening to music.

No. 198 Rue de Rivoli. This was the apartment of collector Victor Chocquet, a surprisingly grand address for a customs official. Chocquet had private means. As the owner of a Delacroix, he found it reassuring to be near the Louvre; it encouraged him to back his hunches with young Renoir, who included the Delacroix on the wall in a portrait of Madame Chocquet. Renoir knew how much it would mean to the struggling Cézanne to meet someone as enthusiastically supportive as Chocquet, who instantly sat for a portrait. The slim, elegant, grey-bearded Chocquet was a masterpiece, one of seventeen Cézannes in the Third Impressionist Show of 1877. Extending the network of generosity among the impressionists, Cézanne arranged for Chocquet to meet Monet, who was going through one of his perennial hard times.

The arcaded entrance to the spot where Monet painted the Tuileries is now typical of the tourist traps along the street, with shops called Paris Chic and Royal Parfum selling costume jewellery and toiletries. Near the gardens are some excellent, reasonably priced places for lunch. I suggest Le Soufflé (Rue du Mont-Thabor), Lescure (Rue Mondovi), or Café Marly (Rue de Rivoli) for lighter fare.

The Tuileries also boast many Maillol statues, sensual nude bronzes placed at the west end of the gardens. Maillol's *Homage to Cézanne* shows three bathers.

Place de la Concorde. While crossing the square on the south side of

A Concert in the Tuileries Gardens (1862) was one of Manet's early Parisian social scenes, more original and less Spanish-influenced, marking him as a vivid depicter of Napoleon III's modern Paris.

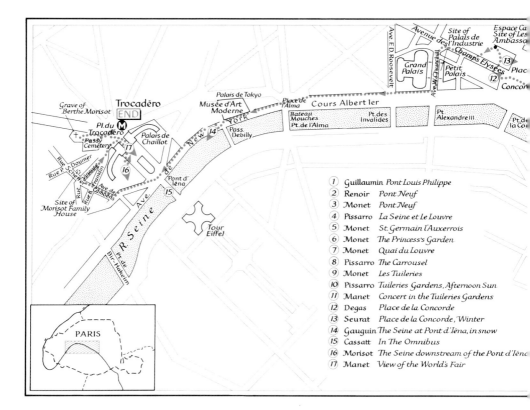

①	Guillaumin	*Pont Louis Philippe*
②	Renoir	*Pont Neuf*
③	Monet	*Pont Neuf*
④	Pissarro	*La Seine et Le Louvre*
⑤	Monet	*St. Germain l'Auxerrois*
⑥	Monet	*The Princess's Garden*
⑦	Monet	*Quai du Louvre*
⑧	Pissarro	*The Carrousel*
⑨	Monet	*Les Tuileries*
⑩	Pissarro	*Tuileries Gardens, Afternoon Sun*
⑪	Manet	*Concert in the Tuileries Gardens*
⑫	Degas	*Place de la Concorde*
⑬	Seurat	*Place de la Concorde, Winter*
⑭	Gauguin	*The Seine at Pont d'Iéna, in snow*
⑮	Cassatt	*In The Omnibus*
⑯	Morisot	*The Seine downstream of the Pont d'Iéna*
⑰	Manet	*View of the World's Fair*

the **Champs-Elysées** I passed the Luxor Obelisk, one of the few pre-Haussmann monuments in a public place. This impressive artefact was offered by the Viceroy of Egypt to Charles X in 1829.

From the beginning of the Champs, Degas captured his engraver friend Vicomte Lepic out for a purposeful walk with two obnoxious-looking little daughters and an amiable dog. The cigar-smoking, dapper viscount seems in a hurry to get somewhere else. Apart from racetracks and café-concerts, Parisian exteriors were a rarity from Degas's brush, and *Place de la Concorde* (1873) shows the alienation of the upper classes from the popular spectacle of the Champs-Elysées with its common crowds, kiosks and candelabra.

Seurat's later crayon drawing is a bleaker *Place de la Concorde, Winter* (1882), with a carriage ploughing through the slush. The new Paris was never depicted sentimentally or picturesquely.

Champs-Elysées. Degas is often mistaken for a snob who preferred the Viscount Lepics to the Guillaumins of the art world, the opera house to the corner bar. Not so. He could slum with the best of them, be it in bordello or at café-concert. And many were his visits to **Les Ambassadeurs** on the north

side of the Champs-Elysées. A path branching right off the main pavement led me to the **Espace Cardin**, a theatre in the trees where the open-air Les Ambassadeurs used to be. One could imagine the singers Degas loved, giving their all in the festive glow of Chinese lanterns and gas footlights: Emilie Bécat's jerky, epileptic gestures illustrating her blatantly bawdy lyrics; Thérésa, whose public sang along with her most famous song *'A bas les pattes, s'il vous plaît'*. A very free translation of a stanza –

'Oh, how I love the whiteness of
  your breasts,
A whiteness like the creamiest of
  cheese!
From your corset's ramparts, doing
  their best
To tumble out when I give them a
  squeeze . . .'
'I've heard that song before, give it a
  rest,
Monsieur, hands off the goods, if you
  please!'

As he quietly observed and memorized, Degas was accompanied by his prudish brother, René. René was something of a liability to the artist, who had already had to bail him out, as a gentlemanly brother of honour did at that time, from bad debts incurred

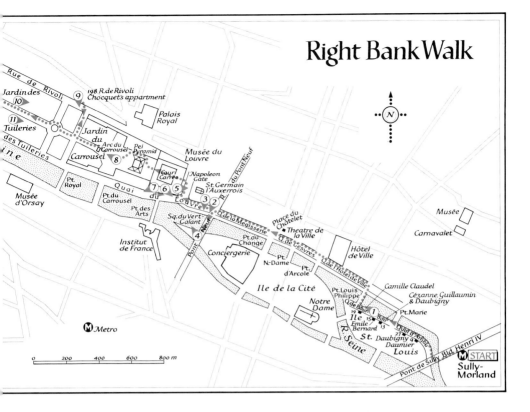

Rue de Rivoli
Jardin des Rivoli
10
198 R.de Rivoli
9 Chocquet's apartment
Palais Royal
11 Tuileries
Jardin du Carrousel
Arc du Carrousel
8 Pei Pyramid
Carrousel
Musée du Louvre
Pt. Royal
Quai du Louvre
Cour Carré
Napoleon Gate
St Germain l'Auxerrois
7 6 5
3 2
Pt. du Carrousel
Pt. des Arts
Sq. du Vert-Galant
4 Quai de la Megisserie
Place du Châtelet
Théâtre de la Ville
Pont Neuf
Qt. de Gesvres
Musée Carnavalet
Musée d'Orsay
Institut de France
Conciergerie
Pt. du Change
Pt. N-Dame
Pt. d'Arcole
Qt. de l'Hôtel de Ville
Hôtel de Ville
Île de la Cité
Camille Claudel
Cézanne, Guillaumin & Daubigny
Notre Dame
Pt. Louis-Philippe
Q.de Bour.
19 1 15
Île
13 Émile Bernard
Pt. Marie
M Metro
Seine
Quai d'Anjou
27
St. Daubigny Daumier Louis
0   200   400   600   800 m
Pont de Sully Bld Henri IV
M START
Sully-Morland

N

in America: after 1875. Degas had to look seriously at his art as a means of support. The café-concert works of 1877–8 were in a more saleable vein than some of his earlier work, though Degas hated selling anything. Ballet scenes were an even better source of income. After his death René suppressed what he considered to be salacious works, unworthy of brother Edgar, done in brothels around the same time. Later dealer Ambroise Vollard unearthed these works and published them in a perfectly respectable illustrated edition of Maupassant's *La Maison Tellier*.

Grand and Petit Palais. Continuing up the Champs, I turned left near La Table du Gouverneur, a Belle Epoque folly of a restaurant, crossed the avenue and headed for **Avenue Winston Churchill**, which runs between the **Grand** and **Petit Palais**. The bombastic stone-steel-and-skylight buildings were constructed for the 1900 World Exhibition. The Grand Palais houses temporary exhibitions, often of impressionists, (most recently Caillebotte and Cézanne). Cézanne longed to make something lasting of impressionism, 'like art in museums'. The Petit Palais Museum has a permanent show, including his *Portrait of Ambroise Vollard* among a small but important collection.

There was no avenue leading to the river in impressionist times. The **Palais de l'Industrie**, scene of the annual **Salon des Beaux-Arts**, was roughly between the two present 'palaces', and was reached on foot from the Champs-Elysées. It resembled London's Crystal Palace. The name of the exhibition derived from the Salon Carré (Square Drawing Room) of the Louvre, where it was formerly held.

The Salon exhibition of contemporary art was, in the 1860s, the only way by which an artist could achieve recognition and make a sale (Introduction, p. 9). Manet, Monet and Renoir always respected its advantages and huge popularity with the public. Zola gives a scarifying account of the Salon world in *L'Oeuvre*, a maelstrom of hype, rages, ribaldry, sneers, inflated egos, corruption, cruelty and hedonistic socializing over terrible food and drink.

I was happy to reach the river and the joyful prancing Pegasus sculptures and clusters of a hundred Venetian lamps on the Pont Alexandre III, a gift from the Tsar for the 1900 World Fair.

Place de l'Alma. The pleasant amble west along the Right Bank of the Seine took me past the *bâteaux-mouches* terminus. Near here, during the 1867 World Fair, Manet boldly followed Courbet's example and set up his own, do-it-yourself exhibition in a purpose-built shed. A few brave souls oohed and aahed at avant-garde shockers such as *The Absinthe Drinker*, *Olympia* and *Le Déjeuner sur l'herbe*.

Avenue de New-York. Continuing along the river, you come to a footbridge. From near here Gauguin did an early work, *The Seine at the Pont d'Iéna, in Snow* (1875). The double-decker road-and-Métro **Pont de Bir-Hakeim**, whose surreal structure appears in the background of Mary Cassatt's Japanese-influenced mother, child and nanny *In the Omnibus* (1891) (American Museum, Giverny), had not yet been built. Gauguin shows the wintry curve of the river and, beyond the **Pont d'Iéna**, the rising slopes of the **Butte Chaillot**, still comparatively countrified.

La Butte Chaillot. Now that it is dominated by the vast twin pavilions of the **Palais de Chaillot**, a 1937 Palace of the People, it is hard to imagine the fashionable Passy street, **Rue Scheffer** (between **Rues Vineuse** and **Franklyn**), ever being suburbanly residential, as it was when the Morisot family inhabited it. Berthe could stroll out, unblocked by the Palais de Chaillot, to do her free, sketchy views of *The Seine Downstream of the Pont d'Iéna* (1866) with its barges and factory chimneys suitably distanced. She painted what she was: a charming Passy *haute bourgeoise*, giving a reassuring picture of young French womanhood, on good terms with their sisters, playing with their children, at their toilette, dressing stylishly, preparing for a ball. A charmed life. And yet she was a loyal fighter for impressionism.

Palais de Chaillot. The platform overlooking the Champ-de-Mars beyond the river is more or less the site of Manet's *View of the Paris World's Fair* (1867). No Eiffel Tower, though. La Butte Chaillot's hillock was reshaped by Haussmann specially for the Fair. Manet shows a straw-hatted gardener with a hose doing his best with a newly planted garden, rude soldiery trampling the young grass, a young masher (Manet's son) with a dog, a Passy gentleman with binoculars viewing the common herd pouring off a steamboat, and a Passy lady pensive on her horse thinking about who's coming to luncheon.

Trocadéro. Berthe Morisot never lived anywhere in the city but the 16th *arrondissement*. Visiting her grave in **Passy Cemetery** (she died of flu in 1895) on the west side of the square is a fitting end to the walk.

A Haussmann bus ride

1 hour

A shorter outing is the round trip by the No. 81, bus which took me through the heart of Haussmann country from **Place du Châtelet** to **Place de Clichy**. The bus follows a slightly different route on the return. Avoid rush-hours and mid-afternoon.

Outward Journey

Place du Châtelet. The 81 leaves from a stop opposite Le La Rochelle Restaurant. Sit on the left side of the bus for good views.

Rue de Rivoli. Driving along the whole length of the **Louvre**, nearly three-quarters of a mile, puts the museum's interior foot-slog into perspective. Impressionists were relegated for years to its antechamber, the Musée du Luxembourg (Chapter Seven, p. 176). Manet's *Olympia* (O) languished there from 1899, before being transferred to the Louvre in 1907.

Avenue de l'Opéra. On my left, facing up the avenue, was the **Grand Hôtel du Louvre**, a nineteenth-century pile from whose balcony Pissarro did fifteen paintings, including one of the **Place du Théâtre-Français** immediately below. By 1898 trouble with his sight had made painting

Above right: Gauguin's The Seine at the Pont d'Iéna, in snow *(1875) is one of his rare cityscapes in pure impressionist mode, giving no indication of the flamboyant colours to come, 'the savage in spite of myself'.*

Below right: Renoir shared a love of grand opera in grand surroundings with Degas and Mary Cassatt. He captured its social nuances in The Box *(1875).*

outdoors for long periods impossible. From his balcony Pissarro did the whole length of *Avenue de l'Opéra, Sunshine, Winter's Morning*.

At **No. 28** was held the Fourth Impressionist Show (1879). This did not include Renoir who, that year, was launched as a portraitist at the Salon with the definitive, charming *Portrait of Madame Charpentier and her Children*. It was also the only year Berthe Morisot did not take part, because she was pregnant.

A glance to the left from the bus revealed **Rue des Pyramides**, where the Fifth Impressionist Show was held at **No. 10** (1880), when Gauguin exhibited for the first time – mostly Oise valley works done while visiting Pissarro (Chapter Five, p. 110).

Place de l'Opéra. Intersection with **Boulevard des Capucines**. This is the hub of Haussmann's cultural and business world, described in the Art and Money Walk (p. 150). The period ambience of the square has changed little since Renoir painted the corner where the Café de la Paix now stands.

The bus now heads, to the right of the Palais Garnier (also described later), into Caillebotte country.

Rue Halévy/Boulevard Haussmann. The short street inspired one of Caillebotte's most adventurous experiments with perspective, *Rue Halévy*, a sixth-floor, bird's-eye view with the street dead centre. After his mother's death he moved to **No. 31 Boulevard Haussmann**, near the intersection of **Rue Gluck** and **Rue Scribe**, from where he did his surrealist *Traffic Island on the Boulevard Haussmann*, described earlier (p. 136). Also influenced by Japanese prints and photography, *Boulevard Seen from Above* (1880) shows Caillebotte's love of modern subjects and daring angles: it is as though spying on two top-hatted men, one sitting on a bench, the other walking near a lightly leafed tree, a delicate image anticipating Bonnard.

Grands magasins. On the outward journey the bus crosses the boulevard, passing nearby *grands magasins*: Galeries-Lafayette, Au Printemps and a rather more recent addition to Paris commerce, Marks et Spencer.

Rue de Clichy. After La Trinité Church and heading up Rue de Clichy, keep a look-out for the monument in **Place de Clichy** to make sure of getting out at the top of the street.

Place de Clichy. The intersection of two more *grands* boulevards, **Batignolles** and **Clichy** (Chapter Two, p. 51), which have seen grander days. They are remembered in Renoir's *Place Clichy* (1880), an audacious close-up of a girl in a bonnet crossing the street, and hazy gentry behind her on the pavement. For once, figures in a cityscape take precedence over the city itself and fix their moment for posterity. Similarly with another evocative close-up by Renoir, *Umbrellas* (1881–6).

Post-impressionist Bonnard's *Boulevard de Clichy* (1911) shows the figurative influence of impressionism still alive and well in the early twentieth century.

Return Journey

Pick up the return bus at **Rue d'Amsterdam**. The following variants on the return journey are worth noting:

Rue d'Amsterdam/Place du Havre. Scene of Pissarro's railway station neighbourhood paintings of 1893 and 1897 (Chapter Two p. 46).

Boulevard Haussman/Rue du Havre. The famous Belle Epoque store, Au Printemps, is on the left before you cross the boulevard.

Rue Auber. Passing the Palais Garnier's west side this time, don't miss the Emperor's Pavilion, **Rue Scribe**, with an entrance big enough for his carriage to enter directly to the royal box. Too bad it never did.

Place de l'Opéra. Passing **Rue de la Paix** on the right you catch a brief glimpse of **Place Vendôme** and Napoleon's column.

Place André-Malraux. Best view of Pissarro's Grand Hôtel du Louvre.

Rue St-Honoré. Another Pissarro subject of 1898. At **No. 251** the Seventh Impressionist Show was held in 1882, with prolific input from Pissarro, Monet, Renoir, Sisley and Gauguin. A decision to bar Degas's cronies led to his abstention that year: his friend Mary Cassatt loyally followed suit. To add to these troubles of their own making, a new Crash

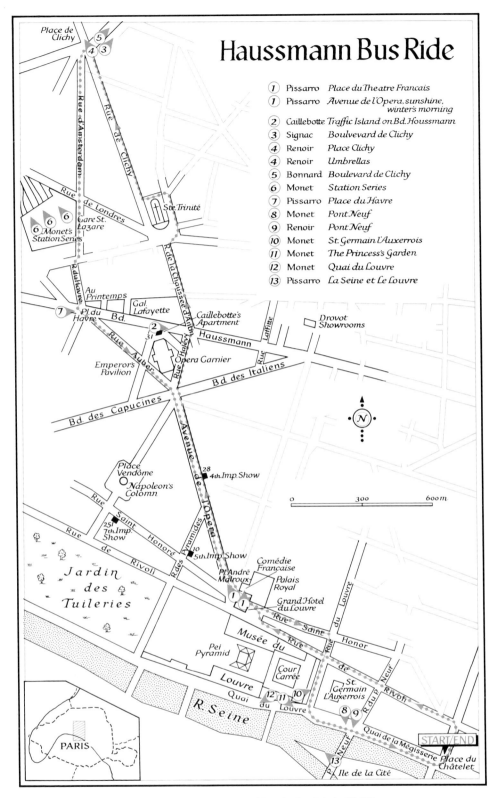

Haussmann Bus Ride

①	Pissarro	Place du Theatre Francais
①	Pissarro	Avenue de l'Opera, sunshine, winter's morning
②	Caillebotte	Traffic Island on Bd. Houssmann
③	Signac	Boulevard de Clichy
④	Renoir	Place Clichy
④	Renoir	Umbrellas
⑤	Bonnard	Boulevard de Clichy
⑥	Monet	Station Series
⑦	Pissarro	Place du Havre
⑧	Monet	Pont Neuf
⑨	Renoir	Pont Neuf
⑩	Monet	St. Germain l'Auxerrois
⑪	Monet	The Princess's Garden
⑫	Monet	Quai du Louvre
⑬	Pissarro	La Seine et Le Louvre

threatened the impressionists' hard working dealer Durand-Ruel with bankruptcy.

Manet, now awarded his coveted Légion d'honneur and still not exhibiting with the others, wrote to the vicious *Figaro* critic Albert Wolff: 'While still in the land of the living, I wouldn't mind reading the marvellous things you'll write about me when I'm dead.' Lucky he didn't: Wolff wrote a bitchy obituary, too.

The bus now returns to **Place du Châtelet**, passing impressionist subjects previously described on the Right Bank Walk: The **Church of St-Germain-l'Auxerrois**, the **Quai du Louvre**, and the **Princess's Garden** (Monet); **Pont Neuf** (Monet, Renoir and Pissarro). **Châtelet** is

Paris's biggest Métro station, with lines to just about everywhere.

Art and Money Walk

half-day

This walk took me into the heart of the Haussmann art world where dealers banked and bankers dealt. The *grands* boulevards were close to Les Batignolles-Pigalle; many of the impressionists had connections with the area, three were born there (Monet, Gauguin, Degas), and it was natural that their exhibitions, when they struck out from the Salon, should be held in the then fashionable part of the town.

Boulevard de la Madeleine. Starting at Métro **Madeleine**, I headed from the colonnaded church up the wide, tree-lined boulevard that becomes **Boulevard des Capucines**. **No. 35** on the right is Arfan, the costume jewellers. The reconstructed seven-storey building has beautifully retained the look of the upper studio with its huge curved window. At the building's angle with **Rue Daunou** the

First Impressionist Show (1874) was held in a second-floor studio that was lent for the occasion by photographer-balloonist Nadar.

A loosely-knit group of artists of varying styles, but sharing a sense of rebellion against the Salon, joined together, mainly under the aegis of the enterprising Monet. Their sales to private collectors in the post-war boom had been rising steadily, and it was time for independence. In a compromise between the dynamic capitalism of the times and Pissarro's anarchy, they formed a joint-stock cooperative with the all-inclusive name *Société des artistes, peintres, sculpteurs, graveurs, etc.*

The 'etc.' included cronies of Degas, such as Lepic and de Nittis, about whose fitness to exhibit there was much argument; as there also was about Cézanne, whose *A Modern Olympia*, a blatant brothel picture, was considered to be too much of a shocker. Renoir exhibited an opera picture, *The Box*, and a graceful young *Dancer* on pointes. And Monet, thanks to a heavily ironic review by critic

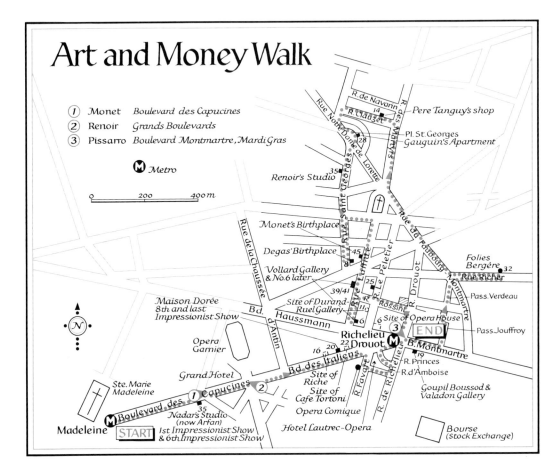

The Palais Garnier opera house.

An early Renoir shows Skating in the Bois de Boulogne *(1868) as an animated social event.*

Leroy, earned the movement its name with *Impression, Sunrise* (Introduction, p. 10).

Monet also exhibited an overhead view of *The Boulevard des Capucines* (1873), done from Nadar's balcony, giving predominance to pedestrians thronging the wide pavement rather than the carriages on the thoroughfare beyond bare trees. The pink balloons of a streetseller provide a focusing splash of colour among the black ant people, blurred like a Japanese print; they could be in dust or snow.

The Sixth Impressionist Show (1881) was also held at this address. At this stage, after much wrangling, Renoir, Monet, Sisley, Cézanne and even Caillebotte (formerly a loyal source of promotion and finance) abstained. Cassatt's mother-and-child pictures were praised for their lack of sentimentality, and *A Cup of Tea* for its sense of Parisian elegance. Gauguin showed a sensual wood-carved medallion of the gorgeous café-concert singer Valérie Roumi.

On the left-hand corner of **Place de l'Opéra** I passed the **Grand Hotel**, which appeared in Renoir's painting *Grands Boulevards*.

Rue Chaussée d'Antin joins the boulevard on the left. It was the fashion centre where Degas's women friends would spend much time *At the Milliner's* (1882). Mary Cassatt tried on feathered hats resembling game birds in a still life, and Renoir's patroness, Madame Charpentier, would demand perfection of her gowns. The couturier Worth was well named. The Worthless could console themselves by window-shopping in comfort on the wide pavements of the outdoor city. **Capucines** becomes **Boulevard des Italiens**, where the Banque Nationale de Paris spreads over a couple of blocks. It has beautifully preserved the **Maison Dorée** (**No. 20**), designed by Lemaire in Louis-Philippe style (1839). The gilded railings and rounded windows once fronted the first-floor restaurant where the Eighth (and final) Impressionist Show was held in 1886. Cassatt's *The Morning Toilet* (Lydia Cassatt plaiting her hair) was received more calmly than Degas's *The Toilet* (nude having hair done), which was thought to be

pornographic. Degas was also in trouble for backing the *pointillistes*, Signac and Seurat. That year Pissarro had experimented with their style. The only works that could be called truly impressionist were by Morisot, Guillaumin and Gauguin. No wonder there were no more shows. At the boulevard cafés, **Tortoni** (**No. 22**) and **Riche** (**No. 16**), formerly the haunts of Manet and Baudelaire, bitchy opinion-makers were crowing over the rout of the impressionists. These now defunct watering-holes were popular with art dealers, bankers and others in the money market (like the young Gauguin), who went there to calm their nerves during the crashes of the 1870s and 1880s. The Bourse was a few minutes' walk away. Degas's *At the Stock Exchange* (1878–9) shows the complicity of brokers doing an insider deal.

Rue Favart/Rue d'Amboise. I turned right off the boulevard down the narrow **Rue Favart**. Just before the Opéra-Comique, where Offenbach launched *La Vie Parisienne*, a left took me into **Rue d'Amboise**. The Hôtel Lautrec-Opéra (**No. 6**) commemorates Lautrec's stay at the street's famous brothel. Lautrec credits another brothel in **Rue des Moulins** more frequently by name, but this was closer to the Bourse for stockbroker or banker to pass a discreet *cinq à sept* in the harem, torture chamber or nunnery cell. Lautrec's subjects reflect harsh reality (*The Boarders Queueing for the Doctor's Weekly Visit*) in a house of dreams. Also an affection for the social outcasts with whom he identified in his compassionate vision of two gay girls, *The Two Friends*, bought by an uninhibited Swiss collector at the beginning of the century. The hotel is a convenient place to stay when visiting Batignolles-Pigalle and Montmartre.

Rue Richelieu. Returning via this street to the boulevard, one can make a short, worthwhile detour through a beautifully restored arcade, **Passage des Princes**, a period piece with globe lamps, glass roof, stylish shops and sunlit courtyard.

Boulevard Montmartre. Turning right at the junction with **Boulevard Haussmann**, I passed the former premises of Goupil, Boussod & Valadon

(**No. 19**), where dealer Theo van Gogh was given a hard time by his bosses for championing the impressionists (Chapter Four, p. 95) In 1884 he bought a Pissarro for 125 francs and then sold it for 150 francs. He never broke faith, buying and selling in all 23 paintings by Degas, 24 Monets, 23 Pissarros, 18 Gauguins, 7 Sisleys, 5 Manets and 1 Cézanne.

On the opposite side of the boulevard, from a balcony of **No. 1 Rue Drouot** (formerly the Grand Hôtel de Russie), Pissarro captured the spirit of *Boulevard Montmartre, Mardi Gras*, with the Shrove Tuesday carnival procession stretching over the hump of **Boulevard Poissonnière**. Streamers decorate the trees, and reds and greens set off the darkness of the crowds on that hazy, wintry day.

I had a similar winter's day. At best, Paris basks in a bowl of brilliant, reflected light; at worst, it is a humid smog trap. Convenient for refreshment if accompanied by children, the Hard Rock Café gives a warning: 'No drugs or nuclear weapons allowed inside.'

Passages Jouffroy/Verdeau. Back in the Belle Epoque, these warren-like, dilapidated old arcades are lined with shops selling antiques, artificial flowers, theatre and cinema books. Also an inexpensive little hotel of great character, Le Chopin.

Rue du Faubourg-Montmartre. Almost immediately to the right, **Rue Richer** leads past Tunisian Jewish food shops and restaurants to the **Folies-Bergère** music-hall. Now art deco, it has no impressionist ambience. More in period is a characterful, inexpensive lunch stop with traditional cuisine at the 1896 brasserie Chartier-Montmartre (**No. 7 Rue du Faubourg-Montmartre**).

The beautiful 1761 shop front of an *épicerie fine*, opposite the entrance of Rue Richer, and a carved-wood façade worthy of Gauguin at Hydrothérapie (**No. 68**) enhance the uphill walk, via **Rue des Martyrs**, to a turn left into **Rue Clauzel**.

Rue Clauzel. At **No. 14** Père Tanguy had his artist's materials emporium. A tough, short Breton fighter with the Commune who was later condemned to two years' hard labour on prison-ships, Tanguy

reckoned that any man who lived on more than fifty centimes per day must be 'a dirty bastard'. Champion of the underdog, he furnished van Gogh with paints in exchange for pictures nobody wanted. If he sold anything, it was by other artists, and never for more than 40–100 francs. Vincent, paranoid about lack of buyers, violently insulted Tanguy's wife, who forbade her husband to have anything more to do with him.

In the 1890s Tanguy's was a store for the works of rejected genius. Cézanne's son Paul, by then grown up and deeply compassionate towards his father's struggle for recognition, got the young dealer Ambroise Vollard to look at paintings *chez* Tanguy. Vollard instantly set up the 1895 Cézanne one-man show.

Rue Clauzel and the parallel Rue Navarin were Degas's red-light district, within walking distance of where he was born in Rue St-Georges and where he died in Boulevard de Clichy. An early photographer, he approached his brothel monotypes as reportage. For once, stillness rather than movement is the key: *les filles*, often women of more than a certain age and of comely girth, slump about in stockings and shifts, endlessly waiting or resting, falsely festive or genuinely so for *The Patronne's Birthday*. Picasso owned this picture, which Vollard described as having 'an air of rejoicing as well as the grandeur of an Egyptian bas-relief'.

Now the downhill walk took me past old friends from the Chapter Two walk: the Gauguins at **No. 28 Place St-Georges**; Renoir at **No. 35 Rue St-Georges**; further down the street, Degas's birthplace at **No. 8**; also **Notre-Dame-de-Lorette**, the artists' neighbourhood church, where his parents were married.

Rue Laffitte, running down from the church's colonnaded façade, has a plethora of impressionist addresses. From **No. 45**, Monet's birthplace, it was a short walk to the church where he was baptized Oscar-Claude. His father, a tradesman of the *quartier*, called him Oscar. But Monet, with his infallible instinct, knew that Oscar Monet hadn't a hope of making it: Claude Monet, on the other hand, had

Mary Cassatt's Woman and Child Driving *(1879) in the Bois de Boulogne shows the adventure of a woman doing a man's job. Degas's niece looks a little nervous with Mary's sister, Lydia, at the reins. The groom sits at the back, admirably unconcerned.*

the right ring, and thirteen years after his father moved to Le Havre to join the family wholesale grocery business, Claude Monet, the 18-year-old local cartoonist, began to be noticed.

Gauguin's dealer, Ambroise Vollard, moved premises from **No. 39/41** to **No. 6** in the same street. It was ironically close to where Gauguin began stockbroking at Bertin's in 1872 (**No. 11**). During the post-war boom years his upwardly mobile progress took him round the corner to the Bourdon Bank (**No. 21 Rue Le Peletier**); later he sold insurance stocks at the Thomereau Agency (**No. 93 Rue Richelieu**). Then came the Crash of 1882. He was out of a job, so he became a full-time artist (Chapter Five, p. 110). And after working in penury for nearly twenty years he arranged with Vollard to be paid a monthly advance of 300 francs against production in Polynesia: 3,600 francs a year. A young, moderately successful stockbroker would have earned about 80,000 francs.

Vollard, himself an islander from Réunion, appreciated the exotic experimentation of Gauguin. He also understood Cézanne (Chapter Two, p. 50). Although the 1895 one-man show sold only to loyal fellow-artists – Monet, Pissarro, Renoir, Degas – at knock-down prices (as low as ten francs!), it got Cézanne talked about and Vollard known as the most brilliant young avant-garde dealer in town. A sociable man, he cooked dinners of spicy Réunionais curries for artists and collectors in the gallery basement. Later his intelligent policy was to sell the surefire post-1900 heavies (Degas, Renoir and Pissarro) to subsidize the upcoming post-impressionists (Picasso, Bonnard, Matisse, Derain, Vlaminck, Braque and Chagall).

Rue Le Peletier runs parallel with Rue Laffitte. In the drab modern street it is hard to imagine Degas in search of *les petits rats* (young ballerinas) at the dance classes of the old opera-house (**No. 6**), which burned down in 1873. Degas worked consistently there between 1867 and 1873. The sombre, heavy male figures of *The Orchestra of the Paris Opéra* (O) in the pit contrast with the lightness of brightly lit ballerinas on stage. Women at play were more Renoir's concern in *The Box*; the glitteringly turned-out lady at the opera is evidently too good for the man, who may have just spotted his mistress with another man through his opera glasses. Manet's *Masked Ball at the Opéra* (1873) took a still sharper look at social foibles: the men all formally dressed in top hat, white tie and tails, the women in fancy dress, indicating that they were ready to lose it. The Bacchanalia lasted from midnight to five.

Equally hard to imagine is the gallery owned by the other great dealer, Paul Durand-Ruel, at **No. 11**. For an idea of how this street once was, finish the walk with lunch at Au Petit Riche (**No. 25**), a marvellously impressionist restaurant (founded 1880), serving classic bourgeois food in a most friendly ambience.

Durand-Ruel was that rarity, a truly international French businessman. He began his long and solid impressionist devotion with an exhibition in London (1872), and, with Mary Cassatt's contacts and Whistler's opinion-making, launched Monet, Renoir, Degas and others in the United States during the 1880s.

Renoir's *Girl with Cat* was among the Monet and Degas works hanging in Durand-Ruel's sumptuous drawing room, decorated by Monet, a ten-minute *fiacre* ride away from the gallery at **No. 35 Rue de Rome**. Durand-Ruel's lifestyle invited resentment, not least from Monet and Degas, who considered his fortune to be outrageous – at their expense.

Degas instructed him acidly: 'For want of big money, send me small . . . I will stuff you with products this winter, and you, for your part, will stuff me with money.'

Monet ungratefully accused his friend of short-changing him on American sales. Largely thanks to Durand-Ruel (and, of course, his own considerable output of saleable works), Monet's income – even in the roller-coaster 1870s – had improved to between 10,000 and 20,000 francs a year, averaging more than a doctor's. By 1891 it had passed the 100,000-franc mark. Yet Monet had little hesitation in wounding his ally or even consorting with the enemy – rival dealers such as the unscrupulous Georges Petit.

The Second Impressionist Show (1876) was held at Durand-Ruel's gallery. Although I have avoided quoting long-outmoded art critics, this diatribe by Albert Wolff in the *Figaro* is too rich to pass up:

Rue Le Peletier has bad luck. After the burning of the Opéra, a new disaster has befallen the neighbourhood. The innocent passer-by, attracted by the flags decorating the entrance, goes in to a monstrous spectacle, terrifying to the beholder: five or six lunatics, one a woman [Degas, Monet, Renoir, Pissarro, Guillaumin, Cézanne, Morisot], a group of unfortunates smitten by mad ambition, have gathered here to exhibit their works. Some people collapse laughing in front of these things. As for me, it breaks my heart.

Rue Drouot. I proceeded to the **Drouot Hôtel des Ventes**, the Paris auction rooms where the impressionists also failed to get a good press. On the corner of the Rues Rossini and Drouot, the modern building combines plate-glass and cascading water with period wrought iron.

The disastrous (financially) First Impressionist Show (1874) and the liquidation of the joint-stock company coincided with a slump in the art market. Durand-Ruel could offer only his professional advice at the auction which the group, to cut their losses, decided to hold at Drouot the following year. Police had to be called to prevent punch-ups, and to protect courageous first-time collectors like Victor Chocquet, who landed an Argenteuil Monet for 100 francs. Prices were rock bottom: Renoir withdrew *The Box* when it reached only 110 francs. Berthe Morisot did best, averaging 250 francs for her twelve paintings, one of which achieved the highest price of all, at 450 francs. Pissarro was the hero of the day: when a spectator yelled 'Whore!' at Morisot, Pissarro turned and, without hesitation, decked him with a surprisingly effective punch – the only time anyone could remember this serene, dignified patriarch resorting to violence.

The neighbourhood abounds with colourful, reasonably priced restaurants. The auction crowds use La Cave Drouot Brasserie, Bistrot le Beaujolais Drouot, and La Brochante. You might also want to browse around the antique shops, mostly selling pricy classics, Louis XIV and XVI. They will give you an idea of how Durand-Ruel's salon looked: the dining-room table was always laid for eighteen, with six wine glasses each, just in case anyone should drop by.

A convenient Métro station is **Richelieu-Drouot** at the junction of the *grands* boulevards.

The Palais Garnier

1 hour

Perhaps the most architecturally spectacular impressionist site visitable today is the Palais Garnier. Even Mary Cassatt, by no means an effusive American-in-Paris, marvelled at the new opera-house's splendour: 'The visitor is advised to sacrifice a whole act of the piece to inspect the building, and a magnificent and curiously shaped lustre containing 340 burners which seen from below presents the appearance of a crown of pearls.'

Since the opening of another, very different new opera-house, Opéra-Bastille, Napoleon III's extravaganza is now devoted entirely to ballet. There are also guided tours during the day. Don't miss the false ceiling, painted by Chagall in 1964.

The **Palais Garnier, Place de l'Opéra**, was built for a spectacle that was every bit as lavish among the audience as on stage. Haussmann, like his Emperor, thought big, and ordered the architect, Charles Garnier, to think big too: a stage big enough for 450 players, an auditorium with a six-ton chandelier, a ten-metre wide staircase with balustrade of onyx, marbles of blue, white, pink, red and green, and Carpeaux statuary everywhere. With the ascendancy of the mid-nineteenth-century bourgeoisie, there was Grand Opéra for neo-grand people in neo-classical surroundings. Garnier knew what would knock the eye out of a Pereire brother and his *dame*. Originality? Forget it. Give them an old-time palace and they'd be happy. Palaces were a Garnier speciality; and when he later saw the Eiffel Tower, a strikingly original structure, he joined in the howls of derision.

Degas, Renoir and Cassatt were lovers of a traditional social occasion. They enjoyed the interval gossip in the long bar, where bottles of champagne never stayed long in the *glacières*, and the plots of dangerous liaisons among the audience were as complicated as a Verdi opera.

Degas manages to endow what is probably a perfectly innocent encounter with an air of tantalizing intrigue in the title *Ludovic Halévy finds Madame Cardinal in an Opera Box* (1880).

Mallarmé's daughter was one of the two prim young ladies in Cassatt's *The Box* (1880), one hiding her mouth decorously behind her fan, the other with a posy of flowers. Meanwhile, the strong, handsome woman in black *At the Opera* knows just what she's doing with those binoculars: while pretending to watch the opera in reality she is wondering who the man is a few boxes away, checking her out with *his* binoculars

The Bois de Boulogne

2 hours, 4 hours with lunch

The No. 63 cross-town bus took me to **Porte de la Muette**, conveniently on the edge of the Bois de Boulogne, the 2224-acre wood that Napoleon III presented to the City of Paris. Haussmann had it landscaped in the manner of Hyde Park, adding Longchamp and Auteuil racetracks, restaurants, lakes and cascades, with later development of the lush Pré Catelan Gardens, incorporating the Shakespeare Garden (plants mentioned in his plays) and a children's amusement park.

In recent years, its amusements have become less childish with the influx of transsexual and other hookers, plying their nocturnal trade in cosy campers and less cosy undergrowth. Pigalle, it seems, has spread its influence into the preserves of Berthe Morisot and Mary Cassatt. By day, however, it remains fit for an Empress Eugénie.

Lac Inférieur. An easy walk from the Porte de la Muette, the Lower Lake is bigger and more spectacular than the Upper Lake, with thickly wooded

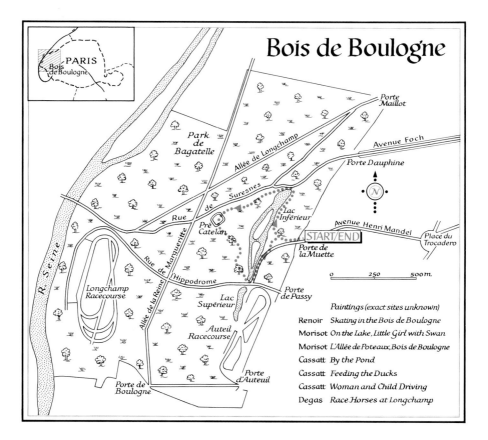

The jockey's bright primary colours – reds, yellows, blues – in Race Horses at Longchamp *(1873-5) are unusually impressionistic for Degas.*

Place de Dublin near the Gare St-Lazare is the easily recognizable junction of Haussmann thoroughfares in Caillebotte's Paris Street; Rain *(1877).*

islands, follies and waterfalls. Taking a boat out is the best way of getting the Morisot and Cassatt ambience.

Morisot's *On the Lake, Little Girl with Swan* (1884) and two little girls playing in the Bois in 1883 (her daughter Julie and niece Nini, who married Paul Valéry), perfectly expressed her 16th *arrondissement* heiress's lifestyle. So does *L'Allée de Poteaux, Bois de Boulogne*, an 1889 watercolour integrating horseback riders and trees. Husband Eugène Manet (brother of Edouard) had masterminded a huge new mansion in **Rue Paul-Valéry** (formerly **Rue Villejust**), a short carriage ride down **Avenue Victor-Hugo** to the Bois. It became the scene of a regular Thursday salon whose A-list guests included Monet, Valéry, Mallarmé, Whistler, Puvis de Chavannes, Caillebotte, Degas, Zola and Renoir.

Mary Cassatt, although not a close friend of Morisot nor half as rich, painted many similar Bois de Boulogne subjects – such as *By the Pond* and *Feeding the Ducks* – in a more naturalistic, Degas-influenced style. Unmarried, supporting herself by her art, Cassatt was a much more liberated woman than Morisot, and contributed to the fight for women's suffrage.

In the gardens a few minutes from the lake, the Michelin 2-star Pré Catelan restaurant is a luxurious summer treat, its Proustian terrace overlooking a vast, 200-year-old copper beech.

Longchamp. An autumn treat is the Arc de Triomphe Grand Prix race meeting on the first Sunday in October. Longchamp is at once chic and democractic, and a wonderful course

for seeing both the people and the horses. Betting is all by Tote (*Pari mutuel*). After the fourth race, if you are decently dressed, you can slip unchecked into the Jockey Club for a glass of champagne, and nobody seems to mind. The Jockey Club, after all, is where you would have seen Degas and Manet.

'It's very good to copy what you see,' Degas said, 'but much better to draw what is only now seen as a memory. This is a transformation during which imagination works in collaboration with memory. You only produce what struck you, what is necessary. At this point, recollection and fantasy are freed from the tyranny of nature's influence.'

In 1866 Degas did his first small gouache and sepia sketches, much admired by Whistler, of turf-mad ladies with binoculars and jockeys preparing for action. *The Parade* (1868) (O) shows horses and jockeys in front of the grandstand at a suburban racetrack, contrasting the elegance of the sunshaded ladies with the slim factory chimneys in the background. *The False Start* (1869) is a skilful evocation of a precise moment of tension: a jockey reining in his horse, the starter with his red flag. *The Wounded Jockey* (1896–8) takes up an old theme – *Steeplechase: the Jockey's Fall* (1866) – with the jockey like a ragdoll on the grass and his wayward steed frisky as a merry-go-round horse. When too blind to paint, Degas made exquisite little equine sculptures in plaster, which after his death were cast in bronze (O). The multiple movements of man and horse were with Degas all his working life.

LEFT BANK

· · · · · · · · · · · · · · ·

This lion stands guard in the Luxembourg Gardens.

The Left Bank, which we now associate with artistic life more than any other part of Paris, scarcely appears at all in impressionist paintings.

Hardly surprising. For Monet, Sisley, Renoir and Pissarro, the Left Bank was school, where they had done time as *rapins*, art students with Gleyre and Suisse. The *intransigeants*, as they called themselves, saw this school as something to be got through, a place to learn as much as possible from before going one's own way. A place of work but not inspiration. 'The fact of having to copy the same model ten times is excellent,' Renoir claimed afterwards. 'It's boring, and if you didn't pay to do it, you wouldn't do it.'

Gleyre's studio was in the heart of Montparnasse at Rue Notre-Dame-des-Champs, a few minutes from the Luxembourg Gardens. Suisse's Academy, beautifully situated on an island quayside near Notre-Dame, was also near the Institut de France, whose Académie des Beaux-Arts mandarins ruled the Paris art world with fists of ham. The Académie de St-Cyr produced officers and gentlemen fit for the French Army; the Académie des Beaux-Arts turned out artists and gentlemen fit to paint a French Empress.

The Left Bank, the heartland of the enemy, has three important roles in our story. Firstly, in those 1860 years of early rebellion against Official Art. Secondly, in the predilection for Left Bank living of the two most avant-garde impressionists: Cézanne, who had six addresses there; and Gauguin, who moved there in 1877, and between journeys to Brittany, Provence and Polynesia spearheaded the 'pure colour' movement away from impressionism towards a less scientific, more mystical way. And thirdly, in the exodus from Montmartre and the development of Montparnasse as the centre of the Paris School of Modern Art, in the lifetimes of Renoir, Degas, Monet, Cassatt and Guillaumin.

Early days saw the formation of a network. It had two distinct branches. One evolved from Manet, born on the Left Bank in Rue Bonaparte near the Seine. Manet studied up the street at the Ecole des Beaux-Arts under Thomas Couture, painter of *Romans in Decadence* (O). Couture was a good teacher, Manet admitted, but when he showed the master his *The Absinthe Drinker* (1859), Couture's crisp comment was: 'My friend, there's only one absinthe drinker there, and that's the painter who perpetrated this insanity.'

In the early 1860s Manet met Degas in the Louvre, establishing the first link in the network. Manet's parents knew Bazille's parents, and he helped Bazille change his studies from medicine to art. At Gleyre's studio Bazille met Renoir and Sisley. They became as close as three musketeers.

Meanwhile, on another branch of the network, Pissarro met Monet, ten years his junior, at the Académie Suisse. There they both met Cézanne, who had become friends with Guillaumin. Later, Monet moved to study at Gleyre's and joined Bazille, Renoir and Sisley. Monet became the fourth musketeer, linking the others to Pissarro, Cézanne and Guillaumin, and all of them to Manet and Degas. By 1862, nine future impressionists knew each other. So the importance of Père Gleyre, a reasonably successful *pompier* who was genuinely Swiss, and Père Suisse, a former model of dubious Swiss origins whose real name was Crébasolles, was considerable.

Gleyre came twice a week to make corrections. Monet recalled Gleyre's comment on physical ugliness when he drew the feet of a model the large size they were in real life: 'Remember, young man, when one renders a body, one thinks classical. Nature, my friend, is all very fine as an element of study, but it has no interest.' When he once accused Renoir of coming there merely to amuse himself, Gleyre was mortified by Renoir's reply: 'Obviously . . . if it didn't amuse me, I wouldn't paint!' Later in life Renoir generously conceded that, even if Gleyre had taught the future impressionists nothing, at least he had left them alone – and even encouraged their expeditions to the forest of Fontainebleau.

'You die with genius, you eat with money!' said Cézanne's banker father, who nevertheless supported his son for fourteen years after his début with Suisse. The homely calm of *Portrait of Louis-Auguste Cézanne* (1866) shows nothing of their fragile relationship. Mme Cézanne was more encouraging.

The singularity of Suisse's male models appealed to Cézanne: a disreputable old *clochard* posing as Moses; a boozy young unemployed workman miraculously holding the world up as Hercules. He saw through to the reality behind the poses, a truth that inspired later works such as *The Negro Scipio* (1866), depicting a male model's bored exhaustion, his black, muscular body leaning forward head on arm.

Cézanne and Pissarro visited the studio Bazille shared with Monet in Rue de Fürstemberg. In the same block lived and worked their anti-establishment god Delacroix. Manet's *copain* Fantin-Latour lived in a studio round the corner, where he did the *Homage to Delacroix* on which Maurice Denis's later *Homage to Cézanne* was based. Courbet dropped by. It was already a small world, with a few enlightened members of an older generation passing on what they knew.

Bazille and Renoir enjoyed walks in the Luxembourg Gardens, where bohemia mixed with bourgeoisie around its bandstand, boating pond and museum. Poets and painters mingled with students and nursemaids. Renoir's attempts to help a panicking nanny whose ward seemed to be choking nearly got him arrested for baby-snatching.

The Closerie des Lilas was between the Luxembourg Gardens and Gleyre's studio. Bazille and Renoir often repaired to the famous bar for a bock. They were joined by Monet, Sisley and Pissarro. Arguments were fierce. Had Fragonard painted genuinely 'what he saw' in those bourgeois ladies on swings, or had he slavishly followed the masters? The *intransigeant* credo was to paint directly, with no reference to the past, an unexplained impression of the present.

Little did Renoir dream of one day being on familiar terms with the Charpentiers at 11 Rue de Grenelle. At Marguerite Charpentier's salons he soon found himself on equal terms with, then overtaking, the *pompier* Carolus-Duran as portraitist of his hostess. *Madame Charpentier and her Children*, Paul and Georgette, not to mention the dog, were available to pose with naturalistic charm for Renoir, a close friend, in the privacy of the drawing room where she entertained her publisher husband's glittering author list – Flaubert, Zola, Maupassant, Daudet. 'Titian at his best' was Proust's crisp comment on Renoir *chez* Charpentier.

The Left Bank was for richer or poorer. In 1891 Guillaumin moved to 20 Rue Servadoni, in the heart of the fashionable 6th *arrondissement* near the church of St-Sulpice. After stealing painting hours from his Department of Bridges and Highways, he struck lucky with a lottery ticket, winning 100,000 francs. He spent the rest of his life painting the countryside of France and Holland in garish, almost fauve colours, and died, aged 86, in 1927 – a year after Monet, who never thought much of him. Guillaumin did for the industrial Seine what Caillebotte did for Haussmann streets; one day, like Caillebotte, he may be revalued for Left Bank images like *Quai de la Gare* and *Place Valhubert*, which even today is pleasantly leafy.

In the riverside exhibition hall on the nearby Quai d'Austerlitz is held the Salon of Erotic Art. At the latter, the young Cézanne would have doubtless found a market for his early soft porn works which he later humorously put down as *couillard* (randy). *Orgy*, a vast, flamboyantly hot-blooded skit on *pompier* works like Couture's *Romans in Decadence*, recalls Juvenal's sixth satire: 'Vice, a scourge more cruel than war, swooped down on Rome to avenge the conquered universe.' Cézanne is tongue-in-cheek, out to shock, whereas Couture is moralistic, out to sell.

Beset by self-doubt, Cézanne chose to isolate himself on the Left Bank, as far away from the Café Guerbois and Nouvelle-Athènes crowd as possible, always on the move: 5 Rue de Chevreuse, 7 Rue des Feuillantines, 53 Rue de Notre-Dame-des-Champs, and 45 Rue de Jussieu, near where he did *Wine Warehouse in Rue Jussieu* (1872), showing barrels covered with snow beneath wintry trees.

Imagine the surprise of his friends when the confirmed bachelor began living with the model Hortense Fiquet and she had his baby. In 1875 the Cézanne family inhabited the same Rue de Vaugirard block as Guillaumin, but bohemian domesticity was not the prickly painter's strong point. Once again he moved – with Guillaumin – to the old Daubigny studio on Ile St-Louis, leaving Hortense and Paul to fend for themselves. Luckily, Hortense enjoyed reading: she had plenty of time for it while her lover shuttled between the Oise, Provence and Paris.

In 1878 Louis-Auguste Cézanne inadvertently found out about his son's clandestine family and, in a fury, slashed his allowance. Zola came to the rescue, virtually supporting Hortense and Paul. Tense relations between the old schoolfriends culminated in a falling-out over Zola's novel *L'Oeuvre* (Chapter Six, p. 139).

The year of its publication, 1886, also had its better moments. Cézanne's father was at last reconciled to Hortense and his 14-year-old grandson, Paul junior. How could he not accept them when he himself had not been married to Cézanne's mother at the time of his own son's birth? Hortense and Paul senior were married in Aix shortly before the death of his father, who left him a considerable fortune. All did not end happily, however. Whatever lonely memories she had, Hortense found life in a Left Bank 'village' had been a lot jollier than in stuffy, heavily bourgeois Aix.

Mette Gauguin was made of sterner stuff. In 1877 Gauguin could hardly have foreseen marital trouble when he moved, 'urged onwards by a terrible itch for the unknown', from the elegance of Place St-Georges to Cité Falguière, an arty cul-de-sac in the 'village' of Vaugirard where the Cézanne family had lived. To Mette, it must have seemed like a move to Polynesia. She did not complain. Gauguin was still working as a stockbroker and they had a comfortable lifestyle: walls adorned with a 17,000-franc personal art collection of impressionists; a house with a garden for the two children; a studio where the landlord, a sculptor called Bouillot, taught Gauguin how to work in wood, in preparation for such marvels as the wooden façade sculpted for the House of Pleasure in the Marquesas Islands (O).

In 1880, with another child on the way, the Gauguins moved again – round the corner to a small, luxurious house at 8 Rue Carcel. Then life changed drastically for Mette. The Crash of 1882 decided her jobless husband, after encouragement from Pissarro and Degas, to become a full-time artist (Chapter Five, p. 110, Chapter Six, p. 154). Mette, pregnant again, had to face a downmarket move to cheaper living outside Paris.

After two miserable years in Rouen and two more in the bourgeois claustrophobia of Mette's native Copenhagen, Gauguin fled back to Paris – with only his son Clovis.

Just up the street from the Montparnasse flat which I lived in for twenty years was Gauguin's Paris refuge. Peeping through a convenient hole in the gate of No. 29 Rue Boulard, I could just see the small house in its garden, typical of a charmed, secret Paris tucked away behind the big Haussmann blocks. It was once the home of his artist friend, portrayed ironically in *Schuffenecker and his Family* (O) (1889). Poor family, Gauguin seems to be saying – having an artist for a breadwinner.

His wanderlust, however, began to find its direction. Between trips to Brittany, Provence and Polynesia, the Left Bank was always his fragile *port d'attache*. He participated in two pacemaking exhibitions: The Synthesist and Impressionist Group at the Café Volpini during the 1889 World Fair, where he exhibited mostly Pont-Aven paintings, much admired by Bonnard, Vuillard and Denis the future Nabis; and the cultural event of 1893 (with Ibsen's *An Enemy of the People*), a one-man show of Polynesian work mounted by Durand-Ruel. Both were *succès d'estime* but commercial disasters.

'One can paint so well in Batignolles,' commented Renoir on Gauguin's obsession with faraway exotica. Not even in Montparnasse did Gauguin find much to inspire him. He painted *Paris in the Snow* (1849), with its vivid oranges, yellows and greens in contrast with the subdued grey, blue and purple of Caillebotte's *View of Rooftops*. That was about it. On his return to Polynesia in 1895 Gauguin was determined to put impressionism behind him:

> 'It was necessary . . . to take up the strongest abstraction, do all that had been forbidden and rebuild more or less successfully, without fear of exaggeration, even with exaggeration. Before his easel, the painter is not the slave either of the past or the present, either of nature or his neighbour. He is himself, still himself, always himself.

To take up the strongest abstraction: the new generation on the Left Bank did just that. Montparnasse cafés like Le Dôme and La Rotonde became the haunts of Picasso, Léger and Braque, celebrating the rapid advance of cubism. Juan Gris's *The Man at the Café* (1912), fragmented as though in a smashed mirror, seemed to have had many petits blancs, suzes and vieux marcs in the years since he was Caillebotte's sober-looking gent *At the Café* (1880).

The last of the impressionists, Guillaumin (1841–1927), entered the world to the sound of Berlioz's *Romeo and Juliet* and exited to the echoes of the jazz band at the Boeuf sur Le Toit in Rue Boissy d'Anglas, where Jean Cocteau sat in on drums.

A WALK
ON
THE LEFT BANK

Nursemaid in the Luxembourg Gardens *by Degas (1872).*

Information

Itinerary

Left Bank Walk (long single day or 2 half-days). Single day. Start: Métro St-Germain-des-Prés. End: Métro Vavin. Half-days. End: Métro Maubert-Mutualité. Start: (second half-day) Métro Odéon.

Lunch: Seine quayside area.

Refreshment, Meals and Overnight

Restaurants, Bars and Cafés

☆ Beaux-Arts, (**C**), 11 Rue Bonaparte. Tel. 01.43.26.92.64.

☆ Lapérouse (gastronomic), (**A**), 51 Quai des Grands-Augustins. Tel. 01.43.26.68.04.

Les Bookinistes, (**B**), (lunch menu **C**), 53 Quai des Grands-Augustins. Tel. 01.43.25.45.94.

L'Ecluse (wine bar), (**C**), 15 Quai des Grands-Augustins.

La Rôtisserie du Beaujolais, (**B**), 19 Quai de la Tournelle. Tel. 01.43.54.17.47.

☆ Closerie des Lilas (bar-brasserie), (**B**), 171 Boulevard Montparnasse. Tel. 01.43.26.70.50.

Le Caméléon, (**B**), 6 Rue de Chevreuse. Tel. 01.43.20.63.43.

Bistrot du Dôme (fish only), (**B**), 1 Rue Delambre. Tel. 01.43.35.32.00.

☆ Café terraces around Place Pablo-Picasso (Carrefour Vavin): Le Dôme, La Rotonde, Le Select, La Coupole.

Hotels

Des Marronniers, (**B**), (no meals), 21 Rue Jacob. Tel. 01.43.25.30.60.

L'Hôtel, (**A**), 13 Rue des Beaux-Arts. Tel. 01.43.25.27.22.

Colbert, (**A**), 7 Rue de l'Hôtel-Colbert. Tel. 01.43.25.85.65.

Relais Médicis, (**A**), (no meals), 23 Rue Racine. Tel. 01.43.26.00.60.

Abbaye St-Germain, (**A**), (no meals), 10 Rue Cassette. Tel. 01.45.44.38.11.

Delavigne, (**C**), (no meals), 1 Rue Casimir-Delavigne. Tel. 01.43.29.31.50.

Villa des Artistes, (**B**), (no meals), 9 Rue Grande-Chaumière. Tel. 01.43.26.60.86.

Museums and Sites

Delacroix Museum, 6 Rue de Fürstemberg. Open daily (except Tues) 9.45–12.30, 2–5.15. Tel. 01.44.41.86.50.

Institute of France, 23 Quai Conti. Mazarin Library open Mon–Fri 10–6. Tel. 01.44.41.44.41.

Luxembourg Museum, 19 Rue Vaugirard. Open daily (except Mon) 1–7. Entry 20F. Tel. 01.42.34.25.95.

Tourist Office

Office du Tourisme, Gare Montparnasse, 75014. Tel. 01.43.22.19.19.

Left Bank Walk

long whole day or 2 half-days

I found this walk one of the most enjoyable, passing through some twenty-three centuries of Paris history. It took me a long whole day: better to take two separate half days. Begin at **St-Germain-des-Prés**. Don't be put off by St-Germain-des-Prêt-à-Porter. Despite a ragtrade overkill, it is still one of the oldest and most beautiful parts of town. Start from **Métro St-Germain-des-Prés**.

Rue de Fürstemberg. Leaving the church on your right, follow **Rue de l'Abbaye** and take the first left into Rue de Fürstemberg. The street is short and sweet, shaded by two magnificent paulownia trees. At **No. 6** is the **Delacroix Museum**, announced outside by a picture of the handsome, romantic hero of the young impressionists. Delacroix crossed swords with Ingres, pillar of the art establishment, for the crimes of rejecting the classical nude and supporting independence of thought, whether it be at the barricades or in the artist's studio.

A gateway leads through the two-storey, late seventeenth-century redbrick building to a cobble-stoned courtyard by which one approached the master's secluded abode. The magnificent, recently refurbished little museum comprises the modest but comfortably furnished apartment, where Delacroix died in 1863, and his studio in a quiet, leafy garden behind.

Works that much influenced the young impressionists are on display: watercolour landscapes of gentle, green hillsides, a broken bridge with two arches, a Turneresque sky at dusk, *The Night of the Flood* with an indigo river; surrealist humour in *The Unmade Bed* (ahead of its time in 1828); sardonic humour in *Man of Letters Reading*; exotica in Algerian harem girls and swarthy Turks; narcissism in a large nude of himself. Delacroix was not known for his modesty.

The youthful Manet was received here somewhat frostily when he went to ask permission to copy *Dante and Virgil* in the Luxembourg Museum. Bazille and Monet once watched Delacroix at work in his studio from a friend's window overlooking the garden, and in 1865 Bazille rented the same studio, which he shared with Monet. They were struck by how Delacroix's model never sat still, always moved about, the master observing and sketching, and sometimes only starting work after the model left. How different from the frozen pose of some wretched, goose-pimpled wood-nymph *chez* Gleyre. 'Beware of colour!' a professor had once warned Renoir. 'You're in danger of becoming another Delacroix!'

The Delacroix Museum was a perfect place to orientate myself before the walk. A limpid, wintry sun slanting into narrow streets made Paris the City of Light and Shade that morning. Which set me wondering why the impressionists had never painted them. Too near school? Or just too picturesque?

First, I took a left into **Rue Jacob**. Hôtel des Marronniers at **No. 21**, small with its own courtyard, could be a convenient, moderately priced place to stay. Then, right into **Rue Bonaparte** for a block, and right again into **Rue Visconti**. Still quite a rough little alley, it once offered cheap living to impecunious young artists. In 1867 Bazille moved studios to **No. 20**. His allowance was no lottery win, but he had no hesitation in giving house-room to his eternally broke friends Renoir and Monet. He even pawned his watch for Monet to buy paints.

No such hardship would seem to threaten the owners of the opulent-looking galleries I passed where I made a double left turn from Rue Visconti via **Rue de Seine** into **Rue des Beaux-Arts**.

Rue des Beaux-Arts. At **No. 8** the impressionists' friend Fantin-Latour lived in a patriotically red-white-and-blue barn. In 1870 Bazille moved here from his Batignolles studio for a short time before his death in the Franco-Prussian War. Four addresses in five years suggests even the relatively well-to-do Bazille had landlord trouble. What must it have been like for Monet, Renoir and Pissarro?

The short street is also famous for the Galerie Claude Bernard, where I once attended the *vernissage* of a Francis Bacon retrospective with the

In carefree Paris before the Franco-Prussian War (1870), Renoir and Monet often worked together, exploring the vibrant reflected light of the Seine. In Pont des Arts (1868), Renoir shows leisurely coming and going on the steamboat pier and footbridge linking Louvre and Institut de France.

artist present in genially inebriated form. Another landmark is L'Hôtel (**No. 13**), the Left Bank's most expensive and starry small hotel-restaurant, formerly the incomparable Alsace where Oscar Wilde lived and died. On the opposite corner, more in keeping with this walk, Restaurant des Beaux-Arts is the perennial, excellent bistro catering for art students from across the street. An atmospheric early lunch stop for those on a tight budget.

Rue Bonaparte. Opposite me were the imposing gates of the **Ecole Supérieure Nationale des Beaux-Arts**, founded in 1648. Here students were sentenced to draw static male nudes until, after many years of good conduct, painting was permitted – but only of historical subjects. Delacroix, six times refused election to the Académie des Beaux-Arts that controlled the school, protested: 'They are taught the beautiful as one teaches algebra.'

However, the coming and going was free and easy, controlled only by a caretaker in uniform and cocked hat. Manet and Degas were on their honour to go and copy the masters in the Grand Gallery of the Louvre. Initiation ceremonies for new boys included standing refreshments all round, jumping from terrifying heights to the sound of hunting-horns, fencing naked with paintbrushes and getting oneself daubed like a Red Indian. The costume balls and rags were the scourge of the area, when wise tradesmen locked up their daughters – and sons.

The *pompier* teachers, however hidebound, had an ability to teach drawing and were far from ogres: Gérôme, dapper and correct; Cabanel, gentle and sympathetic; Couture, eclectic and well informed. You always inscribed 'Pupil of Couture', or whoever was your master, on a canvas submitted to the Salon jury, in hope of easier acceptance and a lucrative commission from a provincial museum.

I half-expected to see Couture ossified in the vast, dilapidated approaches. Nothing much had changed. A mosaic shows *L'Eternel Bénissant le Monde*. The Eternal, while blessing the world, seems to have missed out on this courtyard. Roman statues, bits of antique masonry,

columns and arches make it look like a Hollywood backlot for *Ben Hur*. Only the Italian names on the façade remind one of its worthiness: Cimabue . . . Donatello . . . Giotto – the eternal gods. It was a patch of Renaissance Italy dropped into Paris.

Yet it has a certain dilapidated charm. Penetrate the chapel entrance

on the right, follow the signpost to the Cour du Mûrier, and you reach a courtyard with Italianate cloisters, headless nude statues, and a war memorial to artists of two world wars, overlooked by the art classrooms.

Continuing down **Rue Bonaparte** in the direction of the Seine, I came to Manet's birthplace at **No. 5**. The five-storey Directoire mansion, where the Manets had an apartment, has a plaque on its façade. His father, who wanted Edouard to become a naval officer, was a magistrate at the Palais de Justice across the river on Ile de la Cité, but his son was hardly typical of boys on the block, *haut-bourgeois* swots destined for jobs in law, business

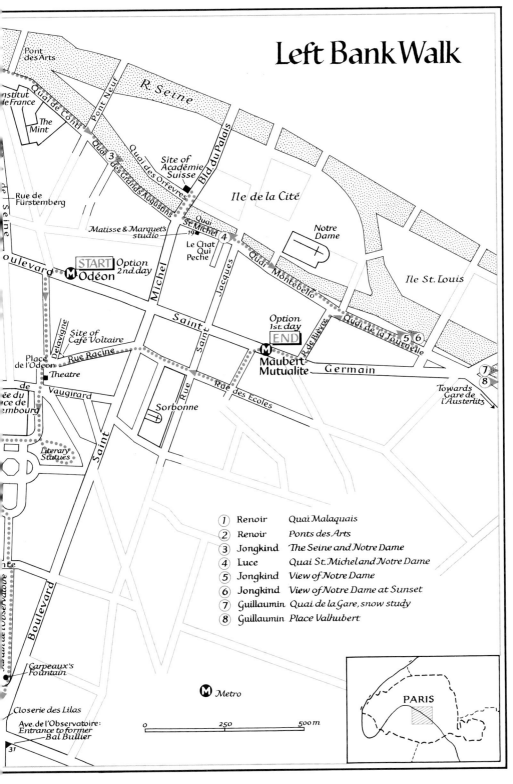

Left Bank Walk

① Renoir   *Quai Malaquais*
② Renoir   *Ponts des Arts*
③ Jongkind   *The Seine and Notre Dame*
④ Luce   *Quai St. Michel and Notre Dame*
⑤ Jongkind   *View of Notre Dame*
⑥ Jongkind   *View of Notre Dame at Sunset*
⑦ Guillaumin   *Quai de la Gare, snow study*
⑧ Guillaumin   *Place Valhubert*

Ⓜ *Metro*

0   250   500 m

PARIS

Cassatt's Young Woman Sewing in a Garden *(1886) can be seen at the Left Bank's Musée d'Orsay.*

Marie dei Medici's waterworks, Luxembourg Gardens.

or the services. A boy who studied the Spanish masters at the Louvre was hardly naval officer material. On failing his exams Manet became a merchant seaman, went to Rio de Janeiro, and contracted syphilis.

In 1850 he returned and entered the Beaux-Arts under Couture. Despite his early avant-garde friends – the poet Baudelaire and the painter Courbet – Manet never identified too closely with the impressionist rebellion. He had enough trouble of his own. He preferred to remain his younger friends' guru, and leave the fighting to others. 'M. Manet has never wished to protest,' wrote his friend and critic, Astruc. 'He has no intention of overthrowing old methods of painting or of creating new ones. He has merely tried to be himself and nobody else.'

Quai Malaquais. The warren of narrow streets finishes at the Seine. I emerged into an explosion of light and traffic hurtling along the quayside. It is easy to see why Renoir chose this point to do two rare Left Bank pictures. A Haussmann openness melds sky and buildings and river.

From the traffic island, looking west, *Quai Malaquais* (1872) even has pedestrians strolling among the carriages in Renoir's hazily impressionist image; today they would be instant mush. On the other side of the road, down on the quay, I found where Renoir did the earlier, more clearly defined, less impressionistic *Pont des Arts* (1868). In the picture Parisians and tourists mill around the steamboat station, enjoying the new, leisurely way of seeing Paris from the river. He worked with Monet on the banks of the Seine, but each would approach the same scene quite differently. 'All too quickly you get into a mutual admiration society,' he said, 'and then it's finished.'

The kind of back-scratching Renoir despised happened at either end of the Pont des Arts, the footbridge built to enable Academicians to pass easily from the Louvre to the **Institut de France**, whose shining dome is on the right of the picture. Neither bridge nor Institute looked much changed.

Institut de France. The walk continues upstream along the quays, passing the august seventeenth-century building with its crescents and colonnaded façade. Designed by Le Vau and created by Richelieu for Louis XIV in 1635, the Institute housed the five Academies that continue to be guardians of French culture and achievement: language, literature, science, fine arts and political sciences.

The 'immortals', as the Académie Française's often obscure members are known, are still arguing over the ninth edition of their dictionary. *Franglais* is their *bête noire*. Among the nineteenth-century writers blackballed were Balzac, Zola, Maupassant and Proust. Meanwhile, the artists rejected by the forty-strong Académie des Beaux-Arts included Corot, Courbet, Delacroix, Daumier and Millet. These heretics were not the sort of chaps to be let loose decorating a university, law court or opera-house, nor to paint flattering portraits of political nonentities. Leave it to the *Chers Maîtres*, as they called each other lovingly – artists such as Cabanel, awarded the glittering Prix de Rome at 21, an Academician by 28, and painter of *The Birth of Venus* (O).

A polite *gardien* stopped me strolling in like any old Academician. I said I wanted to study a dictionary, and was told the Mazarin library was open to the public at 10.00. It is the only way, short of 'immortality', of seeing the magnificent twin porticoes of the courtyard.

Quai des Grands-Augustins. Continuing along **Quai de Conti**, past the Mint, I reached the oldest quay in Paris, built in 1313 for Saint Louis's Augustine monastery. The Lapérouse restaurant (**No. 51**), on the corner of **Rue des Grands-Augustins** where Picasso had his last Parisian studio at **No. 7**, has a seventeenth-century façade with painted glass panels announcing *Bar, Vins, Liqueurs – Salle en Etage*. From the restaurant there is a superb view of the **Ile de la Cité**, the **Pont Neuf** (Chapter Six, p. 139) and the river traffic. More fun is the 'in' bistro for flush young Left Bankers, Les Bookinistes (**No. 53**). Or L'Ecluse wine bar at **No. 15**, serving Pomerol, Graves and Pauillac by the glass. All have reasonably priced lunch menus.

The post-impressionist Marquet painted *The Seine Seen from the Quai des Grands-Augustins* in the depths of

1898's chilly winter, very different from pre-impressionist Jongkind's shimmering sunshine reflected in the water in *The Seine and Notre-Dame-de-Paris* (1864).

Pont St-Michel. A quick detour took me across the bridge to the **Ile de la Cité**, the oldest part of Paris where the Parisii tribe of fishermen and boatmen lived, and where the Romans made a ford across the river in 52BC. At the angle of **Quai des Orfèvres** (famous as Inspector Maigret's HQ) and **Boulevard du Palais** (the Préfecture and Law Courts), the **Académie Suisse** occupied the second floor of a squalid corner house long since gone. It had a sinister metal crossbar with ropes and nooses – not for students who failed the Beaux-Arts to hang themselves, but to help models hold difficult poses. Some were decrepit Italians who students reckoned had posed for Giotto.

Pissarro doubted the benefits of this very free academy, where a banquette was provided for students to sleep on, which they frequently did.

In 1860 Monet and Pissarro escaped Suisse to work together in countryside near the River Marne – in Corot style. While Pissarro continued to explore *pleinairisme*, Monet went off for two years' military service in North Africa, where 'the impressions of light and colour . . . contained the germ of my future researches.' Already the *intransigeants* were leaving the studios for the outdoor experience.

Quai St-Michel. Marquet and his lifelong friend Matisse shared a studio at **No. 19**, a glorious fifth-floor eyrie overlooking river, island and Notre-Dame. There is a happy feeling of *luxe, calme, et volupté* about the young Matisse's *Painter in his Studio, Quai St-Michel*, with its view through the window on to the quay and with the roles wittily reversed – the model clothed and the artist naked.

From the corner of the tiny **Chat-qui-Pêche** alley, pointillist Maximilian Luce did *The Quai St-Michel and Notre-Dame* (1901) (O). The cathedral façade glows golden orange in the sunset while the Seine-side bookstalls attract browsers and a Parisian tradesman humps a heavy load in the cool shadows of evening. The different social milieux of the Left Bank are conveyed with neither heavy moralizing nor sentimentality.

Quai de Montebello. An elegant place to stay at is the beautifully converted seventeenth-century town house, Hôtel Colbert (moderately expensive), off the quay in **Rue de l'Hôtel-Colbert**.

Quai de la Tournelle. It was lunchtime. I resisted the famous panoramic viewpoint known as La Tour d'Argent (**Nos. 15–17**), and headed for La Rôtisserie du Beaujolais (**No. 19**) for proper French bistro food.

Before eating, I took in the riverside gardens downstream of the **Pont de la Tournelle**, where Jongkind did two very different paintings from the same vantage-point. *View of Notre-Dame de Paris* (1863) shows the apse reflected in the sparkling light of a crisp winter's morning, while in the foreground workers are constructing the port. Several months later he returned for *View of Notre-Dame at Sunset* (1864), with the port now complete, and the cathedral a silhouette against a flaming summer sky. Atmospheric conditions at a specific time of day and year were as important as, if not more so than, subject-matter. Monet was to follow Jongkind's example all his life.

Further upstream along the Left Bank, convenient if you happen to be taking a train from the Gare de l'Austerlitz, are the sites of several Guillaumin paintings such as *Quai de la Gare, Snow Study* (O) and *Place Valhubert* (1875) (O).

Montagne Ste-Geneviève. The walk now meanders pleasantly, taking twenty minutes or so to reach **Place de l'Odéon**, without passing any impressionist site. Those who have lunched by the river and are so replete that they wish to pick up the second half of the walk another day, can return from **Métro Maubert-Mutualité**. Otherwise continue left up **Rue Jean-de-Beauvais**; right into **Rue des Ecoles**, passing the Sorbonne university and the Latin quarter's Gallo-Roman remains at the **Cluny Museum**; across the **Boulevard St-Michel** (plenty of student cafés and brasseries for inexpensive snacks); down **Rue Racine** to **Place de l'Odéon**.

Place de l'Odéon. Starting the second half of the walk from here, it's only five minutes from **Métro Odéon** via **Rue de l'Odéon** for those following my two-day recommendation. A cluster of small but quite expensive hotels of charm are near by: Relais St-Germain, Relais Médicis, Abbaye St-Germain. Moderately priced is Hôtel Delavigne.

The noble, semi-circular eighteenth-century square has distinguished literary and theatre connections. The Théâtre de l'Europe plays host to visiting foreign productions such as the Royal Shakespeare Company's, and the publishers Flammarion are in Rue Racine. On the angle with **Rue Casimir-Delavigne (No. 1)** was the **Café Voltaire**, which featured large in Gauguin's life.

It was a regular meeting-place of post-impressionist Symbolists and Nabis – Gauguin, Sérusier, Denis, Redon – under the aegis of the poet Mallarmé, whose distinguished, languid features appear in Gauguin's 1891 etching. Gauguin's constant search to reconcile contradictions (family versus bohemian life, for instance) led him naturally away from the optical phenomena and scientific analysis of impressionism. His ideas came from the unconscious, dreams of a pure, primitive society – which led to yet another conflict when he found that society in decay. In Polynesia his later paintings, though figurative, pose abstract questions. Where do we come from? Why are you angry? What are we? Where do we go? Monet, Renoir, Pissarro and Degas always had concrete titles: a place, a time, an event, a season, a person or persons.

At the Café Voltaire, Mallarmé gave a banquet for Gauguin before he left for the South Seas. On this first journey (1891–3) a vestige of impressionism travelled with him: he would paint nudes and scenes of daily life. Mallarmé's farewell toast included the words: '. . . let us drink to the return of Paul Gauguin, but not before admiring this superbly conscious man, who at the height of his talent is exiling himself to acquire new strength in distant parts and within himself.'

Luxembourg Gardens. Just across **Rue de Vaugirard** is a convenient entrance to the gardens that three pairs of painters used to frequent together: Renoir and Bazille, to amuse themselves; Matisse and Marquet, to work; and Sargent and Whistler, for a bit of both. They also provided inspiration for van Gogh in impressionist mode with *Terrace of the Luxembourg Gardens* (1886) and one of Degas's infrequent Paris exteriors *Nursemaid in the Luxembourg Gardens* (1872).

Today the gardens are much the same. Half closing my eyes, imagining Offenbach playing in the bandstand, I experienced a time-warp among the statues, fountains and shady alleys with, beneath the feet, that special crunch of a Paris park path. I started with the literary lions and one lioness near the Boul' Mich' – a plinth to Stendhal, Flaubert atop a stone, a statue to George Sand. Then I strolled back past Queen Marie dei Medici's elaborate waterworks, only to be denied entrance to the **Palace** that Henri IV built for her. A doorkeeper reminded me, as I strolled blithely in, that this was The Senate and that the Delacroix paintings can only be viewed on a guided tour.

I contented myself with sculptor Dalou's superb monumental fountain to Delacroix: an angel supporting a girl who offers the painter a sheaf of corn (or bunch of gladioli) while another girl claps her hands to get Delacroix's attention as he stares nobly into space. It stands suitably near the **Luxembourg Museum**, once a 'waiting room' for the Louvre.

This was the scene of a major impressionist scandal. Renoir was executor of the Caillebotte legacy. Prescient of an early death, aged 45, Caillebotte had left his entire collection of impressionist paintings to the State, on condition they entered the Louvre within a given time. It was 1894. Already impressionists were commanding prices as high as those of Salon painters. The Louvre could hardly refuse 3 Manets, 4 Cézannes, 7 Degas, 8 Renoirs, 9 Sisleys, 16 Monets, 22 Pissarros. Inevitably, in protest, the powers that be at the Beaux-Arts and the Institut marshalled the heavy artillery. Gérôme blasted off: 'For the State to accept such garbage would be a very great blot on its moral rectitude.'

A commission eventually reached a compromise. Renoir must accept the Luxembourg and not the Louvre, and a reduced selection of paintings: 2 Cézannes, 2 Manets, 6 Renoirs, 6 Sisleys, 7 Pissarros (anti-Semitism played a part in the huge drop from 22), 8 Monets. Only the 7 Degas were accepted in toto. The paintings never did reach the Louvre. They were moved from the Luxembourg to the Jeu de Paume Museum in 1939, and latterly to Orsay, where they can now be seen.

Continuing south across **Rue Auguste-Comte**, the gardens become the **Jardin de l'Observatoire**. By the exit gate Carpeaux's elaborate fountain held me entranced. Turtles spurt water over prancing horses, while three Graces hold up a globe. The water spray hitting their legs to thigh height makes them appear to be wearing black stockings, like *les filles* in a Degas bordello painting. Paris erotica can still have a subtle touch.

Boulevard de Montparnasse. On the right-hand corner of the big intersection is one of the very few remaining impressionist places of refreshment, the **Closerie des Lilas**. With its enclosed garden terrace and trees dominating the pavement, the Closerie is an unmissable landmark.

No wonder it acted like a magnet to Renoir, Bazille, Monet and Sisley after their sessions at Gleyre's. Joined by Pissarro, the doyen, the *intransigeants* thrashed out their beliefs. Food for thought was richer than food on the table. 'I had never been happier,' said Renoir, recalling those hungry Closerie des Lilas days. 'Admittedly, now and again Monet pulled off an invitation to dinner and we gorged ourselves on turkey stuffed with truffles, washed down with chambertin.'

Today's Closerie restaurant is expensive and so-so, hardly worth the glamour of its leafy terrace. Better value is the brasserie, or a drink at the famous bar. Brass plaques commemorate the poor and famous who once frequented the place. From another age, when Picasso and Braque met Max Jacob and Apollinaire there, a pepper steak is still named after Ernest Hemingway, who lived round the corner at **No. 113 Rue Notre-Dame-des-Champs** for two years (1924–6).

Rue de Chevreuse. Turning right into this street two blocks down the boulevard, I passed a favourite, very genuine and moderately priced bistro, Le Caméléon (**No. 6**). Opposite, **No. 5** was one of Cézanne's many, fleeting, Left Bank addresses in the early 1870s.

Rue de Notre-Dame-des-Champs. He was also at **No. 53** of this long, straggly street, a favourite of painters, where he no doubt glowered at and hurried past his establishment neighbours. A left into the street took me past the studios of Bouguereau (**No. 75**), Sargent (down a charming alley, garden on right, **No. 73**), Gérôme (**No. 70bis**), Carolus-Duran (**No. 58**, an early nineteenth-century house that can be visited), Courbet (**No. 61**). For a short time Courbet taught students the naturalist approach – there was even once a live cow in the studio. Not surprisingly, he soon grew bored with clearing up the pats and gave it up.

By contrast, Gleyre, at **No. 70bis**, didn't charge enough to make teaching art profitable, so eventually it gave him up. Student larks were many. Looking at the building today, I thought of the amiable, much-teased Gleyre hastily ripping from the wall drawings of erect, outsize phalli, a few paces ahead of the Dutch ambassador who had come to assess the suitability of Gleyre's as an academy for his art-student daughter.

Gleyre was a Swiss puritan who tried to keep his act clean. An impossible task, given the humour of the likes of Sisley, Bazille, Renoir and Monet. Gleyre always insisted that the male models kept their underpants on. 'Monsieur Gleyre,' a young British *milady* commanded once. 'Please ask the gentlemen to disrobe.' When he refused, she protested: 'I do know what it's like, you know. I have a lover!' On another occasion Monet's grand airs and lace-cuffed shirts earned him a pass from a pushy Parisian *bourgeoise* who mistook him for a sprig of the nobility. 'I only ever make love,' he said, 'to maids or duchesses. Preferably the maid of a duchess.'

Right: Gauguin's Nevermore (1892) shows the revolutionary development of the nude in the relatively short time since Manet's Olympia shocked Paris in 1865.

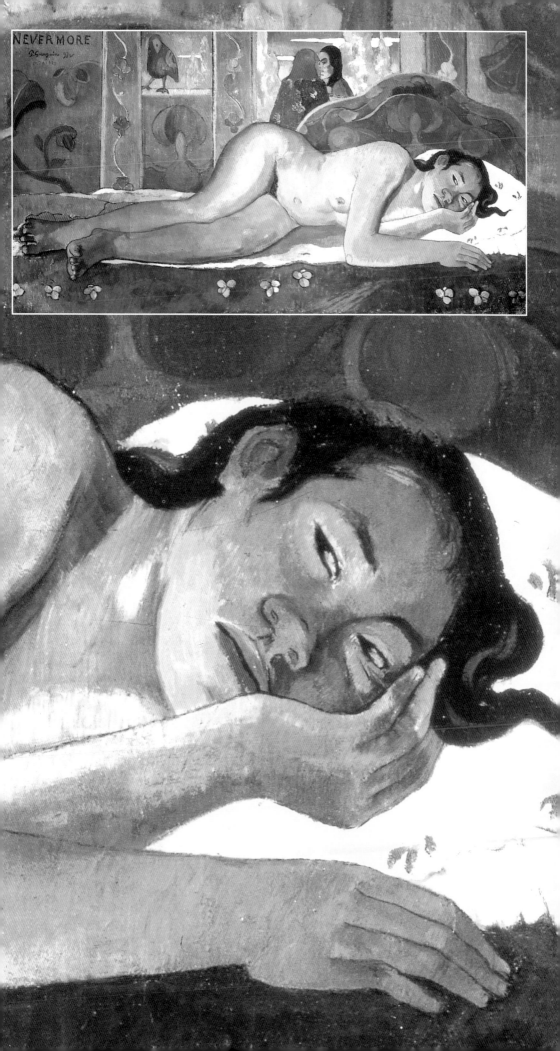

Rue de la Grande-Chaumière.
Gauguin's love life was tumultuous
after his return from Tahiti in 1893,
when he took up residence at **No. 13**,
two rooms over La Crémerie, where the
shopfront of *la patronne*, Madame
Charlotte, had been decorated by the
art nouveau artist Alphonse Mucha.
Gauguin knew the street; he had been
at art school at the **Académie
Colarossi (No. 10)**. I penetrated the
front door of what is now Académie
Charpentier to find there is still a
studio and a little garden at the back.

Mucha generously shared his studio
at **No. 8** with the wild-living Gauguin,
who had much work to do on the
Tahitian paintings for Durand-Ruel,
but no money for a studio of his own.
A keen photographer, Mucha took a
photo of Gauguin in his underpants
playing the harmonium, and another,
later, of Gauguin's volatile mistress,
Annah the Javanese. The music of love
was not so sweet, however. When
Ambroise Vollard introduced Annah
(born in Ceylon, not Java) to Gauguin,
she was thirteen; four years later, in
Mucha's photo, she looks thirty. It was
a fast life.

At another Montparnasse
apartment, which combined
beachcomber's shanty and artist's tip,
Annah played hostess at Gauguin's
musical evenings to such unlikely
guests as the playwright Strindberg,
whom Gauguin asked to write the
preface to his 1893 exhibition
catalogue. Strindberg regretfully
declined. Gauguin's nude portrait of
Annah shows her brown body on a
royal-blue chair, her orange monkey at
her feet. It was an exotic dream world,
and Paris didn't really take to it, any
more than Gauguin took to Paris. To
add to his disillusion, after a row
Annah pillaged the flat of wood
carvings and furniture, leaving him
only the paintings.

His love life in disarray, his family
estranged, his exhibition a disaster,
what was left for him in Paris? In 1895
Gauguin left for the Marquesas Islands
for the last time. *Nevermore*, showing a
naked Polynesian girl reflecting, was
one of his most poignant images. His
melancholy vision was the epitaph of a
disappearing culture, the death of the
mythic noble savage.

At the Boulevard de Montparnasse
end of Rue de la Grande-Chaumière, a
model market was held each Monday,
where Gérôme shopped for 'soldiers'
for his *Execution of Maréchal Ney*
(1867) and Bouguereau for 'widows' to
lay wreaths in *Day of the Dead* (1859).
The Marquesas Islands and *Te tamari
no Atua* (*The Birth of the God*, 1896)
seem to belong to another planet.

Place Pablo-Picasso, as the
Carrefour Vavin is now called, is the
perfect place for end-of-walk
refreshment. Cafés and restaurants
haunted by the impressionists' heirs,
each catching the sun or shade at
different times of day, are still extant:
Le Dôme, the café where the 1903
regulars were known as *Dômiers*, now
also an elegant fish restaurant with a
less expensive bistro round the corner
in Rue Delambre; **La Rotonde**, where
Modigliani and Picasso were photo-
graphed by Cocteau in 1916, not so
long after Picasso had shocked high-
brows by doing décor for Diaghilev's
Les Ballets Russes; **Le Select**, the first
bar to stay open all night, still with its
original décor; **La Coupole**, now
preserving only the pillars of its original décor by 31 Montparnasse artists,
once the best brasserie in town but
fallen from grace since its 1988 refit.

Here was the crossroads of the art
world from 1910 to the Second World
War. Within a few minutes' walk lived,
at some time or other, Picasso at **No.
242 Boulevard Raspail**, up the road
from Modigliani at **No. 216**; Brancusi
at **No. 54 Rue de Montparnasse**;
Léger at **No. 66 Rue Notre-Dame-
des-Champs**; Soutine at **No. 9
Boulevard Edgar-Quinet**; and the
American Dadaist photographer Man
Ray at **No. 31bis Rue Campagne-
Première**, near his favourite model
Kiki at **No. 5 Rue Delambre**.

Kiki, Queen of Montparnasse,
arrived aged thirteen with her mother,
and gave up work as a bookbinder's
apprentice at seventeen to model for
Soutine, Kisling, Foujita and Man Ray,
whose lover she was for several years.
'All the peoples on earth have pitched
their tent here,' Kiki said, 'and yet it's
like one big family.' The support
system of the impressionists, it seemed,
had been passed on to the founders of
modern art.

GIVERNY

· · · · · · · · · · · ·

Monet's garden at Giverny.

'I have embarked on things that are impossible to do,' said Monet, pushing himself hard until the end of his days. 'Water with grass waving below the surface . . . beautiful to look at, but a desire to paint it can drive you out of your mind. That is the kind of thing I've always wanted to try!'

Not far from the Seine, on the watery borders of Ile-de-France and Normandy, was my last destination: Giverny, the house and gardens where Monet lived from the upturn in his fortunes in 1883 to his death as a wealthy man in 1926.

This stirring coda begins on a dissonant note. Have the gardens of Giverny worn better than the painting they and their surroundings inspired? Is late Monet overrated? Too scientific in execution, too decorative in result? Was his flower garden really about flowers, or rather a painter's colour laboratory? Proust, writing in 1907, suspected this after merely looking at the paintings.

'If one day I am able to see Claude Monet's garden, I feel that I shall find in it a garden of tones and colours much more than flowers, a garden which needs to be less of the traditional flower-garden than a colourist's garden, if you can call it that, with flowers arranged as a whole, not exactly according to nature since they have been planted in such a manner that only those whose subtleties go together flower at the same time, in harmony with an infinite stretch of blue or pink, following the painter's powerfully expressed intention to dematerialize everything which is not colour.'

Similarly with the 'series' pictures. A haystack, a row of poplars, a cathedral façade are of little importance in themselves; what counts is the atmospheric conditions at, say, 4.15pm on a sunny December day. At 4.45pm Monet would pack up, or change to another canvas if the ensuing sunset effect looked promising. 'My strength is to stop in time,' Monet said. 'No painter can work more than half an hour on the same subject out of doors if he wishes to remain faithful to nature. When the subject changes, stop.'

In addition to nature, Giverny saw the culmination of another great influence on Monet's work, Japanese art. After the 1854 opening up of Japan by the Americans, Japanese prints on silk and rice-paper became a colourful spin-off from the new steamship trade with Europe. As early as 1856 Monet bought the first of what would become a collection, hot off the boat at Le Havre. He was even ahead of the Parisian avant-garde such as the engraver Bracquemond, who had found a Hokusai used as wrapping paper in a packing case. Baudelaire, Whistler, Manet and Zola draped their loved ones in kimonos, ate off blue-and-white china, and hung images of contemporary Japanese life on their walls. Whereas Degas was influenced by the 'Floating World' of Ukiyo-e masters, depicting geishas and other entertainers, Monet's highly original perspectives of Paris boulevards were a complex synthesis of early photography and Japanese prints. Flashily derivative portraits like *La Japonaise* gave way, as his Giverny collection of prints increased, to something much more his own, largely through the inspiration of the Japanese water garden that obsessed him in later life.

The Giverny water garden, with its gentle flow of water from the stream, is blessed with a perpetual movement of changing effects and reflections. Sensitive to the vibrations of light reflected by water lilies and irises, Monet made of them what friend and neighbour Georges Clemenceau described as a 'dusty haze'. By 1923, when Monet was 83, the 'dusty haze' had become almost total abstraction; in a painting helpfully titled *The Japanese Bridge* we would not be able to recognize those strong, pulsating red and yellow swirls as any kind of bridge if it had a contemporary title like *Giverny IV*. Poor sight in late life may have contributed to it, but this was a Monet no one had ever seen before. He cared little for new movements in art. He hated Gauguin's work and was only peripherally aware of the new intellectual approach to art of the Paris School. Yet Kandinsky said of his colours: 'They gave painting a fantastic strength and brilliance. But, unconsciously, the object, as indispensable element of painting, was also discredited.' Later Jackson Pollock and Sam Francis also recognized in late Monet an instinctive abstract painter in the making.

A long convergence of time and place is established by his work. For Monet the magic of this part of the Seine valley, where the river snakes spectacularly below chalk cliffs, through lush meadows, and is divided by secret wooded islands, dates back to the 1860s, when he worked at the hamlet of Gloton, near Bennecourt, three miles away. Deeply in love with Camille Doncieux, he painted her *By the Water's Edge* (1868) on the Island of Pleasures, opposite the rustic inn of Père Dumont that is reflected in the water along with the other cottages of the riverside hamlet.

Ten years later Monet was to face the bleakest period of his life at Vétheuil, a peaceful village further upstream. It reads like a nineteenth-century novel.

In the summer of 1878 the Monets and the Hoschedés shared a rented family house near the river. The Hoschedés were more than just good friends of the Monets. Previously Ernest Hoschedé, a Paris store-owner of seemingly unlimited funds, had commissioned Claude to decorate his château. While he was in Paris minding the store, his neglected wife Alice and Claude had an affair. Alice became pregnant. It was her sixth child, but Ernest had more drastic worries than its paternity. Through some bad business decisions he suddenly found himself bankrupt.

Things became tense at Vétheuil as the house-sharing continued into the following year. Monets and Hoschedés alike were pushed for money. Claude and Alice had to hide their feelings for each other from Camille, who was pregnant. And whenever Ernest paid a visit from wherever he was working (now as a journalist), Claude felt obliged to leave the house.

The birth of Camille's second son Michel was difficult. She became seriously ill and cancer of the uterus was diagnosed. Claude found himself with a house full of eight children, a sick wife, and a mistress nursing her devotedly day and night.

Work, as always, was his escape. With dogged detachment he produced such tranquil masterpieces of shimmering light and shade as *The Seine at Vétheuil* (1879) (O). Who could guess at the anguish in that sunlit, red-roofed village across the river, where a bumbling doctor did little to relieve Camille's suffering? In September she died. Again a certain detachment overtook Claude's sadness as he became intrigued by the changing pigmentation of his wife's face: *Camille on her Deathbed*, as though her shrouded face is emerging from a gentle sprinkling of bluish snow, is a touching image of peace after agony.

Rigorous work eased his grief in the cold winter that followed. Alice looked after the children, while Claude made use of the unusual temperatures (−25° at Christmas) to depict the frozen Seine, and the ice breaking up when the thaw came.

Then, at the age of 42, his life changed. The Hoschedés officially separated. In 1883 Claude and Alice and their eight children installed themselves at Giverny, in a house known as La Maison du Pressoir (the press-house), where Norman cider had once been made. It had two and a half acres sloping down from the top of the village towards a stream called Le Ru, a tributary of the River Epte, which itself flowed into the Seine. Claude and Alice went to work on the garden, planting flowers that would provide indoor still-life subjects on wet days.

On fine days he would be up early to catch the dawn. After bacon and eggs and hot chocolate, the stocky, tweedy, beaver-bearded figure would stump off through the garden, the aroma of the first of the day's forty cigarettes mingling with the dewy perfumes. Followed by servants carrying up to fourteen canvases to be worked on in the changing conditions of the day, he crossed damp-grassed meadows to the misty riverbank. Then he rowed his skiff to the painting-boat moored to its island and, from there, went in search of a single *pleinair* motif that could become a series. For *Poplars, Haystacks* or *Mornings on the Seine*, the canvas would change every half-hour, as the master worked feverishly, and cigarettes would be tossed half-smoked into the reeds.

Lunch was at eleven. A bell rang twice. God help a child who was late. The entire family had to be seated when the master returned – glowering if the morning had gone badly, which it frequently had. ('Last autumn I burned six paintings with the dead leaves in my garden.') A heavy silence would fall in the yellow dining room, and the scene could have been painted with the irony of Caillebotte. Alice, the headstrong former millionaire's wife, had turned a rebel into a *grand seigneur*.

Alice was not happy, though. The village frowned and gossiped about their unmarried status and eight children. Feuds about what flowers to plant where became bitter. To escape, Claude made trips, mostly without Alice, painting the Italian Riviera, tulips in Holland, the town of Antibes, the cliffs of Etretat, the rocks of Belle-Ile, and the Creuse valley. Yet daily letters, insisted on by Alice, said how much he missed her, the family and Giverny. Partly true.

It was a lyrical painting place. In between trips, *Boat at Giverny* (1887) shows his stepdaughters Germaine, Suzanne and Blanche line-fishing on the River Epte, their soft-focus blue figures in straw hats making a mirror image in water without a ripple. Remembering Camille shaded by her parasol and accompanied by young Jean in a summery field (*The Walk* – 1875), he did *Woman with Parasol* (1886), in which Suzanne seems to be gliding across another summery field, a scarf billowing on a gentle breeze behind her.

In 1892 Suzanne married the American painter Theodore Butler in the village church. Already Giverny was beginning to be invaded by foreign artists who were later to drive Monet mad. At this turning-point in his career, however, he was only too glad of American buyers for the *Haystacks* and *Poplars* series.

Marital life became easier, too. At this timely moment Ernest Hoschedé had the grace to die, leaving Alice a free woman. A few weeks after Suzanne's marriage Claude married her mother in the same village church. Alice felt herself to be respectable at last. The village felt otherwise. Especially when Jean Monet married Blanche Hoschedé: the village had always thought of them as brother and sister, and continued to do so.

The mayor, little caring what went on at the Monets' as long as they paid their taxes (which they frequently had not), was pleased to hear of Monet's new richesse: the water garden, begun in 1893, meant work for the locals. Monet already employed eight full-time gardeners. He was the true master at last – and showed it. For *Cathedrals*, which he considered to be his most original work so far, he savagely blackmailed the loyal Durand-Ruel by playing him off against two other dealers to push the price up to 15,000 francs a picture. In the end he settled for 12,000 francs each for twenty *Cathedrals*, exhibited by Durand-Ruel in 1895. And the 1900 first series of *Water Lilies* made him internationally famous.

Alice and Claude continued to quarrel, more amiably now, about the Japanese cherry trees and winter heliotropes. He built a garage for his Panhard motor car, and together they motored to Madrid – quite a drive in those days – to see the paintings in the Prado. A dark-room was constructed for his photography. After a lavish luncheon in the yellow dining room, guests such as Renoir, Cézanne, Rodin, Matisse and the playwright Sacha Guitry would be proudly shown the water garden, which was to preoccupy Monet for his last twenty years.

Once more, hard work was much-needed therapy. Deaths of friends – Morisot (1895), Sisley (1899), Pissarro (1903), Cézanne (1906) – left him feeling more and more isolated. Between 1899 and 1914 he successively lost his stepdaughter Suzanne, his wife Alice and his son Jean. Throughout the First World War he sensed the triviality of wielding a paintbrush while other men were being bayoneted in the trenches.

Blanche, Jean's widow, now devoted herself to her demanding, irrepressible stepfather-in-law, and neighbour 'Tiger' Clemenceau dropped by most days to boost the old man's morale. Monet had proposed dedicating two vast panels, then being painted in the new Water Lily Studio constructed in 1916, to the State to celebrate the 1918 victory. 'Tiger' clawed his way through the objections from the usual Beaux-Arts Academicians, but the actual donation was not signed until 1922. Infuriated by the delay, Monet refused to allow the complete set of panels to be delivered to the Orangerie until after his death.

The problem was: would he ever finish the *Water Lilies*? He had been resisting an operation for glaucoma, and the increasingly blurred vision resulted in a predominance of yellow on the canvas. Clemenceau, trained as a doctor, prevailed; in 1923 Monet had a cataract operation, and near-perfect vision was restored by specially strong glasses.

Nothing, however, could cure Monet's depression at two final deaths. In 1917 Degas departed. Two years later Renoir, last of the original group, also died. 'What a sad end for me!' said Monet. But the fighting spirit never left him. By 1924 his paintings were commanding prices of between 40,000 and 50,000 francs, sums that astonished even the often greedy Monet. 'I'm working as never before,' he wrote the year before his death, 'happy with what I'm doing and, if my new glasses are even better, I only ask to live to a hundred.' He died at Giverny on 5 December 1926, aged 86.

WALKS AND DRIVES
······················· AT ·······················
GIVERNY

Grandes Décorations *for the Orangerie by Monet, inaugurated in 1927,*
the year after his death.

INFORMATION

Itinerary

Long day trip. Advisable to spend one night nearby. Allow 1hr 15mins from Paris.

Paris–Vernon via autoroute A13 to Vernon exit. Cross Seine. Vernon–Giverny by D5.

Visit Claude Monet House and Garden (half-day).

Lunch.

Visit American Art Museum (2 hours).

Giverny–Gloton (via Bennecourt) by D5 and D201.

Gloton–Vétheuil (via La Roche-Guyon) by D100 and D913.

Visit Vétheuil (1 hour).

Vétheuil–Mantes by D145.

Mantes–Paris by autoroute A13.

Refreshment, Meals and Overnight

Hotels and B & B

Château de Brécourt, (range of rooms from **C** to **A**). Douains (Pacy-sur-Eure).
Tel. 02.32.52.40.50.

Normandy, (**C**), 1 Avenue P. Mendès-France, Vernon.
Tel. 02.32.51.97.97.

Mme Lefèbre (b & b), (**C**) 1 Rue Grande, 27510 Tilly.
Tel. 02.32.53.56.17.

Restaurants

Les Fleurs (value-for-money food and wine), (**C**), 71 Rue Carnot, Vernon. Tel. 02.32.51.16.80.

La Gueulardière (gastronomic), (**B**) (lunch **C**), Port-Villez.
Tel. 01.34.76.22.12.

Les Jardins de Giverny, (**B**), Giverny. Tel. 02.32.21.60.80.

La Pierre à Poisson (fish), (**B**), Vétheuil. Tel. 01.34.78.18.71.

Museums

Claude Monet (house, gardens and water garden), Giverny. Open Apr–Oct, daily 10–6 (except Mon). Entry: 35F.
Tel. 02.32.51.28.21.

American Art, 99 Rue Claude Monet, Giverny. Open Apr–Oct, daily 10–6 (except Mon). Entry: 35F. Good cafeteria.
Tel. 02.32.51.94.65.

Tourist Office

Office du Tourisme, 36 Rue Carnot, 27200 Vernon.
Tel. 02.32.51.39.60.

An Itinerary for Giverny

long whole day or stay overnight

Fifty miles on the A13 autoroute brought me, in just over an hour from central Paris, to the **Vernon** exit. An intentionally slow speed across the bridge (with an impatient Giverny tour bus blasting off behind) was rewarded with expansive Monet-like views of the Seine in either direction. On the right bank, just upstream of the bridge, I strolled down to the riverside spot where Monet painted several views of the Seine with the ninth-century town and its Romanesque church opposite.

For once the stroll had to be quick, because friends had advised me to arrive at **Giverny**, just over a mile south-east of Vernon on the D5, well before the ten o'clock opening. It had become, they warned, the Disneyland of art, a popular family outing best avoided between Saturday midday and Monday morning. In June the car park opposite, shady for picnics, was already nearly full before opening time, but a fast-moving queue meant only a twenty-minute wait.

The House. Early visitors are advised to start indoors, as it gets crowded before the gardens. The solid two-storey Norman farmhouse, with a raised wooden terrace stretching along it where Monet liked to dine on summer evenings, has apple-green doors and shutters set against a pink-and-white façade. An impressionist painting in itself.

Inside, I was struck by the smallness of the rooms and the prevalence of simple, cane furniture, light-wood furnishings, pale tones. Everywhere colours are blended as subtly as in the garden – delicate pinky grey with olive green, graceful mouldings picked out in dark blue against a light blue background. Marble fireplaces and tiled floors make it a house for all seasons. A designer's dream house with no designer but the master – and the bossy complicity of Alice.

Garden and house seemed to converge in the master's bedroom with the huge windows thrown open, flowers indoors and out. From a photo by Nadar above the bed, Alice seems to be keeping a fierce watch over her footloose husband as much as us intruders. Near a beautiful bureau with eighteenth-century marquetry I found the perfect place to orientate myself between house and garden. Outside, the deceptively haphazard abundance of the **Clos Normand** gardens sloped away down to the Chemin du Roy, a road where narrow-gauge trains once chuffed and clattered by. Beyond the road was the delicate, oriental order of the **Water Garden**.

Inside the house the many Japanese among us felt thoroughly at home. Nowhere in France is the connection between eastern and western art more

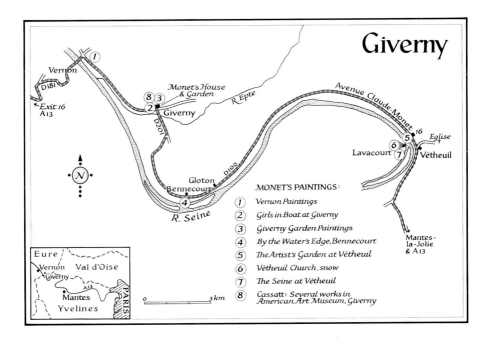

MONET'S PAINTINGS:

1. Vernon Paintings
2. Girls in Boat at Giverny
3. Giverny Garden Paintings
4. By the Water's Edge, Bennecourt
5. The Artist's Garden at Vétheuil
6. Vétheuil Church, snow
7. The Seine at Vétheuil
8. Cassatt: Several works in American Art Museum, Giverny

Above: The Alley of Rosebushes *(1920–22) at Giverny where Monet spent much time in the contemplation of nature's cycle and its changes.*

Above: Originally influenced by Japanese lithographs, Monet continued experimenting to the end of his life, with more than a touch of abstract art in The Japanese Bridge *(1918–24).*

Right: A sketch for Cassatt's The Banjo Lesson *(1894) is from a small, excellent collection of her work at the American Art Museum, Giverny.*

personal. Lightly greeting them from wall after wall, Japanese engravings are reminders of the influence on Monet already mentioned. There is a link between Hokusai's waves and Monet's storm-tossed Norman seas, between a river with fishing boats and the Seine at Argenteuil, Vétheuil and Honfleur. Kitagawa's *A Young Woman Combs her Hair and Feeds her Distracted Child* is a feat of domesticity that Degas and Cassatt might have achieved together in a single joint work. Hiroshige, Yoshitori and others were only two generations pre-impressionist, as important an influence from abroad as Turner and Constable.

The studio cum drawing room that Monet had built in the barn was for both work and relaxation. Replicas from his personal collection are like pages from a very grand scrapbook: Renoir's *Madame Monet reading Figaro*, a memento of Camille, and Cézanne's *The Negro Scipio*, a souvenir of the Académie Suisse (Chapter Seven, p. 167). Most touching of the visuals is a modest photo of Jean Monet's and Suzanne Hoschedé's marriages, attended by Pierre and Jeanne Sisley. After their father's penurious death Monet raised funds for the children by first putting his own Sisleys up for sale and then persuading friends like Morisot to do the same.

The yellow dining room and kitchen, the apotheosis of the house tour, made me long to have been a lunch guest, eating off Limoges china, surrounded by blue-and-white delft tiles, faience tobacco jars, an ormolu clock, with a glimpse of green balcony and red tulips beyond the draped net curtains. Delicious course after course, chosen and supervised by the gastronome Monet, would emerge from a kitchen equipped with thirty different copper pans, a huge fish kettle, a black range with big brass watertaps – even a chicken run for fresh eggs at the back door.

Clos Normand. Garden perfumes were fragrant after close body contact in narrow corridors and small rooms. Like the other bodies, I was suddenly swept into a Monet masterpiece and could happily get lost in it. 'I am good for nothing but painting and gardening,' he said. The words echo the garden's informality, as though he had hastily 'tossed off' the garden, as he was often accused of doing his painting; in fact, both were the result of much planning. A colour laboratory indeed – as Proust suspected. With Monet's eye and love of nature, however, also a place of beauty.

It is a bee-loud, rambling paradise of alleys, arbours, pergolas, lawns and flowerbeds. Go down the path on the left of the house first. At least six colours of clematis. Apples in bloom along runners. Multi-coloured tulips from cream to purple-black, white pansies, hollyhocks and azaleas mingling with unassuming daisies. A wallflower corner with its tumultuous splash of reds, mauves and yellows was like another Monet picture. Paintings came at me from all sides until, dizzy in the sunshine, I had to sit quietly for a few minutes on a green garden seat under blue jacaranda trees. And close my eyes.

The best view is by the central entrance gate, looking up towards the house with its backdrop of sloping, wooded hill and green meadow. They echo the apple green of the half-hoops that span the path, making arcades of roses at intervals along the beds of gentians, phlox, sweet peas and creeping nasturtium. I was lucky. June is the month for the roses in all their multitudinous variety. *The Alley of Rosebushes* (1920–2) is one of Monet's most abstract works. But from April to October, when Giverny is now open to the public, he had colours changing with the season. Spring narcissi gave way to wistaria, rhododendrons, lilacs and Monet's favourite irises. Come autumn, sunflowers turned their heads; dahlias, marigolds, asters and zinnias flourished; and the central pathway was lined with nasturtiums. In the winter he established three hothouses where exotic orchids, ferns and climbing begonias continued the cycle.

The Water Garden is reached by a tunnel under the Chemin du Roy. Its Japanese finesse hardly goes with our gawping presence. I felt gross there, out of scale with its delicacy. Children on the famous green Japanese bridge seem to fit it better than obese tourists snapping each other. Monet, unlike us, would come here to do nothing. Nothing, that is, in the Zen manner, which is far from nothing. In fallow periods he would sit contemplating in a wicker armchair, just looking, absorbing, replenishing, studying the myriad tones of one fern stem or the expanding pink petals of a water lily.

A young gardener with a gentle smile asked me politely not to stand on the grass to take my photograph of the bridge in the five precious seconds it was people-free. I missed the snap but didn't care. I thought, oh, to be a Giverny gardener in another life!

I followed the boundary path. Two different Monet views appeared: in one direction, lush meadows stretching to where the Epte joins the Seine: in the other, the water garden with its perfectly placed willows, may trees, alders, copper beech, a miniature landscape reflected in the lily pond with its two Japanese bridges. Drifting around the pond and attempting to detach myself, Monet-like, from the multitude of others doing the same, I contemplated feather ferns, explosions of azalea, tamarisk, wistaria, peonies like those sent to Monet by friends in Japan, Judas trees and laburnum copses, a forest of bamboo, and, on the gently moving surface of the water, every known variety of water lily.

'I grew them without thinking of painting them,' Monet said. 'It was revealed to me how magical my pond is. And since then, I have hardly had any other model.'

The Water Lily Studio. To the right of the house, this vast hangar of a studio was built specifically for working on *grandes décorations* for the Orangerie. I was happy to find reproductions of some of his other large canvases, particularly *Le Déjeuner sur l'herbe* (O).

The Claude Monet boutique is where you queue thirty minutes for postcards, reproductions, table sets, sweatshirts, souvenir matches, or a money-box in the shape of the house. There are Claude Monet calendars, Claude Monet garden and gastronomy books, Claude Monet scarves by Christian Dior – even an eau-de-toilette, 'Les Fleurs de Claude Monet'. You name it, Claude Monet is on it.

It was getting on for the rush hour. I left as fast as I could through the oncoming waves of nuns and schoolchildren, accents of Kyoto, Leeds, Stuttgart and Seattle, groups of hyped-up French senior citizens out for the money's worth they would most certainly get. Visit in late October, when the leaves of the water garden are pink, green and yellow, and have the place to yourself.

The American Art Museum. No visit to Giverny is complete without taking in this fine one-storey, California-style building, opened in 1992, just 300 yards up the road from Monet's house. Its modernity blends inoffensively into the wooded hillside behind.

The museum celebrates the twenty-four pioneer American impressionist painters who, at some time or other in Monet's day, made a pilgrimage to Giverny. Some of them stayed on, and the **Hôtel Baudy** housed a flourishing American colony between 1887 and 1900. The best known is Theodore Robinson, who painted the marriage of his colleague Theodore Butler to Monet's stepdaughter Suzanne. Breck did haystacks in the Monet manner, Metcalf many paintings of the River Epte, Frieske a bourgeois woman serving tea from a silver pot, and the Millet-influenced watercolourist Winslow Homer spent a highly productive 1866 in France.

Women are represented by Lilla Cabot-Perry, Mary Fairchild MacMonnies and, of course, Mary Cassatt. Lovers of Cassatt will be glad to find – finally – a decent display of her work in the Paris region. *Feeding the Ducks, By the Pond* and *Summertime* are all 1894 Bois de Boulogne works (Chapter Six, p. 158). Many are in her Japanese-engraving style (colour, drypoint and etching) with flattened perspective and clear line, as in the definitive *In the Omnibus* (1890–1), which is also sometimes called *Tramway Ride*. *The Banjo Lesson* (1894) and *Afternoon Tea Party* (1891) show an artist in tune with her time. The 1890s were Cassatt's most productive period.

In 1891 she was excluded from exhibiting with French artists because she was a foreigner, along with West Indies-born Pissarro, who sarcastically

In The Artist's Garden at Vétheuil *(1881), the sunny, lyrical image seems to reflect Monet's recovery from Camille's death and his new family life with Alice Hoschedé.*

called the others 'the patriots'. In 1904 France officially recognized her with the Légion d'honneur. Cassatt's old age, which brought a falling-out with Degas, a nervous breakdown after the death of her brother, and eventual blindness, led her to become a crotchety, hard-swearing, dog-obsessed recluse. She died a few months before Monet in 1926 at her seventeenth-century Château de Beaufresne in the valley of the Oise.

For an overnight stay in the Giverny area, a hotel of charm is the Château de Brécourt at Pacy-sur-Eure, near Vernon, or there is the modern Normandy in Vernon itself. To find a bed and breakfast ask at the Giverny tourist office. On my day trip I took a picnic, but Les Fleurs (Vernon) and Les Jardins de Giverny (Giverny) are moderately priced lunch suggestions, while the gastronomic, expensive La Gueulardière (Port-Villez) has a special lunch menu.

I headed back towards Paris along the serpentine Seine, reached from Giverny by the D5 and D201. From **Bennecourt** and **Gloton**, where Monet painted Camille *On the Water's Edge*, the D100 to **La Roche-Guyon** passes the former **Auberge du Père Dumont (No. 47 Rue Emile-Zola)** – now a riverside bakery – where the couple stayed in 1868.

Continuing via La Roche-Guyon on the D913 to **Vétheuil**, I found the house the Monets shared with the Hoschedés on the western approaches of the village, **No. 16 Avenue Claude-Monet**. A plaque announces that 'Claude Monet, Creator of Impressionism, lived in this house (1878–1881), where his wife Camille Doncieux died.' The three-storey house, built into the chalk cliffs with great vaults for cider barrels, is a pinky terracotta with green shutters resembling the Giverny colour scheme.

On the Seine side of the road a track descends to a wide, public meadow running along the riverbank. Looking back up towards the house, I found the exact slope where the younger Hoschedé children are playing in the lyrical *Artist's Garden at Vétheuil* (1881). Camille was buried in the cemetery of the Gothic **Church** dominating the town, which looks rather less ugly in Monet's *Vétheuil Church, Snow* (1878), done from the other side of the river in **Lavacourt**. The inn where Monet used often to eat is now the Restaurant Saint-Christophe in **Place de la Mairie**. An alternative is down by the river, the moderately priced La Pierre à Poisson at **No. 4 Rue de Seine**, with its charming winter garden. Also worth a visit is Antiquités de Grand-Papa, where you can buy anything from rural antiques to homemade jams. To return to Paris, head for **Mantes-la-Jolie**, where you can pick up the A13 autoroute again.

MUSEUMS

Apart from those included in the Walks and Drives itineraries, a number of Paris museums are worth separate visits. Many of the works mentioned in the book are on show.

Prices quoted are the standard entry; check out youth reductions, group and other deals including free days.

MUSÉE D'ORSAY

Love it or loathe it as a building, Orsay houses the biggest collection of French art created between 1848 and 1914. It is essential to arm yourself with a map, which is free. Better still, invest in the excellent English catalogue. The layout is confusing, and finding a loo or the right elevator or escalator for the floor you want requires the IQ of an Einstein. Pictograms and arrows often indicate the best way to get lost.

I began on the Ground Floor with pre-impressionist influences like Delacroix's sketch in wild, bold, swirling reds and oranges for *The Lion Hunt*, and what the impressionists were rebelling against in *pompier* works like Cabanel's *The Birth of Venus*, perfectly well-crafted classical nudity with absolutely no relevance to his century.

Also on the Ground Floor are more positive influences: Daubigny's *Snow* – pink sky, wintry landscape, cold crows settling on a bare, snow-dusted tree; realist Courbet's *The Bathers* – sensual nudes with accurate flesh tones, a woman in kaftan with bare breasts and necklace – and his monumental *The Studio*, which inspired Bazille and Fantin-Latour to paint similar group portraits; and characteristic landscapes by Barbizon painters, Millet, Corot, Rousseau and Diaz.

Still on the Ground Floor, pre-1870 impressionist works include Degas's *The Parade* of racehorses at Longchamp; Manet's *Olympia* and *Portrait of Emile Zola*; Monet's *Le Déjeuner sur l'herbe* (Manet's is on the Upper Level for comparison); Bazille's *Forest of Fontainebleau*, in Barbizon style; and Renoir's charming portrait of the dashing Bazille at his studio easel.

If the Ground Floor is the hors-d'oeuvres, the Upper Level is the feast proper. Manet continues to provoke with his luscious *Blonde Girl with Bare Breasts*, wearing a revolutionary hat, and *Portrait of Berthe Morisot*, hiding teasingly behind a fan.

Nobody understood the difficulties of painting snow and ice better than Monet, who admitted that it nearly defeated him in Norway. Here he succeeds brilliantly with *Hoar Frost*, *Floating Ice on the Seine* and *The Church at Vétheuil*, seen from across the river in winter. The sheer range dazzles: from the simple, clear line and use of light in *Women in the Garden* and *The Train in the Country*, via the broader brushstrokes of the archetypal impressionist Argenteuil output and more realist surprises such as *Unloading Coal*; through to the pyrotechnics of the water lily, haystack and Rouen Cathedral series.

Manual labour such as unloading coal from a barge is rarely depicted by the impressionists. Caillebotte's *Planing a Floor* shows the sensitivity of a man who, though a millionaire, built boats and knew what it was to sweat; a sustaining bottle of wine stands near the planers. And, of course, there are Degas's hardworked laundresses encountered farther on.

The many Sisleys include key pictures *The Chemin de la Machine* and *Floods at Port-Marly*. Even better is *Rest on the Edge of the Forest* – the springtime pleasures of a girl propped against a tree, reading by a stream with sunlight filtering through green leaves.

Pissarro's subdued, earthy landscapes show *Chestnut Trees at Louveciennes, The Hermitage, Barrow in an Orchard* and *Wash-Place at Port-Marly*. Three Cézannes, following work with Pissarro at Pontoise, are *Doctor Gachet's House*, *Courtyard of a Farm at Auvers* and *The House of the Hanged Man*. Even more important in the artist's development is *The Bridge at Maincy*, a totally original vision with cubist tendencies ahead of their time.

Guillaumin's *Self-Portrait* – less diabolically challenging than his friend Cézanne's, whose black beard covers a sharp-tongued mouth – shows an amiable young man with nothing to hide. His *Sunset at Ivry*, where the Marne flows into the Seine, the evening glow silhouetting factory chimneys, reveals an underrated artist at his best.

Like local government employee Guillaumin somehow finding time to paint, wife/mother/society-hostess Berthe Morisot in *The Cradle* has her sister Edma watching over a newborn baby with much tenderness. In *Butterfly Hunt* and *Young Woman in a Ball Gown*, featuring her daughter Julie at different ages, Morisot is surely the most romantic of impressionists.

And Degas the least. *The Pedicure* illuminates a banal domestic scene of a girl, draped in white, having her toe-nails clipped. During the hard work of *Girls Ironing* one of them yawns, after doing her ninety-second dress that day, while another presses down on her iron, face featureless and contorted, presaging Francis Bacon. And, if not exactly hard labour, muscle-testing bodily exertion is needed for *Ballet Rehearsal on Stage*. The *maître de ballet* gave Degas permission to paint him choreographing *The Dancing Class*, a backstage evocation of the multiple different postures of ballerinas in rehearsal. 'A pretext for painting fabrics and representing movement,' Degas claimed, but he was more accurate with the costumes than the *entrechats*. One can follow Degas's whole development from restrained, realistic ballet dresses to – as he later began to lose his sight – the startlingly pure, almost Gauguin-like colours in *Blue Dancers*.

Degas's musical scenes include *The Orchestra of the Paris Opéra*, with his bassoonist friend, Désiré Dihau, well to the fore; *Mademoiselle Dihau*, the bassoonist's sister, playing the piano – the painting Lautrec presented to dinner guests as their dessert (Chapter Four, p. 98); and *Lorenzo Pagans*, a Spanish tenor playing the guitar and singing, with Degas's father listening.

Besides *Dancing at the Moulin de le Galette*, a pair of terpsichorean Renoirs are matched: *Dance in the Country*, showing a couple of down-dressed Parisians (Aline Charigot and Paul Lhote) at a *guinguette*; and *Dance in the City*, with the dancers (Suzanne Valadon and Paul Lhote) in evening dress against a background of potted palms. Spirit of place flows from his rainbow palette, be it riverside restaurant or fashionable drawing room: *Alphonsine Fournaise*, winning in her straw hat with a sailboat in the background; or *Madame Charpentier*, elegantly at home in the splendours of her Rue de Grenelle mansion.

A collection of small sculptures by Renoir and Degas are displayed in cases – nudes, ballerinas, racehorses.

Post-impressionist Paris and surroundings appear in Lautrec's panels for La Goulue's booth and various *Elles* brothel lithographs; van Gogh's *The Church at Auvers*, *Portrait of Doctor Gachet* and *Restaurant de la Sirène*; Gauguin's *Schuffenecker's Studio*; Vlaminck's *Street in Chatou*.

On the Middle Level, Les Nabis – Bonnard, Vuillard, Denis and Vallotton – have moved still further away from impressionism with their Japanese and medieval stylization. 'Give us walls to decorate!' they cried. In panels such as Vuillard's *Public Gardens*, Vallotton's child playing with a ball in a park, or even a Bonnard opera box, Paris is hardly recognizable any more. Not that it matters. I heard a small British boy, enchanted by a Bonnard cat, exclaim: 'Oh my gosh, look at that cat, Mum!' It appeared to come to life, stretching and preening at a child's wonder.

Orsay needs at least two visits, or eyes boggle and feet scream. There are plenty of places to sit and ponder in, plus an outside terrace beneath the original station clock, overlooking the Seine. There is a good cafeteria, and the restaurant, in an ornate Third Republic décor, serves reasonable, popularly priced lunches. It also has one of the best art bookshops in Paris.

Those with more time can take in art nouveau decorative exhibits, early movies and photography, the building of the Palais Garnier, and sculptures by Carpeaux, Dalou and Rodin.

Information
Orsay, 1 Rue Bellechasse (Métro Solférino, RER Musée d'Orsay). Open daily (except Mon) 10–6; Thurs until 9.45pm, Sun opens 9am. Entry: 36F. Tel. 01.40.49.48.48.

LE PETIT PALAIS

The small museum of important pre-impressionist and impressionist works begins, in the South Gallery, with monumental *pompier* paintings. Bouguereau's *Virgin with Angels* shows pink-and-white nymphet angels in virginal white – insipid, sentimental. Near it, however, a proof that Salon official art was not all bad, merely conventional: Gleyre's *Whitsun* is the painterly work of a good draughtsman who taught – or tried to – Monet, Bazille, Renoir and Sisley.

Sisley's *Alley of Chestnut Trees near La Celle-St-Cloud* is an early work, accepted by the Salon of 1868 – a dark, sombre alley, with the subtle play of sunlight on the tops of trees, while fleecy clouds in the blue sky suggest a slight breeze.

The treats are in the Zoubaloff Gallery. A daring Courbet shows *Two Girls Sleeping*, evidently gay, their legs amorously intertwined. Female intimacy, such a strong suit of Morisot and Cassatt, continues with more modesty in Morisot's *Portrait of a Young Girl*, apprehensive, in a décolleté dress, about to go to a ball; and Cassatt's portrait of sister Lydia, a pensive, more resigned girl than Morisot's, sitting on a bright green park bench among autumnal trees.

Another twinning comprises the two portraits of Ambroise Vollard by Renoir and Cézanne. Renoir's is exotic – a Réunionais 'pirate', swarthy in a dashing turban; Cézanne's is sober – a thoughtful, serious young art dealer in suit and waistcoat.

A pre-impressionist Jongkind of Notre-Dame in summer, highly detailed, showing workers constructing a port on the Seine with the cathedral's apse behind, was an important influence on Monet. Monet is represented by a marvellous Seine picture, too: *Sunset at Lavacourt*, with fishermen's boats and village in the blues of a misty evening. And a late Pissarro shows *The Pont Royal and Pavillon de Flore*, the south-west tower of the Louvre with a tugboat appearing under the bridge.

Information
Petit Palais, Avenue Winston-Churchill (Métro Champs-Elysées-Clemenceau). Open daily (except Mon and hols) 10–5.40. Entry: 27F. Tel. 01.42.65.12.73.

L'ORANGERIE DES TUILERIES

Eclectic and transitional, the small, varied collection covers the change from impressionism to modern art.

Among the 24 Renoirs is the enchanting *Young Girls at the Piano*, a sketch for the finished version at Orsay. One girl puzzles out a phrase, while the other listens encouragingly. His son, Claude Renoir, dressed as a clown, is another warm 'family' picture; whereas *Recumbent Nude* is an Amazon with belly folds, hams of arms, and a dull, lifeless face.

There is no sin in finding Renoir's late nudes ugly and macho. In old age his view of the female body seems to have coarsened since *The Bather with Long Hair*. She is the adorable little Montmartroise, the unmistakable Renoir girl, natural, open, gold hair shining, with peach-blossom cheeks and sensual mouth.

A touching *Portrait of Paul Cézanne*, the artist's son, reminded me of his illegitimate birth, so elaborately hidden from Cézanne's father. Young Paul's strong face indicates the later support he would be for Cézanne, a link with the younger generation of artists like Les Nabis, who so admired his father. Among the fourteen Cézannes, yet another *Déjeuner sur l'herbe*, predictably weirder than Manet's or Monet's, shows the artist fully dressed at a spartan picnic where a naked 'Eve' is offering him one of three apples.

There are post-impressionist works by Matisse, 'Douanier' Rousseau,

Derain, Soutine, Picasso and Marie Laurencin.

In the oval basement are Monet's water lily panels, which he worked on at Giverny (Chapter Eight, p. 191). Inauguration of this gift to the State did not take place until 1927, a year after Monet's death. Now, for all their intricacy and adventurous abstraction, they seem too blandly decorative in this setting. Official art, tucked away, in a basement. Heresy, I admit, but shared with Degas, who held Monet's later work to be 'that of a skilful but not profound decorator'.

Information

Orangerie des Tuileries, Place de la Concorde (Métro Concorde). Open daily (except Tues) 9.45– 5.15. Entry: 27F. Tel. 01.42.97.48.16.

MARMOTTAN–CLAUDE MONET

Nothing fustian about this collection of Monet and his Friends, a state-of-the-art display in an old Paris mansion refurbished by Nippon Network Television. Here superbly lit *Water Lilies* – a choice selection ranged round a horseshoe-shaped room – can be viewed from a big octagonal settee.

There's a rediscovered Monet masterpiece (*Pont de l'Europe, Gare St-Lazare*), and a version of his seminal painting *Impression, Sunrise* that gave the impressionist group their misnomer. What, for instance, could be more naturalistic than Caillebotte's earnest ladies in black at the piano? Berthe Morisot's pretty girl with a fan, waiting to be asked to dance, is more of an impression, certainly. By the late 1890s, however, only Monet, Sisley and Pissarro were still working impressionistically. Sisley shows the Loing Canal, Pissarro the exterior boulevards of Paris under snow.

Other Monet friends in this de luxe museum are Renoir, Manet, Boudin, Guillaumin, Jongkind and Rodin.

Information

Marmottan–Claude Monet, 2 Rue Louis-Boilly (Métro Muette). Open daily (except Mon) 10–5.30. Entry: 35F. Tel. 01.42.24.07.02.

RODIN

Though they collected each other's works, Monet and Rodin had a serious disagreement during a joint 1889 exhibition. Outside the gallery, Rodin's *Burghers of Calais* sculpture group upstaged Monet's advertisement, blocking his name from view.

The *Burghers of Calais* is one of the Rodin groups gracing the beautifully kept, peaceful gardens of the Hôtel Biron, which basks elegantly in the golden glow of the Invalides dome. Inside, Monet and Renoir feature among the sculptor's personal collection, but the main reason for the visit is the *Portrait of Père Tanguy*, one of van Gogh's most intimate, affectionate portrayals of a friend.

Information

Rodin, 77 Rue de Varenne (Métro Varenne). Open Apr–Sep: daily (except Mon) 9.30–5.45; Oct–Mar: closes 4.45. Entry: 28F. Tel. 01.47.05.01.34.

PICASSO

Housed in the heart of the Marais at the Hôtel Salé, Picasso's early Paris work shows the link back to Degas via the tough expressionism of Steinlen and Lautrec (cabarets, brothels, street life). *The Death of Casegenas* (1901) – a Catalan artist friend, after suicide – and a Blue Period self-portrait reveal the downside of a struggling young artist's life in a foreign city. Elsewhere, in *Family of Acrobats with Monkey* and *Woman Ironing*, he takes in and absorbs Paris at its moment of impact, just as the impressionists had done. Even the subject-matter is familiar.

Picasso's personal collection of impressionists is notable for Cézanne's *Five Bathers*, Degas's *In the Salon* (a brothel monotype), and Renoir's sensual *Bather Seated in a Landscape*. In the 1950s he reinterpreted Manet's *Le Déjeuner sur l'herbe*. Impressionist eroticism appealed to Picasso; under its influence he produced his own brothel painting, *Les Demoiselles d'Avignon*.

Picasso, 5 Rue de Thorigny (Métros Chemin Vert or Saint-Paul). Open daily (except Tues) 9.30–5.30. Entry: 28F. Tel. 01.42.71.25.21.

AN IMPRESSIONIST WHO'S WHO

The impressionists, in the accepted definition of art historian John Rewald, were those artists who contributed to the eight independent group shows in Paris between 1874 and 1886. Two others were not represented in those exhibitions: Manet who, though supporting the cause, seldom deserted the official Salon; and Bazille, killed in action during the Franco-Prussian War (1870).

Abbreviations: b=born, d=died, f=family background, m=married, c=children, e=education, i=influences, p=places of inspiration, s=subjects, o=other interests, w=works (selected to show range).

BAZILLE Frédéric. b: 1841 near Montpellier. d: 1870 Beaune-la-Rolande. f: Prosperous Hérault winemakers. e: Medical faculty, then Gleyre's studio. i: Delacroix, Courbet. p: Hérault family home, Honfleur, Fontainebleau forest, Paris. s: Social events, portraits, landscapes. o: Wagner, contemporary literature, financing Monet and Renoir. w: *Family Reunion* (1867) (O), *The Artist's Studio, Rue de la Condamine* (1870) (O).

CAILLEBOTTE, Gustave. b: 1848 Paris. d: 1894 Gennevilliers. f: Well-to-do Parisians; his inheritance made him a millionaire. e: Law school, then Ecole des Beaux-Arts. i: Degas, Monet. p: Paris, Yerres (Ile-de-France), River Seine. s: Haussmann's new city, upper-middle-class interiors with workmen, family or friends, regattas and boating, gardens, still-life fruit and flowers. o: Gardening, boat-building, collecting impressionists, organizing group shows. w: *Planing a Floor* (1875) (O), *Paris Street; Rain* (1877), *Boat Outing* (1877).

CASSATT, Mary. b: 1844 Pittsburgh, Pennsylvania. d: 1926 Château de Beaufresne, near Paris. f: Father American businessman; her family followed her to Paris. e: Pennsylvania Academy of Fine Arts. i: Degas, Japanese prints. p: Paris parks, opera, homes. s: Social events, mother-and-child, women at their toilet, modern transport. o: Feminism, wellbeing of her family, promotion of impressionists in America, love-hate for Degas. w: *At the Opéra* (1880), *The Omnibus* (1891) (American Museum), *Young Woman Sewing in a Garden* (1886) (O), *Mother and Boy* (1901).

CEZANNE, Paul. b: 1839 Aix-en-Provence. d: 1906 Aix-en-Provence. f: Father hatter then banker; his inheritance made him the richest impressionist. m: 1886 model Hortense Fiquet after living with her seventeen years. c: one son. e: Law in Aix, then art in Paris at Académie Suisse. i: Provençal erotic and romantic art, Delacroix, Daumier, Pissarro. p: Aix, Paris, Oise valley, Fontainebleau forest, Lake Annecy, L'Estaque, Le Tholonnet, Montagne Ste-Victoire. s: Sex and violence, friends and family, sun, water, sky, country buildings, fruit, skulls, nude bathers. o: Baudelaire and Virgil, Beethoven and Wagner, shocking the *bourgeoisie*, friendship and falling out with Emile Zola, keeping secret of son's birth from father. w: *The House of the Hanged Man* (1873–4) (O), *Portrait of Victor Chocquet* (1876–7), *Apples and Biscuits* (1879–82), *The Card Players* (1891) (O), *Château-Noir* (1904–6).

DEGAS, Edgar. b: De Gas, 1834 Paris. d: 1917 Paris. f: Father from banking family married into Neapolitan aristocracy, mother from cotton-rich New Orleans family. e: Ecole des Beaux-Arts, travels in Italy. i: Leonardo da Vinci, Mantegna, Ingres, Muybridge (photography), Manet. p: Naples, Dieppe, New Orleans, Paris, Le Ménil-Hubert (Normandy), St-Valéry-sur-Somme (Picardy). s: Domestic portraits, seascapes, landscapes, jockeys, horses, race-goers, ballet dancers, musicians, laundresses, absinthe drinkers, women at their toilet, women and clients in brothels, cabaret singers, acrobats. o: Bitchy *bons mots*, quarrels with and encouragement of fellow artists, bold experiments with print-making, photography and sculpture. w: *The Bellelli Family* (1858–60) (O), *Absinthe* (1875–6) (O), *La Patronne's Birthday* (1876–7), *Young Dancer of Fourteen* (1881) (O), *The Tub* (1886) (O), *The Wounded Jockey* (1895–8).

GAUGUIN, Paul. b: 1848 Paris. d: 1903 Hiva Hoa, Marquesas Islands. f: Father French journalist, mother Peruvian Creole, childhood in Lima, Peru. m: 1873 Danish Mette Gad. c: three sons, one daughter. e: Naval college, seeing the world as merchant seaman. i: Primitive art, Ingres, Pissarro, Degas. p: Paris, Oise valley, Dieppe, Pont-Aven, Le Pouldu, Arles, Martinique, Tahiti, Marquesas Islands. s: Interiors of Paris homes, his wife and children, cabaret singers, landscapes, Breton women, religious symbolism, mistress Annah La Javanaise, Polynesian loves and life. o: Collecting impressionists, stockbroking, love-hate for Mette, search for primitive values, founding of Pont-Aven group, sculpture in wood, symbolist poetry of Mallarmé, fighting with French colonials, writing *Noa Noa* about Tahitian life and myth. w: *Sleeping Child* (1885), *Jacob Wrestling with the Angel* (1888), *Nevermore* (1897), *Riders on the Beach* (1902).

GUILLAUMIN, Armand. b: 1841 Paris. d: 1927 Paris. f: Moulins shopkeepers; he was fired from his uncle's Paris haberdashery store, also by the Paris-Orleans Railway. e: Self-taught and Académie Suisse (with Pissarro and Cézanne). p: Montmartre, Oise valley, Paris, Creuse valley. s: Paris suburbs and quaysides at different times of day and year, rural landscapes. o: Employment with Department of Bridges and Highways, winning lottery to paint full-time, long loyalty to impressionist cause and one of the most frequent exhibitors in group shows. w: *Sunset at Ivry* (1873) (O), *Place Valhubert* (1875), *The Pont Louis-Philippe* (1875) (O).

MANET, Edouard. b: 1832 Paris. d: 1883 Paris. f: Father Parisian magistrate and mayor of Gennevilliers, where family owned large property near Seine. m: 1863 Dutch pianist Suzanne Leenhoff. c: one son. e: Sea voyage as naval apprentice, then Ecole des Beaux-Arts. i: Velasquez, Zurburan, Dutch masters, Morisot, Monet. p: Boulogne-sur-Mer, Paris, Spain, Holland, Argenteuil. s: Spanish dancers, social events, contemporary history, portraits of friends and family, prostitutes, café and cabaret life, street singers, race meetings. o: Guru of younger impressionists, dandy, gentleman bohemian, womanizer, politically radical, eager for Légion d'honneur. w: *Olympia* (1863) (O), *The Execution of Emperor Maximilian* (1864), *Portrait of Emile Zola* (1868) (O), *Claude Monet and Wife in his Painting-Boat* (1874), *Blonde with Bare Breasts* (1878) (O), *A Bar at the Folies-Bergère* (1882).

MONET, Claude. b: 1840 Paris. d: 1926 Giverny. f: Father shopkeeper, moved to Le Havre when Monet was five. m: (1) 1870 model Camille Doncieux, after living with her five years (d. 1879). (2) 1892 Alice Hoschedé, widow of store owner and collector Ernest Hoschedé (d. 1911). c: two sons by Camille. e: Académie Suisse (with Pissarro), Gleyre's studio (with Renoir, Sisley and Bazille). i: Corot, Daubigny, Delacroix, Courbet, Boudin, Jongkind, Japanese prints. p: Le Havre, Honfleur, Normandy coast, Fontainebleau forest, Seine valley, Paris, London, Argenteuil, Belle-Ile, French and Italian Rivieras, Creuse valley, Norway, Venice, Giverny. s: Cartoons, elegant forest picnics, smartly dressed women in a garden, wild seas, snowy mountains, frozen rivers, cathedrals and churches, regattas, railways and bridges, steam, fog, city boulevards, haystacks, poplars, water lilies. o: Gardening, wheedling money out of Bazille, Caillebotte and Manet, generosity with fellow artists, mulish dedication to his work, natural leadership of group. w: *The Terrace at Sainte-Adresse* (1867), *Train in the Country* (1870), *Impression, Sunrise* (1872) (Marmottan-Monet), *Parisians in the*

Parc Monceau (1878), *Camille Monet on her Deathbed* (1879), *The Boat at Giverny* (1887), *London, the Houses of Parliament* (1904), *The Japanese Bridge* (1923) (O).

MORISOT, Berthe. b: 1841 Bourges. d: 1895 Paris. f: Father prosperous civil servant who gave her and sister Edma drawing lessons. m: 1874 Eugène Manet, brother of the artist. c: one daughter. e: Privately. i: Corot, Daubigny, Manet. p: Paris (Passy and Bois de Boulogne), Oise valley, Bougival, Gennevilliers. s: Domestic scenes of upper-middle-class Parisian life, cityscapes, children boating, cherry-picking and catching butterflies, her daughter Julie at all ages. o: Regular contributor to group shows (she only missed one owing to pregnancy), hostess at regular Thursday salons, keen walker and naturalist, clever combiner of marriage, motherhood and career. w: *Paris Seen from the Trocadéro* (1866), *The Cradle* (1873) (O), *Young Woman Dressed for a Ball* (1879) (O), *The Hydrangea* (1894) (O).

PISSARRO, Camille, b: 1830 St-Thomas, West Indies. d: 1903 Paris. f: Father well-to-do Jewish store owner, intended Pissarro for family business but agreed to his studying art. m: 1870 Julie Vellay, formerly the artist's mother's maid, after living with her ten years and having his allowance cut off. c: five sons, three daughters. e: Académie Suisse (with Monet). i: Delacroix, Corot, Seurat. p: Paris, River Marne, Montmorency forest, Pontoise, Louveciennes, London, Osny, Eragny-sur-Epte, Montfoucault (Mayenne). s: Village streets and houses, market towns, orchards, factories in countryside, country people at work, landscapes and cityscapes at different times of year and day. o: Anarchist, ecologist, experimenter in engraving and pointillism, hospitable on very little money, generous with advice to fellow artists. w: *The Jallais Hillside at Pontoise* (1867), *Entrance of the Village of Voisins* (1872), *Woman in a Small Field, Spring Sunshine in the Meadow at Eragny* (1887) (O), *Charing Cross Bridge, London* (1890), *Avenue de l'Opéra, Sunshine, Winter's Morning* (1898).

RENOIR, Pierre-Auguste. b: 1841 Limoges. d: 1919 Cagnes-sur-Mer. f: Father tailor, mother dressmaker, moved to Paris when Renoir was three. m: 1890 model Aline Charigot after living with her nine years. c: three sons. e: Porcelain decoration, Gleyre's studio (with Monet and Sisley), Ecole des Beaux-Arts. i: Poussin, Corot, Diaz, Italian and Spanish masters. p: Paris, Montmartre, Bougival, Chatou, Argenteuil, Essoyes (Burgundy), Algiers, Italy, Brittany, Spain, French Riviera. s: Boulevards, parks, riverside pleasure-grounds, dance-halls and dancers, circus acts, portraits of society women, children, servants, friends and family, voluptuous nudes. o: Music (Wagner, Chabrier, Offenbach), charity (for street children), gastronomy, hygiene. w: *La Grenouillère* (1869), *The Pont Neuf* (1872), *The Swing* (1876) (O), *Luncheon of the Boating Party* (1881), *Gabrielle with Jewels* (1910), *The Bathers* (1918–19).

SEURAT, Georges. b: 1859 Paris. d: 1891 Paris. f: Parents middle-class, reasonably well-off Parisians. e: Ecole des Beaux-Arts. i: Louvre masters, Chevreul (chemist specializing in colour experiments), Pissarro. p: Paris, Oise valley, Seine estuary, Asnières, La Grande-Jatte island. s: Street life, circuses, harbours and boats, river bathers, contemporary figures in a leisured landscape. o: Neo-impressionism – scientific experiment in colour, pointillism, otherwise known as divisionism (painting with dots), which split other impressionists into pro- and anti- camps at the last group show (1886) and finally broke it up. w: *Bathing Party at Asnières* (1883–4), *La Maria, Honfleur* (1886), *Sunday Afternoon on the Island of La Grande Jatte* (1886), *Circus* (1891) (O).

SISLEY, Alfred. b: 1839 Paris. d: 1899 Moret-sur-Loing. f: Father expatriate British manufacturer bankrupted by Franco-Prussian War (1870). m: 1897 model Marie Lescouezec (at Cardiff) after living with her 23 years. c: one son, one daughter. e: Gleyre's studio (with Monet, Bazille and Renoir). i: Turner, Constable, Bonington, Courbet, Daubigny. p: Paris, London, Fontainebleau forest, Seine valley,

Marly-le-Roi, Louveciennes, Normandy, Wales, Moret-sur-Loing. s: Effects of sky, cloud and water, canals, rivers, river transport, floods, landscapes at different times of day and year, churches and village houses. o: Recluse in middle age after gregarious youth. w: *View of Montmartre* (1869), *Snow at Louveciennes* (1874) (O), *Beneath Hampton Court Bridge* (1874), *The Flood at Port-Marly* (1876) (O), *The Loing Canal* (1892) (O).

A selection of others associated with the movement . . .

PRE-IMPRESSIONIST ARTISTS

BOUDIN, Eugène (1824–1898). Norman bookseller's son, self-taught painter. Seascapes of Seine estuary. Landscapes near Paris and Honfleur. Great influence on the young Monet. Exhibited in first Impressionist Show. w: *The Beach at Trouville* (1864) (O), *Drinkers at Saint-Siméon* (1869), *Sailing Boats* (1885–90) (O).

COROT, Camille (1796–1875). After work in Norman father's textile business, followed Claude and Poussin traditional landscapes with his own lyrical, poetic style. On fringe of Barbizon group. The greatest pre-impressionist influence on Morisot, Monet, Renoir and Pissarro. w: *Nymphs Dancing* (1850) (O) *Rocks in the Forest of Fontainebleau* (1874).

COURBET, Gustave (1819–1877). Family prosperous winemakers in Franche-Comté. Led realist movement in Paris, depicting people in contemporary surroundings. Rebellion against art establishment much admired by young impressionists. w: *Burial at Ornans* (1855) (O), *The Young Stonebreaker* (1865), *The Spring* (1868) (O).

DAUBIGNY, Charles-François (1817–1878). Taught by artist father, was associated with the Barbizon school. River paintings and landscapes in Oise valley. As Salon jury member, influential in getting early impressionist works accepted (Bazille, Monet, Manet, Pissarro, Renoir, Sisley). w: *Harvest Time* (1852) (O), *Snow* (1873) (O).

DELACROIX, Eugène (1798–1863). General's son, influenced by British landscape painters Bonington and Constable. Highly original colourist, specializing in romantic and exotic subjects. Violently anti-establishment and opposed to classicism of Ingres. Freedom of technique a powerful influence on young impressionists, notably Renoir. w: *The Lion Hunt* (1854) (O), *The Night of the Flood* (Delacroix), *Crossing a Ford in Morocco* (1858) (O).

MILLET, Jean-François (1814–1875). Norman farmer's son, member of the realist Barbizon school. Not a *pleinairiste*, he worked in his studio, depicting country scenes and peasant labour with a certain idealized Christian meekness. His socialist principles appealed to Pissarro, his art to Monet, van Gogh and Seurat. w: *The Angelus* (1858–9) (O), *Gleaners* (1857) (O).

ROUSSEAU, Théodore (1812–1867). With Millet, a leader of the Barbizon school. Early experimenter with light and shade in natural surroundings. Influence on Pissarro. w: *The Forest in Winter at Sunset* (1846), *Road in the Forest of Fontainebleau, Storm Effect* (1860–5).

POST-IMPRESSIONIST ARTISTS

BERNARD, Emile (1868–1941). Symbolist painter, associated with Gauguin and Sérusier in the Pont-Aven group. Better remembered as catalyst than artist. In articles, a dedicated rooter for Cézanne. Also arranged van Gogh's posthumous first Paris exhibition (1893). w: *Madeleine in the Bois d'Amour* (1888) (O).

DENIS, Maurice (1870–1943). Leader of Les Nabis ('The Prophets') – **Vuillard, Bonnard, Vallotton** – from his home at St-Germain-en-Laye. Moved from impressionism towards a more decorative, pure art form where design on a flat surface was more important than subject-matter. Acknowledged debt to the (then) least-known impressionist, Cézanne. w: *The Muses* (1893) (O), *Homage to Cézanne* (1901).

DERAIN, André (1880–1954). Son of a wealthy shopkeeper at Chatou, where he was a founder of Les Fauves ('The Wild Beasts'), who took the pure colour of Gauguin a stage further. w: *Port of Collioure, with White Horse* (1905), *The Two Barges* (1906), *Westminster Bridge* (1906).

LUCE, Maximilien (1858–1941). Underestimated neo-impressionist associated with Seurat and Signac in pioneering pointillist techniques. Specialized in Paris scenes with social comment. Admired Pissarro for his anarchistic ideals. w: *The House of Suzanne Valadon* (1895),*The Quai St-Michel and Notre-Dame* (1901) (O).

MATISSE, Henri (1869–1954). Born in Northern France, studied with Marquet in Paris, later at Gustave Moreau's art class. Advised by Pissarro to study Turner in London. With Marquet, joined the fauve group: **Derain, Vlaminck, Dufy, Braque, Friesz, Van Dongen**. Influenced by southern sun of Collioure and Biskra. Later moved from representational post-impressionism to variations on his more abstract 'Odalisque' theme. w: *The Painter in his Paris Studio, Quai St-Michel* (1899), *Luxe, Calme et Volupté* (1904) (O), *Open Window at Collioure* (1905).

SIGNAC, Paul (1863–1935). Son of well-off parents who wanted him to be an architect. Began painting as an impressionist under Monet's influence. With close friend Seurat, turned to neo-impressionism. Though not exhibited in the last Impressionist Show (1886), was associated with the group's final break-up after the controversy about pointillism. A keen yachtsman, he moved to St-Tropez, followed by fauve disciples such as Marquet, Matisse and Derain. w: *The Road to Gennevilliers* (1883) (O), *Red Buoy* (1895) (O).

TOULOUSE-LAUTREC, Henri de (1864–1901). Born in Albi of an old aristocratic family with artistic talents. Rare bone disease stunted growth of his legs after two fractures. Studied at Cormon's studio in Paris with van Gogh. Influenced by Degas's show-business pictures. His earthy rendition of nightlife, circuses and brothels was more expressionistic than Degas's. Involvement with such artistes as La Goulue, Jane Avril and Yvette Guilbert – and living in a brothel – resulted in a certain intimacy, a frankness tempered with tenderness. Pioneer of poster and sheet-music, an important influence on German expressionists and Picasso. Burned out by wild living and hard work, he died at 37. w: *Dancing at the Moulin Rouge* (1890), *Poster for the Divan Japonais* (1892), *Moorish Dance* (1895) (O), *Redhead Washing* (1896) (O).

VALADON, Suzanne (1867–1938). High-wire artist who became artist's model after a fall. Posed for Renoir, Puvis de Chavannes and Lautrec, whom she wanted to marry. Degas encouraged her drawing. Mother of Maurice Utrillo, she became a talented artist in her own right, rendering Montmartre life and landscapes with a realism learnt from her friend Degas. w: *Rue Cortot* (1900).

VAN GOGH, Vincent (1853–1890). A Dutch pastor's son, he was a preacher among the poor and later an art dealer before contentrating on his own art. Early grim, realistic images of miners, poverty and religious life. Arrival in Paris (1886) led to a lightening of his palette and subject-matter under impressionist influence. Met Lautrec at art school, was encouraged by art-shop owner Père Tanguy. Developed his own expressionistic, flamboyantly coloured style, often imbued with a deep spirituality. Moved to Arles (1888); during visit by Gauguin his mental instability and wild drinking led to cutting off part of his ear in a brothel. Last two years of frenetic output were also spent fighting madness in asylums at St-Rémy and at Auvers, where he died after a suicide attempt. w: *The Moulin de la Galette seen from Rue Girardon* (1886), *Portrait of Père Tanguy* (1887–8) (Rodin), *van Gogh's Bedroom at Arles* (1889) (O), *Wheatfield under Threatening Skies with crows* (1890).

VLAMINCK, Maurice de
(1876–1958). Former Paris delivery
boy and street musician of Dutch
origin, working with Derain at Chatou.
Admirer of van Gogh. The wildest
member of the fauve group, with a
violent intensity of colour and high
drama in his treatment of raw,
primitive nature. w: *Country Outing*
(1905), *Tugboat at Chatou* (1906),
Landscape with Red Trees (1906–7).

COLLECTORS

CHOCQUET, Victor (1821–1891).
Customs officer with private money
spent on Delacroix and commissioning
portraits from Renoir and Cézanne.

GACHET, Doctor Paul (1828–1909).
Versatile doctor, also engraver. Lived at
Auvers-sur-Oise, encouraged Cézanne,
attended van Gogh's death. Collection
can be seen in Orsay.

MURER, Eugène (1845–1906).
Pastry-cook, restaurateur. Schoolfriend
of Guillaumin and collector of Renoir,
Cézanne, Pissarro, Monet, Sisley – and,
of course, Guillaumin (22 pictures).

TANGUY, Julien (1825–1894). Owner
of paint-shop, known as 'Père' Tanguy.
First met Renoir, Pissarro and Monet in
Fontainebleau forest. Generous to
struggling artists, exchanged paint for
(then) unsaleable pictures. Through
Pissarro, met and collected Cézanne.
Also helped van Gogh, who painted
two portraits of him.

DEALERS

DURAND-RUEL, Paul
(1831–1922).While running family
gallery in London during Franco-
Prussian War he met Monet through
Pissarro. Valiant battler for
impressionist cause, while equally
battling with his artists, especially
Monet and Degas, who suspected his
opulent lifestyle of being achieved at
their expense. Launched
impressionists in America.

PETIT, Georges (1835–1900). Society
gallery owner, who ruthlessly poached

Monet and Renoir from Durand-Ruel
for some works. Introduced them to
useful contacts that resulted in better
sales. Sisley contracted with him.
Organizer of successful Monet–Rodin
Exhibition (1889).

VAN GOGH, Theo (1857–1891).
Pressure of loyally looking after his
unstable genius of an elder brother,
Vincent, and holding down his job at
the Goupil, Boussod & Valadon gallery
ended in premature death at 34.
Dedicated his short life to promoting
Pissarro, Renoir, Monet, Sisley,
Gauguin, Cézanne, Manet and Degas –
against the philistine discouragement
of his bosses.

VOLLARD, Ambroise (1868–1939).
From the French island of Réunion,
perhaps the most perceptive and
eccentric of dealers. Cooked spicy
curries for Degas, Pissarro and Renoir
on his gallery premises. Always in the
avant-garde, he was the first to achieve
success with Cézanne, who painted a
superb portrait of him, as did Renoir
(Petit Palais). Later, moved on to even
greater success with post-
impressionists van Gogh, Bonnard,
Vuillard, Matisse and Picasso.

CRITICS

ASTRUC, Zacharie (1833–1907).
Himself a sculptor and painter, he
launched art journal for Salon des
Refusés (1863), proclaiming Manet a
genius. Also hailed Pissarro and Monet
in print.

CHAMPFLEURY, Jules (1821–1889).
Great supporter of Courbet's realism,
paving way for impressionists, whom
he later collected.

LEROY, Louis (1812–1885). Writing
in *Le Charivari*, made fun of Monet's
Impression Sunrise and coined the
word 'impressionism'.

WOLFF, Albert (1835–1891). Savage
attacker of impressionists in the
Figaro, even panning Manet in his
obituary.

SELECTED BIBLIOGRAPHY

Marie Berhaut, *Caillebotte, Catalogue Raisoné*, Paris, Bibliotheque des Arts 1977.

Maria and Godfrey Blunden, *The Impressionist Revolution*, Geneva, Skira 1991.

Pascal Bonafoux, *Van Gogh*, Paris, Gallimard 1987.

Françoise Cachin, *Gauguin*, Paris, Gallimard 1989.

T. J. Clark, *The Painting of Modern Life: Paris in the Art of Manet and his Followers*, New York, Albert A. Knopf 1985.

Jean-Paul Crespelle, *Guide de la France Impressioniste*, Paris, Hazan 1990.

Jean-Paul Crespelle, *La Vie Quotidienne des Impressionistes*, Paris, Hachette 1981.

Bernard Denvir, *Encyclopaedia of Impressionism*, London, Thames & Hudson 1990

T. J. Edelstein, *Perspectives on Morisot*, New York, Hudson Hills Press (undated).

Docteur Paul Gachet, *Lettres Impressionistes au Docteur Gachet et à Mürer*, Paris, Grasset 1957.

Guide Artistique de France, Paris, Hachette 1968.

Guide to the Musée d'Orsay, Paris, Réunion des Musées Nationaux 1992.

Robert L. Herbert, *Impressionism: Art, Leisure and Parisian Society*, New Haven, London, Yale University Press, 1988.

Michel Hoog, *Cézanne*, Paris, Gallimard 1989.

Jean Leymarie, *Le Fauvisme*, Geneva, Skira 1991.

Henri Loyrette, *Degas*, Paris, Gallimard 1989.

Pattie Lurie, *Guide to Impressionist Paris*, Parigram 1996.

Guy de Maupassant, *Contes et Nouvelles*, Paris, Gallimard 1974.

Sylvia Patin, *Monet*, Paris, Gallimard 1974.

Yann le Pichon, *Les Peintres du Bonheur*, Paris, Robert Laffont 1988.

Camille Pissarro, *Lettres à Mon Fils*, Paris, Albin Michel 1950.

Théry and Waks Puydebat, *Les Impressionistes autour de Paris*, S.E.M. Chateau d'Auvers 1993.

Jean Renoir, *Pierre-Auguste Renoir, Mon Père*, Paris, Gallimard 1974.

John Rewald, *The History of Impressionism*, New York, Museum of Modern Art 1946.

Maurice Raynal, *Modern Painting*, Lausanne, Albert Skira 1956.

Jay Roudebush, *Mary Cassatt*, New York, Crown Art Library 1979.

John Russell, *Seurat*, Paris, Thames & Hudson 1989.

L. Venturi, *De Manet à Lautrec*, Paris, Albin Michel 1953.

Emile Zola, *L'Oeuvre*, (novel in Les Rougon-Macquart series), Paris Gallimard 1860–67.

INDEX

Page references in **bold** indicate reproduction of the paintings.

Picture credits

Bridgeman Art Library, London: pp: 17, Musée de la Ville de Paris, Musée du Petit-Palais, Giraudon; 20–1, Louvre, Paris; 24T Musée de L'Orangerie, Laurois-Giraudon, Paris; 25, 28, 32–3, Musée D'Orsay, Paris, Giraudon; 41, National Gallery of Art, Washington, DC; 44T, Musée D'Orsay; 44B, Private Collection; 48–9, Petit Palais, Geneva; 53, Mellon Collection, National Gallery of Art, Washington; 61, 64, Musée D'Orsay; 65, Museum of Fine Arts, Boston; 68T, Fitzwilliam Museum, University of Cambridge; 68B, National Museum of Wales, Cardiff; 73T, Phillips Collection, Washington; 76T, Neue Pinakothek, Munich; 76B, Musée D'Orsay; 80, Art Institute of Chicago; 89, 92, Musée D'Orsay; 100T, Philadelphia Museum of Art, Pennsylvania; 101B, Courtauld Institute Galleries, University of London; 113, 116T, 117B, 124–5, 137, Musée D'Orsay; 140, National Gallery, London; 145T, Musée D'Orsay; 145B, Courtauld Institute; 149B, Private Collection; 152–3, Philadelphia Museum of Art; 157T, Musée D'Orsay; 157B, Musée Marmottan, Paris; 172T, Musée D'Orsay; 177, Courtauld Institute; 184, Musée De L'Orangerie; 188T, Musée Marmottan; 188B, Galerie Daniel Maligue, Paris; 189, Agnew & Sons, London; 192, National Gallery of Art, Washington. Musée D'Orsay/© RMN, Paris: p: 128–9. Musée Fabre, Montpellier: p: 165. Norton Simon Foundation, Pasadena: p: 168–9.

Jacket: Bridgeman Art Library: front (from top): Art Institute of Chicago; Musée D'Orsay, Musée D'Orsay; back (from top): Pushkin Museum, Moscow; Musée Marmottan, Paris; Philadelphia Museum of Art.